Restorative Justice In Practice

Restorative justice has made significant progress in recent years and now plays an increasingly important role in and alongside the criminal justice systems of a number of countries in different parts of the world. In many cases, however, successes and failures, strengths and weaknesses have not been evaluated sufficiently systematically and comprehensively, and it has been difficult to gain an accurate picture of its implementation and the lessons to be drawn from this.

Restorative Justice in Practice addresses this need, analysing the results of the implementation of three restorative justice schemes in England and Wales in the largest and most complete trial of restorative justice with adult offenders worldwide. It aims to bring out the practicalities of setting up and running restorative justice schemes in connection with criminal justice, the costs of doing so and the key professional and ethical issues involved.

At the same time the book situates these findings within the growing international academic and policy debates about restorative justice, addressing a number of key issues for criminal justice and penology, including:

- how far victim expectations of justice are and can be met by restorative justice aligned with criminal justice;
- whether 'community' is involved in restorative justice for adult offenders and how this relates to social capital;
- how far restorative justice events relate to processes of desistance (giving up crime), promote reductions in reoffending and link to resettlement;
- what stages of criminal justice may be most suitable for restorative justice and how this relates to victim and offender needs;
- the usefulness of conferencing and mediation as forms of restorative justice with adults.

Restorative Justice in Practice will be essential reading for both students and practitioners, and a key contribution to the restorative justice debate.

Joanna Shapland is Professor of Criminal Justice in the School of Law, University of Sheffield, and Head of the School of Law; **Gwen Robinson** is Reader in Criminal Justice in the School of Law at the University of Sheffield; **Angela Sorsby** is a freelance criminologist specialising in data analysis and statistics.

Restorative Justice in Practice

Restorative Justice in Practice

Evaluating what works for victims and offenders

Joanna Shapland, Gwen Robinson and Angela Sorsby

LONDON AND NEW YORK

First published 2011 by Routledge
2 Park Square, Milton Park, Abingdon, Oxon, OX14 4RN

Simultaneously published in the USA and Canada
by Routledge
711 Third Avenue, New York, NY 10017

Routledge is an imprint of the Taylor & Francis Group, an informa business

Typeset in Times New Roman
by GCS, Leighton Buzzard, Bedfordshire
Printed and bound in Great Britain by the MPG Books Group

British Library Cataloguing in Publication Data
A catalogue record for this book is available from the British Library

Library of Congress Cataloguing in Publication Data
A catalog record for this book has been requested

ISBN: 978-1-84392-846-1 (hbk)
ISBN: 978-1-84392-845-4 (pbk)
ISBN: 978-0-203-80610-4 (ebk)

Contents

List of tables and figure

Tables

Figure

List of abbreviations

CARAT	Counselling, Assessment, Referral, Advice and Throughcare
CoE	Council of Europe
CRP	Crime Reduction Programme
ILPS	Inner London Probation Service
JRC	Justice Research Consortium
NACRO	National Association for the Care and Resettlement of Offenders
NI	Northern Ireland
NZ	New Zealand
RCT	randomised controlled trial
RISE	Reintegrative Shaming Experiments
SACRO	Safeguarding Communities – Reducing Offending
SAJJ	South Australian Juvenile Justice Conferencing
SMART PS	Specific, Measurable, Achievable, Relevant, Timed, Proportionate and Supervised
TJA	Transformative Justice Australia
UN	United Nations
VOM	victim-offender mediation
YOT	Youth Offending Team

Acknowledgments

There are many people who contributed, directly or indirectly, to the research project which is at the heart of this book and to whom we would like to extend our thanks.

The study itself was funded by the Home Office (and, after 2007, the Ministry of Justice), which also provided funding for the three restorative justice schemes we evaluated. We would particularly like to acknowledge the support provided by the senior research staff at the Home Office and Ministry of Justice who were responsible for managing the evaluation: Robert Street, Blair Turner, Robin Elliott-Marshall and Rachel Walmsley, as well as those in the Economics Unit of the Home Office and elsewhere who provided specific help.

We are also indebted to the managers, researchers and practitioners of the three schemes which we evaluated, without whose cooperation and support the project would not have been possible. There are too many to name individually, but we would like in particular to thank Professor Larry Sherman and Dr Heather Strang (Justice Research Consortium), Philip Gilbert (REMEDI) and Ben Lyon (CONNECT). Staff from all three schemes gave generously of their time and many allowed us to observe their practice (we hope as unobtrusively as possible).

We also wish to acknowledge the hard work of all of those who, as members of our research team at the University of Sheffield, contributed to the research reported in this book. There are many of them, reflecting the considerable scope and longevity of the project. They are: Anne Atkinson, Helen Atkinson, Becca Chapman, Emily Colledge, Jim Dignan, Lucy Edwards, Jeremy Hibbert, Marie Howes, Jennifer Johnstone and Rachel Pennant. Thanks are also due to Jenny Chambers and Jackie McKay who provided administrative support and to NFO System Three Social Research whose fieldworkers carried out many of the interviews with victims and offenders.

Finally, we would like to thank all of those who, during the course of the project, took part in the restorative justice schemes we evaluated, whether as victims, offenders or their supporters. Particular thanks go to those individuals who responded to questionnaires or agreed to be interviewed by us about their experiences of restorative and criminal justice. All of them helped us to get inside the 'black box' of restorative justice and to begin to answer the key question which is at the heart of this book, namely: what works for victims and offenders?

Developing restorative justice with adults

1 Setting the scene

Introduction

Few would dispute the observation that the ideas, theories and practices which we have come to understand as 'restorative justice' have in the last 25 years or so grown considerably in their spread and influence. This remarkable development, which has been evident in many parts of the world and has spanned a variety of social and cultural contexts, is perhaps most evident in the burgeoning academic literature on the subject. Writing in 2004, Daly observed that in the previous decade some 60 books on restorative justice had been published in English alone, and it is fair to say that this crescendo of scholarly activity shows no sign of abating. This book, of course, simply contributes to and confirms that trend.

Much of the development of restorative justice as a response to offending, however, has been with young offenders, with practice often featuring diversion from formal criminal justice procedures to restorative justice processes. The research we have been undertaking from 2001 to 2008 in England, however, was primarily in relation to restorative justice schemes dealing with adult offenders – and often serious offences. Because the work of the schemes did relate to the serious end of the criminal justice spectrum, it was inappropriate for them to feature diversion for most offences. Restorative justice took place in conjunction with criminal justice – either pre-sentence, during sentence, at pre-release from prison or as diversion. Undertaking restorative justice in these circumstances raised a number of questions which have not always been prominent in previous practice with predominantly young offenders. How can (or should) restorative justice account to criminal justice as well as to participants for what has happened? Should justice be open to view? What is the effect on reoffending? Is restorative justice ever criminogenic? What would victims of serious offences feel about participation in restorative justice? Is restorative justice value for money? How can a new restorative justice service, so associated with criminal justice, be set up and receive sufficient cases? Does conferencing produce different effects to mediation? How can restorative justice outcomes occur when offenders are likely to be sent to prison?

The opportunity of evaluating several different restorative justice initiatives which were designed and funded primarily to work with adult offenders and in relation to serious offences allows us to start to address these questions. First, however, we need to set the scene in relation to the development of restorative justice internationally and how the schemes we evaluated in England relate to those developments.

The theoretical and practical development of restorative justice

The restorative justice agenda or 'movement', as it is often described, encompasses a very broad range of practices and approaches, such that a definitive definition has proven elusive. We take the view that restorative justice is best described as a 'conceptual umbrella' under which a number of different practices, adopted in a variety of contexts, have found common ground (Shapland *et al.* 2006b). At its broadest, restorative justice can be understood as a strategy or set of strategies oriented toward the resolution of conflicts or disputes between parties, with applications in a number of arenas: civil, corporate, criminal and political. Thus restorative justice has inspired solutions to issues ranging from school bullying to large-scale political conflicts (for examples of restorative justice in all of these 'regulatory arenas', see Roche 2006). It is, however, the criminal arena that specifically concerns us in this book.

As a response to offending, restorative justice has a history that is complicated by the parallel development of its theoretical and practical expressions or dimensions. As Daly and Immarigeon (1998: 21) have explained, restorative justice has 'sprung from sites of activism, academia, and justice system workplaces' so that the influences of social movements, academic theorising and real-world practices have tended to overlap and, to a large degree, influence each other. The history of restorative justice is also bound up with a 'rediscovery' of apparently ancient practices of dispute resolution among indigenous populations and in (western) pre-modern societies (e.g. Van Ness and Strong 1997; Braithwaite 2002a), although aspects of this 'prehistory' have been challenged (e.g. Daly 2001, 2002; Bottoms 2003).

Notwithstanding some resemblance between certain 'traditional' approaches to dispute resolution and more recent practices, the 'birth' of restorative justice in late-modern western societies is often located in Kitchener, Ontario, where in 1974 a probation officer introduced two young offenders to the victims whose property they had vandalised, with the consent of the judge in their case (Peachey 1989). Also in Canada, 'circle sentencing' emerged in the early 1990s as a means of responding to crime specifically within indigenous communities (Stuart 1996; Lilles 2001). However, restorative justice arguably has multiple birthplaces (Roche 2006). Others include New Zealand, which in the 1980s sought to establish new principles and procedures for responding to juvenile crime (and more broadly child welfare/protection issues), culminating in the 1989 Children, Young People and Their Families Act. This established the family group conference as the principal mechanism through which juvenile offending was to be dealt with (Maxwell and Morris 1993). At about the same time, the small Australian town of Wagga Wagga in New South Wales was the birthplace of another (police-led) model of conferencing which was initially used in the context of a police caution. From these multiple points of origin, the various models of restorative justice spread to other parts of the world where they were sometimes adapted or modified and where they became more or less 'established'.

Although the term itself has been traced back to the 1970s (Eglash 1977),[1] it was not until the 1990s that these developments came to be grouped together and described as operational examples of 'restorative justice' by writers such as Zehr (1985, 1990), Wright (1991) and Van Ness and Strong (1997), among others. By the end of that decade, a working definition had emerged which sought to capture the 'shared essence' of the various manifestations of restorative justice as a response to offending around the world:

> Restorative justice is a process whereby all parties with a stake in a particular offence come together to resolve collectively how to deal with the aftermath of the offence and its implications for the future.
>
> (Marshall 1999: 5)

Marshall's definition has not, however, proven entirely unproblematic. As a number of commentators have observed, Marshall's is a 'process-focused' definition, which emphasises the processes of 'coming together' and 'collective resolution' but has less to say about the desired 'ends' of that process or the values that might usefully or appropriately inform it. Others have preferred definitions which emphasise *values* or *outcomes* (e.g. see Braithwaite and Strang 2001; Zernova and Wright 2007; Walgrave 2007). Walgrave, for example, has adopted an 'outcome-focused' definition of restorative justice as every action that is primarily oriented toward repairing the harm that has been caused by crime. Still others have sought to generate multi-dimensional definitions, in which processes, values and outcomes are all important (e.g. Dignan 2005).

To a large extent, disagreement about how best to define restorative justice has reflected the multiple theoretical roots of and influences on restorative justice, which have in turn generated a variety of 'visions' of the restorative justice enterprise, each with their own emphases and ideas about what 'counts' as restorative justice. This variety is evident in and goes some way toward explaining the range of practices currently in operation under the guise of 'restorative justice' in the criminal arena. So, for example, the emergence of victim-offender mediation in North America is generally linked with the Christian Mennonite movement, which sought to promote the personal reconciliation of victims and 'their' offenders. Howard Zehr, perhaps the best known writer in this tradition, advocates ways of bringing victims and offenders together to discuss the offence and seek resolutions capable of repairing any harm caused, thus encouraging the healing and reconciliation of the main parties (Zehr 1985, 1990). The spread of mediation in Europe, however, owes more to the influence of Nils Christie's writing (Dignan 2005). In his classic paper 'Conflicts as Property', Christie (1977) famously argued that in taking responsibility for prosecution, the modern state has 'stolen' the conflict from victims, denying them the right to full participation in their case and its resolution. Christie advocated the 'de-professionalisation' of responses to crime, so that responsibility for resolving conflicts associated with crime should be returned to those with a personal stake in such matters.

Other restorative justice approaches have been linked more with attempts to develop culturally appropriate responses to criminal behaviour which are capable of including a wider range of 'stakeholders'. One of the most important factors which inspired the development of family group conferencing in New Zealand was a perceived 'legitimacy deficit' in respect of the existing criminal justice and child and family welfare systems in their dealings with minority groups: specifically the Maori population and Pacific Island Polynesians (Maxwell and Morris 1993; Daly 2001; Bottoms 2003). The same is true of circle sentencing in the Canadian context (e.g. Lilles 2001). Daly describes the development of family group conferencing in New Zealand as both a 'bottom-up' and a 'top-down' initiative, which 'splices white, bureaucratic forms of justice with elements of informal justice that may include non-white (or non-Western) values or methods of judgment' (2001: 65). In contrast, the development of police-led ('Wagga Wagga model') conferencing in Australia was very much led by professionals and administrators, who sought to bring some of the features of the New Zealand model to bear on the development of police cautioning practices in New South Wales. There then followed a process of drawing more explicitly upon Braithwaite's (1989) theory of reintegrative shaming, which had been developed in parallel with conferencing initiatives but in relative isolation from them (Daly 2001). With its explicit focus on the reduction of reoffending and central thesis of the superiority of informal crime control methods involving the offender's 'significant others' (whose role is to induce 'shame' in offenders as a precursor to acceptance and reintegration), Braithwaite's theory seemed to offer a constructive solution to the problem of juvenile crime and it has continued to be the key theoretical influence behind police-led conferencing as this has developed in other parts of the world (e.g. Young 2001).

Although the above analysis does not of course capture every theoretical influence on restorative justice practices (see, for example, Daly and Immarigeon (1998) for a wide-ranging discussion of the multiple 'streams of influence' on restorative justice in North America), it nonetheless gives a flavour of some of the key ideas at work. To the extent that these can be said to have a common source or point of reference, one element lies in their focus upon bringing people together and empowering them to discuss the offence, its aftermath and, sometimes, the future. Another is in their dissatisfaction with some aspects of modern, predominantly western, criminal justice systems, processes or outcomes.

In relation to the comparison with criminal justice, although to a large degree their critiques have tended to overlap, different theoretical 'streams' have tended to emphasise different 'justice deficits'. So, for example, Braithwaite's (1989) theory of reintegrative shaming can be understood principally as a critique of criminal justice's poor performance in respect of crime reduction outcomes, whereas for the Christian Mennonite movement it is the typically adversarial nature of criminal justice which has aroused critique. Dignan (2005) has described the Mennonite tradition as part of a collection of perspectives which share in common a desire to 'civilise' criminal justice, in two senses of the word: first, by reconceptualising crime as a 'civil wrong' (rather than an offence against the state), thereby creating a meaningful role for victims; and second, by pursuing more humane and constructive 'justice outcomes'. Others have gone further, seeking to involve members of communities (variously understood) beyond the immediate victim and offender in responses to crime. Elements of this 'communitarian' perspective (Dignan 2005) are to be found in the work of both Christie and Braithwaite, among others. Perceptions of procedural justice deficits (Tyler 1990, 2006) in criminal justice processes also feature, implicitly or explicitly, across a number of theoretical 'streams'.

To the extent that restorative justice which seeks to respond to offending can be understood as a critique of criminal justice, it is hardly surprising that the relationship(s) between these two 'families' of justice responses has ignited considerable debate and disagreement among advocates and commentators (for example, see von Hirsch *et al*. 2003). For some advocates, restorative justice has been conceived as an alternative, 'third way' between traditions of retributive and rehabilitative justice; others have argued that restorative justice contains elements of one or both of these approaches (e.g. Daly 2000; Duff 2003; Roche 2007). In the 'real world', of course, the development of restorative justice has tended to take place in the context of, rather than outside, 'mainstream' criminal justice – albeit not always at active 'decision points' in the criminal justice process.[2] Restorative justice has, thus, been deployed as a diversionary measure (e.g. with a police caution or warning), between conviction and sentence, as part of a sentence, and following the imposition and completion of a sentence. However, the extent to which restorative justice has become a 'mainstream' response to offending and/or received statutory backing has varied considerably between jurisdictions (e.g. Dignan and Lowey 2000: Ch. 3). For example, in New Zealand conferencing has become an integral part of the criminal justice process for juveniles, while in Australia some states have introduced restorative justice on a legislated basis whereas others have not (Daly 2001).

The development of restorative justice in England and Wales

The story of restorative justice in England and Wales is one of peaks and troughs of activity over the last thirty years or so. The 1980s saw the emergence, on an ad hoc basis, of a number of police- and probation-led schemes offering victim-offender mediation. While the majority of these schemes deployed mediation in conjunction with a police caution and tended to target juvenile offenders who had committed relatively minor offences, a smaller number of schemes focused their attention on adult offenders and sometimes quite serious offences (Marshall 1984). In the mid-1980s, in the context of a growing interest in victims and reparation, the Home Office funded a small number of experimental schemes based in Cumbria, Wolverhampton, Coventry and Leeds; however, 'official' interest in – and funding for – the schemes was not sustained (Davis 1992). The schemes looked elsewhere for funding and, over the next ten years, some victim-offender mediation schemes flourished while others floundered.

However, restorative justice in the youth justice realm was to receive a significant boost in the late 1990s, when the incoming 'New Labour' government announced plans to put restorative justice principles at the heart of a reformed youth justice system (Home Office 1997). The 'new youth justice' sought to implement restorative justice principles in three main ways: through the introduction of two new penalties (the Reparation Order and the Action Plan Order) and the reform of the system of cautioning (Holdaway *et al.* 2001). All three initiatives were conceived with a strong emphasis on reparation to victims (including an apology) (Bottoms and Dignan 2004). Subsequently the Youth Justice and Criminal Evidence Act 1999 introduced the Referral Order: a mandatory sanction for most 10–17-year-olds pleading guilty and convicted by the courts for the first time. The Referral Order involves the referral of a young offender by the court to a panel made up of two trained volunteers (intended to be from the local community) and a professional from the Youth Offending Team, who seek to develop an appropriate action plan/agreement for the offender. Victims may also be invited to panel meetings (Crawford and Newburn 2003). At about the same time, the Thames Valley police service, which had been developing restorative justice initiatives for a number of years, decided to move wholesale toward a model of 'restorative cautioning', along the lines of the police-led (Wagga Wagga style) conferencing model described above (Hoyle *et al.* 2002). These developments, albeit significant, shared in common a clear focus on young offenders and less serious offending. All have received some critical attention regarding their 'restorative' credentials (e.g. Young 2001; Gray 2005).

In 2001, the Home Office decided to provide funding to a number of restorative justice schemes under the auspices of its Crime Reduction Programme (CRP). The CRP was a major initiative on the part of the government in England and Wales which sought to develop evidence-based practice in a variety of areas of crime prevention and criminal justice and which generated an unprecedented level of funding for pilot projects of various kinds, as well as a number of large-scale, independent evaluations of their performance.[3] Having invited bids from schemes (organisations, partnerships or consortia) wishing to pilot or develop restorative justice, and following a review of seven existing restorative justice projects in England also commissioned under the CRP (Miers *et al.* 2001) the Home Office selected three schemes which all commenced work in mid-2001. Schemes were funded until 2003/4. It is the resulting work of these three schemes, and the independent evaluation we (and colleagues) conducted, which comprise the focus of this book.

The CRP-funded schemes

The three schemes which the Home Office decided to support were CONNECT, the Justice Research Consortium (JRC) and REMEDI. Of these, only REMEDI was an existing scheme: a charitable organisation with an existing base in Sheffield. The new funding was to support an expansion of REMEDI's mediation service to the whole of the county of South Yorkshire. The CONNECT scheme arose from a joint bid from the National Association for the Care and Resettlement of Offenders (NACRO) and what was at that time the Inner London Probation Service (ILPS), which subsequently became part of the National Probation Service for England and Wales.

The Justice Research Consortium, the largest of the three schemes in terms of personnel and scope, was based at the Jerry Lee Center of Criminology at the University of Pennsylvania, in partnership with the Australian National University. Led by Professor Lawrence Sherman and Professor Heather Strang from these respective institutions, the JRC scheme had operational sites in London, Thames Valley and Northumbria and partnerships with (in London) the Metropolitan Police; (in Thames Valley) the National Probation Service, HM Prison Bullingdon, Thames Valley Police and Oxford Community Mediation Service; and (in Northumbria) Northumbria Police. Between them, the schemes aimed to offer a range of models of restorative justice, including:

- *conferencing* – involving a face-to-face meeting between offender and victim, with one or more mediators or facilitators, and including one or more supporters of the offender and victim also invited to attend (CONNECT and JRC);[4]
- *direct mediation* – involving a face-to-face meeting between offender and victim, with one or more mediators or facilitators (CONNECT and REMEDI);
- *indirect (or 'shuttle') mediation* – involving the passing of information, by one or more mediators or facilitators, between offender and victim (CONNECT and REMEDI).

In preparing their bids for funding, applicants were invited to consider the potential for restorative justice with adult offenders and in respect of a range of offences, including serious offences and 'high-volume' crimes such as burglary (Shapland *et al.* 2004a). As we saw above, the three schemes which secured funding were thus destined to depart from the bulk of previous restorative justice projects which had been deployed in England and Wales (and indeed internationally) in four main ways.

First, they all sought to focus upon cases involving adult offenders, albeit that some young offenders were also included by JRC and REMEDI. Second, all three schemes were intended to operate as an integral part of 'regular' criminal justice processes. In other words, the cases they sought to work with would all originate at and be referred from 'formal' decision points in that process.

This included offering restorative justice in the context of a police caution (or, in the case of juveniles, a 'final warning'),[5] during a community sentence or a custodial sentence and, in some cases, between conviction and sentence. Third, all of the schemes sought to establish a substantial flow of referrals, so that there would be a 'presumption in favour' of restorative justice when cases met eligibility criteria. The fourth point of departure from earlier projects very much followed on from the other three, and that was an intention to include some of the more serious offences, such as residential burglary, robbery and violent offences (Shapland *et al.* 2004a).

The fact that the schemes all sought to 'stage' restorative justice against the backdrop of criminal justice processes (Dignan *et al.* 2007) placed a number of constraints and pressures on the schemes. In respect of the typology of 'implementation strategies' described by Dignan and Lowey (2000), the three schemes – notwithstanding their diversity – were all examples of the 'stand-alone' model – that is, intended to supplement rather than replace existing criminal justice processes – and functioned in the absence of specific statutory authorisation. In this regard they conformed to the history of stand-alone schemes outlined by Dignan and Lowey, which has encompassed most attempts to 'extend the boundaries' of restorative justice by applying it to atypical groups or types of cases (Dignan and Lowey 2000: 48).

The evaluation

In 2001 a team of researchers based at the University of Sheffield was appointed to conduct an independent evaluation of the work of the three schemes. The authors of this book comprise the lead researcher (Shapland) and two of the members of the evaluation team who worked on the project for its duration. Initially it was envisaged that the evaluation would run until the end of 2006, but it was in fact extended until March 2008 in order to allow sufficient time for the schemes to amass a substantial number of referrals and still to have a two-year period in which to study reconviction. The evaluation was designed to include an element of action research, so that there was consultation with schemes in the design of research instruments, and every effort was made to regularly feed back our findings to the schemes in order to inform their development.

The definition of restorative justice, originally set out by the Home Office for both the schemes and the evaluation team, was Marshall's (1999) process definition, discussed above. However, it was necessary to acknowledge in designing the evaluation that it would be necessary to consider the *outcomes* as well as the *processes* of restorative justice, not least because the Home Office/Ministry of Justice[6] was clearly interested in outcomes of various kinds. There were two stated outcome measures, originally set out as equal in importance:

- reoffending outcomes (consistent with the Crime Reduction Programme funding which supported both the schemes and the evaluation);
- meeting the needs of victims.

Subsequent governmental emphasis tended to shift towards reoffending as the main outcome, but the schemes and ourselves as the evaluation team continued to see both outcomes as equally important.

As evaluators we also considered it important to draw some boundaries around what we would and what we would not count as restorative justice (Shapland *et al*. 2004a). This was necessary because the schemes were proposing to deliver a wide range of interventions, both direct and indirect, not all of which could be unproblematically included under the umbrella of restorative justice practices. We included all examples of face-to-face mediation and conferencing but decided to exclude from the evaluation any practice which did not involve an element of information exchange in *both* directions between offender and victim (so we excluded writing a letter of apology which was not sent to the victim, or cases in which the offender or victim could not be contacted or refused to participate). Where a conference had been convened but the victim failed to attend having agreed to do so, we included this as a 'victim-absent' conference.

Research methods and analyses

Spanning some seven years, the evaluation incorporated the collection and analysis of a range of quantitative and qualitative data from a variety of sources. Our principal research methods and the main analyses we conducted were as follows.

At the initial stage of the evaluation we were involved in the design and development of databases to capture details of all cases referred to the schemes while they were in receipt of Home Office/Ministry of Justice funding.

We also sought to observe, as far as possible, the processes of setting up (or, in the case of REMEDI, expanding) the schemes as well as their operational activities. This involved the collection of literature produced by the schemes about their work, attending staff training events and attending meetings of scheme personnel and steering groups. We also conducted observations in the magistrates' courts involved with CONNECT and the JRC (Northumbria) scheme.

Interviews with both scheme personnel and representatives of the main agencies working with or alongside the schemes were conducted towards the end of the first year and at the end of the schemes' funding period. These were a combination of one-to-one and group interviews, addressing (among other issues) experiences of working in or with the scheme, views about restorative justice and information about costs. Agency representatives included court personnel (judges, magistrates and justices' clerks), and managers from both prisons and the National Probation Service. The first round of interviews (n = 77) comprised 9 for CONNECT, 59 for JRC and 9 for REMEDI; the second round (n = 62) comprised 7 for CONNECT, 48 for JRC and 7 for REMEDI.

We observed a total of 285 restorative justice events, the majority of which were conferences run by JRC, the largest of the three schemes.[7] Twenty-one of the conferences observed were victim-absent conferences but the remaining 259 included at least one offender and victim. We were able to observe five direct mediations: four run by REMEDI and one by CONNECT. It was not possible to observe indirect mediation.[8] Observations were recorded by means of an observation schedule developed by us but informed by similar schedules used in a number of other evaluations of restorative justice, most notably RISE in Canberra (Strang *et al.* 1999), Kathleen Daly's evaluation in South Australia (Daly 1998, 2001) and the evaluation by Miers *et al.* (2001) in England and Wales. Our schedule included both objective and subjective measures and ratings, and both quantitative and qualitative information (including a free text summary of the event). The latter summaries were analysed using a qualitative data analysis package (MAXqda); quantitative data were analysed in SPSS.

We also collected and analysed all of the agreements drawn up by participants at the end of conferences or direct mediations, in conjunction with data from databases and case files pertaining to completion of agreements and follow-up by facilitators or mediators after the restorative justice event (REMEDI produced 11 such agreements and JRC produced written agreements in 98 per cent of conferences).

In respect of the views of participants we sought, as far as possible, to seek their views both prior to and after taking part in restorative justice. Prior to restorative justice, we conducted brief pre-conference interviews with 54 victims and 62 offenders in the 'pilot' phase of the JRC scheme.[9] For CONNECT and REMEDI, participants were asked to complete a questionnaire prior to taking part in restorative justice. A total of 207 questionnaires were completed for REMEDI, of which 157 were completed by the offender and 50 by victims, representing response rates of 26 per cent and 19 per cent respectively. Only three questionnaires were returned for CONNECT.

In addition we sought to interview all victims and offenders who had taken part in restorative justice, and (for JRC only) all victims and offenders who had been allocated to a control group. An exception was REMEDI cases involving a young offender, where questionnaires were sent to both parties. Interviews usually took place some months after the restorative justice event and were conducted in a variety of locations by members of the research team or (for JRC cases only) trained interviewers from NFO System 3 Research (now TNS Research). For CONNECT, interviews were conducted with 4 offenders and 11 victims. For JRC, interviews were conducted with 152 offenders and 216 victims who took part in a conference, as well as 118 offenders and 166 victims in the control group. For REMEDI, 21 offenders and 23 victims were interviewed and questionnaires were completed by 3 offenders and 9 victims. Details of response rates can be found in Shapland *et al.* (2007).

Finally, reconviction data were obtained for offenders who took part in restorative justice and for control groups of offenders. For JRC, control groups were available due to the experimental (RCT) design utilised by the scheme; for CONNECT and REMEDI control groups were created by the research team by individually matching each case according to a number of relevant static variables (for further details see Shapland *et al.* 2008). It was possible to find matched controls for 47 of the 49 CONNECT offenders and all 81 REMEDI offenders.

A note about terminology

Throughout the book, we will use a number of terms which may be unfamiliar to readers or otherwise require clarification. Where we refer to a 'scheme', we mean one of the three organisations or partnerships which were awarded Home Office/Ministry of Justice funding to develop restorative justice under the CRP (i.e. CONNECT, JRC or REMEDI). In other words, a 'scheme' denotes a discrete 'managerial entity', which may be operational in more than one place or 'site'. Thus, when we refer to a 'site', we mean a geographical location in which a scheme was working. For example, JRC was a single scheme, but it operated in three sites: London, Northumbria and Thames Valley. A 'case' is what was treated by the scheme as one event. It might include more than one offender (for example, where several co-offenders committed an offence together) and more than one victim. A restorative justice 'event' describes a temporally defined mediation or conference attended by the lay participants (offender(s), victim(s), supporters of each as appropriate) and facilitated by one or more facilitators.

Where we use the term 'facilitator' we mean any person employed by any scheme to participate in a restorative justice event for an individual case as a neutral party, whether in the context of conferencing, or direct or indirect mediation. 'Facilitators' will thus be used to include those trained to conduct a variety of operational examples of restorative justice and, in the context of our schemes, include police, prison and probation staff seconded to work with schemes as well as professional mediators with no specific criminal justice training. The word 'facilitator' therefore includes all those working as 'mediators' in any case.

Finally, where statistical analyses were performed, we worked to the standard $p = 0.05$ level or less, so that a 'statistically significant difference' means that the likelihood of having obtained the result by chance is once in 20 times or less.

The layout of the book

The first section of the book focuses upon how previous schemes working with adult offenders have fared and the activities needed to set up and run restorative justice schemes. Chapter 2 considers the international development of major schemes which have sought to use restorative justice mediation or conferencing with adult offenders, together with the major schemes working with young offenders. Where these schemes have been subject to evaluation, the results of those evaluations are given, to set the scene for the discussion of the development of the three schemes we evaluated in England and Wales. Chapter 3 looks at how the three schemes started and what obstacles they faced in setting up or expanding within the context of the English criminal justice system and its multi-agency ethos. Chapter 4 turns to the key aspects of accountability and regulation which the schemes found to be important, now that adult offenders were the foci of restorative justice run in parallel with the adult criminal justice system. Often, evaluations have focused solely on outcomes of initiatives. The history of restorative justice initiatives, like that of other new initiatives in criminal justice, shows, however, that the way in which schemes set themselves up and deal with other parts of criminal justice are key to their success and their ability to acquire the right number of suitable cases. We hope that this chapter will not only aid those developing future schemes, but also point up aspects of scheme management and liaison which assume added importance when one is thinking in terms of working with adult offenders rather than young offenders.

The second section of the book considers the experiences of participants in the three schemes. Experiences and reactions are linked to expectations when agreeing to take part in restorative justice (and indeed all other forms of justice processes). We hence first consider in Chapter 5 how participants were approached, why they wanted to take part and what they thought would occur. Chapter 6 uses a single case study method to set out in some detail what happened in a number of cases undertaken by JRC.[10] Restorative justice schemes vary considerably in the details of the processes they adopt and the order of what happens during conferences. We think it is important that readers are able to see what kinds of issues were raised at what point and what then happened, in order to set the reactions of victims and offenders in context. No restorative justice case is 'typical', because each restorative justice event involves a unique set of participants. However, we have tried to illustrate a range of scenarios. Chapter 7 then uses both the quantitative and qualitative data we have for conferences and direct and indirect mediation to consider whether the main elements which theoretical approaches to restorative justice have proposed are occurring during these events.

The third section then looks back at the experience of restorative justice from the perspective of victims and offenders and at effects on reoffending and to what extent the schemes proved to be value for money. Chapter 8 considers victim reactions and the extent to which victims felt the process had affected them. Chapter 9 analyses the outcome agreements for restorative justice events which ended with the making of such an agreement and what then happened after the event. It also addresses the extent to which outcome agreements were followed up and were tied up with criminal justice decision making, and potential links with resettlement of offenders. Chapter 10 looks at the extent to which the aim of reducing reoffending was met, considering the likelihood of reoffending, its occurrence, its frequency, its severity and its cost. The cost of running the three schemes and the value for money they represented are then considered.

Finally, we look back in Chapter 11 at the three schemes and their experiences of running restorative justice for primarily adult offenders with serious offences. We consider the different theoretical justifications for restorative justice and see which might be considered to be met and whether the results show that restorative justice should be made more widely available for such cases and in what ways.

2 Setting the schemes in context: a review of the aims, histories and results of restorative justice

As we saw in Chapter 1, the theoretical development of restorative justice has followed a number of different, though connected, streams, each of which has emphasised somewhat different aims and objectives for restorative justice in practice. The aims for restorative justice initiatives should thus reflect the theoretical tradition of restorative justice from which the scheme itself has developed. They are also likely, however, to be influenced by the prevailing justice climate. Indeed, because participants in restorative justice events are key decision-makers as to what is raised during the event and what may be put in any outcome agreement, we have argued that the cultural views about justice of the participants – their 'justice values' – will necessarily shape what happens (Shapland *et al.* 2006b). Similarly, it is possible to argue that those who are setting up restorative justice schemes – and those who are funding them – will be influenced by the prevailing views about what justice should be achieving in that society at that time.

It is therefore no surprise that key themes relating to criminal justice surface within restorative justice schemes which deal with criminal offences as they are set up and run in practice. Recent criminal justice themes have included the importance of human rights; the idea of just deserts and of proportionality in sentencing (offenders should suffer that amount of punishment which is proportional to the severity of the offence and their part in it); and, for some societies, including the United Kingdom, populist punitiveness (Bottoms 1995) – the idea that politicians are increasingly referring to what they call 'public opinion' to justify or buttress their own views of the need for increasing punitiveness and, often, of treating offenders as different from the 'law-abiding citizen'. The latter two themes can be in tension with restorative justice values, which emphasise individualism in restorative event outcomes, inclusiveness in bringing people together to talk, and the idea that offenders, if they acknowledge wrongdoing, should be reintegrated as far as possible into the community. Most recently, there has been a major emphasis in European criminal justice to reduce reoffending, whether this be done by long prison sentences, cognitive behavioural programmes, teaching offenders skills so that they can find work or other rehabilitative or deterrent means. But this has been tempered for young offenders by the need also to consider the young person's development and the best interests of the child.[1]

The result of all these influences is that the aims of restorative justice schemes tend to vary widely, depending upon the theoretical stream they are following, the priorities of criminal justice at the time and their closeness (or not) to criminal justice. Assessing how effective schemes have been must mean assessing them in relation to their own aims. If, for example, one scheme has managed to reduce reoffending significantly, this is a benefit – but it is only an intended benefit if the scheme's aims included reducing reoffending.

The aims and achievements of restorative justice with adult offenders

It is helpful to consider the aims of those restorative justice schemes which have been subject to evaluation and to which we shall be referring later when we compare our own results with theirs. This also gives an idea of the context in which restorative justice has been developing, primarily for young offenders, but occasionally for adult offenders. As we said in Chapter 1, there are few evaluations of restorative justice with adult offenders, though schemes have occurred in the United States, Canada and New Zealand, as well as in England and Wales. The review below is in approximate chronological order.

The Brooklyn Dispute Resolution Center

An early pioneer of restorative justice for adult offenders was the Brooklyn Dispute Resolution Center in New York, evaluated by the Vera Institute of Justice (Davis *et al.* 1980). This was a diversionary programme designed to deal with disputes 'between persons who knew each other, which had erupted into criminal offenses for which arrests were made' (p. ii) through offering mediation or arbitration. It was hence dealing primarily with domestic violence or harassment, areas which have only rarely been seen as suitable for restorative justice more recently. Most offences were assault or burglary. Screening was done by the arresting officer, the prosecutor and scheme staff, with the victim, the offender and the judge needing at arraignment to agree to participation in restorative justice. About 10 per cent of all felony arrests with civilian complainants (30 per cent where complainant and offender knew each other) were allocated to the scheme (465 cases from four months in 1977). This was victim-offender mediation, with active participation by the mediator. Its aims were to secure a resolution of the underlying dispute, the satisfaction of both parties and a reduction in the recurrence of subsequent hostilities (Davis *et al.* 1980). The control sample (prosecuted) was randomly assigned after the screening process (259 cases to the restorative justice group and 209 to the control group).

In fact, it was clear that most cases would have been dismissed at court (only 28 per cent of control cases resulted in an actual prosecution). The mediation was completed in only 56 per cent of the assigned cases, with one or both disputants failing to turn up in most of the remainder. Outcome agreements were made in all cases completing mediation. Complainants who did complete mediation felt they had a greater opportunity to participate than if the case had been prosecuted, that the mediator was fairer, and that the outcome was fairer and more satisfactory (all statistically significant at $p < 0.05$ or less). Defendants felt similarly, but to a lesser extent (the results on the defendant feeling their story had been heard by the judge or mediator and that the outcome was fair were statistically significant). In the four months afterwards, complainants reported being significantly less angry at or fearful of defendants and were more likely to believe the defendant's behaviour had changed for the better. However, in terms of subsequent 'hostilities' over a four-month follow-up period, there was no difference between the restorative justice and control groups (reports of the same number of subsequent calls to the police etc.) and there was no difference in terms of the subsequent frequency of arrests of one party on the complaint of the other – though the number of arrests in both groups was very low (only 4 per cent in both groups).

The Leeds Mediation Service

Another early pilot of restorative justice with adult offenders was the Leeds Mediation Service (Wynne 1996; Marshall and Merry 1990). Initially, this was one of four schemes set up with Home Office funding, its aim being 'to test whether mediation/reparation was a valid way of working with high tariff offenders and whether it was possible to reduce the numbers of offenders in this group receiving custodial sentences' (Wynne 1996: 446). These are primarily offender-centred aims. Mediation was victim-offender direct mediation, taking place pre-sentence, with offenders being assessed on the 'genuineness of their remorse' and reports made to the judge before sentencing. Referral rates ran at about 9.5 per month, the highest level of the English schemes at this period. However, the aims of the various agencies involved were rather different.

Though the evaluation found that victims who took part in mediation were less punitive towards offenders and more likely to feel that they had obtained justice, there was little diversion away from custody (Marshall and Merry 1990). As a result, the funders lost interest, but Leeds Probation Service recognised the wider benefits and stepped in to fund the service, delivered at 'arm's length' from probation by paid community mediators. At the same time, the scope of the scheme was widened to include referrals from all sources, all stages of criminal justice and young offenders. With the widening of the scheme came a broadening of its aims, so that mediation was seen as 'a process of communication which allows victims to express their needs and feelings and offenders to accept and act on their responsibilities' (Wynne 1996). The process now involved contacting victims and offenders, in a process of indirect mediation, with direct mediation only following if both were willing and the offender acknowledged guilt. In its later years,[2] the majority of offenders were young offenders. Around 48 per cent of referrals resulted in mediation.

Miers *et al.* (2001) looked at reconviction data over the following two years and found that 44 per cent of those offenders with whom the scheme did some mediation work were reconvicted, which was significant compared to 56 per cent of those where the referral did not lead to an intervention (the most common reason being that the victim declined to participate). The results held when prior likelihood of reconviction (due to previous convictions etc. and measured using OGRS2, the nationally validated group likelihood of reconviction scale) was controlled, but mediation appeared to be most successful with those with the lowest risk of reconviction. There was also a statistically significant reduced frequency of reconviction over the two years, amounting to a decrease of 28 per cent in frequency of the mediation group compared to the convictions in the control group. There was also some evidence that reconviction for the mediation group was for less serious offences than that for the control group, seriousness being ranked according to maximum penalty available, but this was not significant.

The Coventry Reparation Scheme

Roberts and Umbreit (1996) report on a cross-national evaluation which involved both the Leeds Mediation and Reparation Service (described above) and the Coventry Reparation Scheme, another of the four original Home Office-funded projects (Marshall and Merry 1990; Miers *et al.* 2001). The aims of the scheme stressed communication through mediation, described as:

> a method of providing a framework within which a victim and offender can communicate with one another through the involvement of the mediator who has an equal concern for both parties … the primary aim … is to help both parties come to terms with the aftermath of the crime and discuss issues relating to it. In addition mediation can be a process used by victim and offender in order to reach a personal agreement as to how the offender might make some amends for the harm he has caused.
>
> (Marshall and Merry 1990: 60)

The scheme worked at various stages of criminal justice, but primarily pre-sentence at the magistrates' court with young adult offenders.

There were, however, differences between criminal justice agencies as to their priorities for the scheme:

> Expectations were varied – the government was looking for a new method of dealing with some offenders that could possibly achieve a punitive objective while also recompensing the victim in a practical way; the probation service's interest lay in reducing sentences, possibly providing an alternative to custody, and in offender learning; the mediation movement … was increasingly interested in mediation and reparation as a complete alternative to the formal justice system which had failed to resolve the personal nature of crime and its consequences for both parties.
>
> (Ruddick 1989: 96)

Achieving referrals from the courts was difficult, with the project staff needing to keep a visible presence constantly. As in Leeds in its later stages, most mediation was indirect, whereby information was conveyed between victim and offender by a mediator. Roberts and Umbreit (1996) found that victims and offenders who participated in mediation were more likely to be satisfied than those whose cases were referred but who did not experience mediation. Mediation victims were less fearful of being revictimised by the same offender, with victims who experienced direct mediation being even less fearful than those who experienced indirect mediation.

Roberts and Umbreit concluded that direct mediation victims benefited considerably more than victims who experienced indirect mediation, with direct mediation victims being 'more likely to feel they participated voluntarily, to express satisfaction with the justice system's response to their case, to be satisfied with the outcome of mediation, to be less fearful, and to indicate they experienced fairness in the justice system's response to their case'. However, only 16 per cent of the total cases involved in mediation were direct mediation. Comparing direct and indirect mediation, offenders' views were more mixed: direct mediation offenders were more likely to feel they participated voluntarily and to express satisfaction with the outcome, but indirect mediation offenders were more likely to express satisfaction and a perception of fairness in the justice system's response to their case. Roberts and Umbreit concluded that both schemes should encourage direct mediation, using a 'more assertive, encouraging and supportive approach to victims and offenders during the pre-mediation phase … while still respecting and honouring the importance of each party making an informed and voluntary choice'.

Miers *et al.* (2001) included the Coventry scheme in their assessment of seven restorative justice schemes which received funding from the Home Office in the late 1990s from its Crime Reduction Programme. At this point, the Coventry scheme was operating pre-sentence, primarily with young adult offenders. In the 1996/7 year, there were relatively few cases, with 166 cases being referred by judges or magistrates pre-sentence, but only five cases of direct mediation and eight of indirect mediation being completed.[3] Miers *et al.* say the main reason for the paucity of completed cases was lack of resources, with probation officers being instructed not to refer cases even if they were suitable for mediation. If an offender indicated willingness to meet the victim, this was included in pre-sentence reports as a mitigating factor and might lead to a reduction in sentence, seen by the scheme as an end in itself. We would comment that this seems to be a rather justice system-oriented and indeed offender-oriented practice, which overlooks the benefit a meeting might bring to both victim and offender and also offenders' potential negative reactions if no meeting was attempted. By 1998, Miers *et al.* say that the Scheme had 'all but ceased work' on mediation (p. 26).

The Probation West Midlands website indicates that its Victims Unit in Coventry in 2008 offers victim-offender mediation in cases where the offender has already been sentenced, and is also intending to pilot it at the magistrates' court in cases where sentenced is deferred.[4]

The Essex, Totton and Wolverhampton early schemes

In parallel with the Leeds and Coventry schemes described above, court-based schemes were also set up by Essex Probation Service, Hampshire Probation Service and a voluntary association in Wolverhampton (Marshall and Merry 1990). All were relatively poorly funded and had difficulty in obtaining referrals. Wolverhampton achieved around 5.8 referrals per month, Essex around 2.1 and Totton 1. As far as we are aware, the schemes are no longer in existence.

The Essex scheme had strong associations with Victim Support and stressed victim benefits from mediation, with the aims being:

- to allow victims of criminal offences to meet the offenders;
- to provide an opportunity for an offender to offer an apology for the offence;
- to enable the offender, if appropriate, to perform some task to remedy the wrong or make recompense for the loss.

(Marshall and Merry 1990: 70)

The Hampshire scheme at Totton was unusual in operating before a court hearing took place, through the supervising officer being granted access to charges and summonses which were to be heard at the magistrates' court. The difficulty was that it was not clear whether the offender would plead guilty. The scheme mostly operated at the low end of the tariff.

The Wolverhampton scheme worked primarily with the magistrates' court, though it also accepted referrals from the youth court (juvenile court) and Crown Court. Because of low referrals, project staff started to use lists of cases remanded for pre-sentence reports (social enquiry reports) to pick up cases. Its aims were communication between the parties and making amends: 'the provision of an opportunity for all parties involved in an incident to converse with each other with the assistance of a trained mediator who has a neutral stance in the operation ... The objective is ... to achieve some agreement upon common ground, usually for future conduct or payment of compensation, in an effort for the party at fault to make amends to the victim' (Marshall and Merry 1990: 73). Though reparation was initially an important element of the scheme, it was found that victims generally saw it as 'unimportant' and the emphasis changed to discussion and apology.

The evaluation undertook a number of interviews with victims and offenders, which produced evidence of considerable satisfaction with the scheme processes. It was not able to undertake reconviction analysis on sufficiently large samples to consider whether decreases were significant.

New Zealand court-referred pilots

New Zealand is very well known for its statutory youth conferencing, but it has also experimented with the use of restorative justice for other groups. In a pilot scheme which commenced in 2001, judges referred adult cases from four district courts in New Zealand, with the evaluation looking at all cases referred in one year from 4 February 2002 (Crime and Justice Research Centre, with Triggs, 2005). The offender had to have pleaded guilty, with victims being approached as to whether they would wish to participate after offender consent and judgment by the coordinator of the scheme that the case was suitable. Cases were primarily conferencing rather than mediation, with offender and victim supporters present. A report was provided to the judge prior to sentencing, with judges able to take into account or not the conference agreement, but also to adjourn cases until outcome agreements were completed.

The aims of the scheme were to:

- increase resolution of the effects of crime for victims who participate in restorative justice conferences;
- increase victim satisfaction with the criminal justice process; and
- reduce the rate of offending by offenders referred to restorative justice conferences compared with offenders dealt with through conventional criminal justice processes.

(Crime and Justice Research Centre, with Triggs, 2005: 18)

The results showed that almost all the victims interviewed said that their needs were met, at least partly, through the conference agreement. Both at initial interviews, shortly after the conference and at interviews 12 months later, most pilot victims were satisfied with the conference, the outcome agreement and the sentence given to the offender, but a fifth said that something had happened since the conference which made them regret taking part – normally failure to know what had been done by the offender about the outcome agreement or failure to pay reparation. About a third of pilot victims said that they felt more positively about the criminal justice system as a result of participating.

In a two-year follow-up reconviction study of 193 offenders, offenders' likelihood of reconviction and the seriousness of reconvictions were compared against predicted rates and against several control groups (the frequency of reconviction was not measured) (Triggs 2005). Judges were more likely to refer less serious cases to the pilot compared to the average of cases going through the district court (fewer previous convictions, more traffic offences). Participating offenders were slightly less likely to be reconvicted during the following two years, both against predicted rates and against control groups (at a level of 4 per cent decrease on a 45 per cent likelihood of reconviction), but this was not a statistically significant effect. There was no difference on seriousness of reoffending.

Maxwell and Morris (2001) report on an initial pilot of two community panel adult pre-trial schemes: Project Turnaround and *Te Whanau Awhina*. Project Turnaround operated in a town in South Island, from council/police premises in a shopping mall, using volunteers from the town to form the panel. Offenders were largely New Zealand European and were referred by the court to the proceedings, which deployed conferencing. If the referral was successful and the offender completed the agreed work, the police withdrew their evidence and the case did not proceed further. For *Te Whanau Awhina*, offenders were all Maori and panel members were *marae* members,[5] with one elder chairing the meeting. Victims were only rarely present, with the focus being on confronting offenders with the consequences of their offending for themselves, their victims, their family, their *whanau* (extended family) and the Maori community, followed by 'embrace' – reintegrating the offender back into the *whanau* and finding employment. Cases went back to court for sentence after the panel meeting and a regular court sentence could be imposed. For both schemes, most offences were property offences and appear to be of medium or low seriousness. The most common outcomes of the meetings for both were apologies or work in the community, as well as programmes being arranged for offenders.

The processes of the two schemes were therefore different. Their aims are not set out clearly, but both stress participation in the meetings, the importance of remorse on the part of offenders and the reintegration of the offender into the community. Offenders themselves mostly felt the meetings were positive, fair and that they had received support, but a minority interviewed about Project Turnaround felt it was negative – they were not listened to or they felt shamed by or worried about the large number of people present. Looking at reconviction after one year, participants in both projects were significantly less likely to have been reconvicted than matched control samples.

Restorative justice conferencing for adult offenders in New Zealand is now available at 30 District Courts and can also be done by the police as part of police diversion (Ministry of Justice 2007, 2008). The Sentencing, Parole and Victims Rights Act 2002 encourages its use and requires judges to take account of the outcome of restorative justice in sentencing.

The Restorative Resolutions Project in Winnipeg

The Restorative Resolutions Project was run by a voluntary sector agency, the John Howard Society of Manitoba, in Winnipeg and started in 1993 (Bonta *et al.* 1998). Its progress was evaluated in 1995, but very few offenders had been referred and many victims were reluctant to participate. Evaluation over a longer time scale, to 1997, allowed more detailed description of the programme's progress and of its effects on recidivism.

The project was designed to be a community-based alternative to imprisonment, with referrals from criminal justice agencies (corrections, attorneys, judges, family members and offenders). For referral, the prosecution had to be recommending a sentence of at least six months, the offender must have pleaded guilty and the offender needed to be motivated to meet the victim. Sexual assaults, domestic violence and drug/gang-related crime were excluded. The aims were to target appropriate offenders, arrange victim-offender meetings, provide an alternative to imprisonment and reduce recidivism. They were, hence, primarily offender-oriented goals, reflecting the aims of the Society itself.

There were considerable difficulties in acquiring a reasonable number of suitable referrals (94 out of 297 referrals had offenders not meeting the criteria). Of the 297 offenders, reoffending could only be looked at for 94, because only this number had made restorative plans which were accepted by the judge and had been at risk in the community for at least one year. However, these were overwhelmingly from the target group otherwise likely to be sent to prison – though 19 per cent received a custodial sentence in addition to the programme! Victims were both businesses and individuals and many were difficult to contact or did not wish to meet the offender: only 25 of the 243 victims met the offender, though 79 per cent provided victim impact statements and 24 per cent received written apologies from the offender. Restorative plans included restitution to victims but also counselling or treatment services for offenders.

Reoffending was measured by whether a new arrest led to a custodial sentence and also whether there had been new arrests over two years. Matched control groups were used. It was found that the offenders on the programme were significantly less likely to have received a prison sentence following rearrest than the prison control group ($p < 0.05$) and also to have been rearrested ($p < 0.05$). Compared to a group undertaking probation which included paying restitution or community work over 18 months the programme offenders showed a significantly lower likelihood of being rearrested ($p < 0.001$).

Restorative Resolutions is still running in Winnipeg as a community-based sentencing programme.

Victim-offender mediation projects with adult offenders in Canada

Victim-offender mediation (VOM) has become widespread throughout North America, though normally with young offenders. Umbreit *et al.* (2000) found 289 programmes operating in the United States, most of which were community-based, privately-funded programmes. Of these, 57 worked with adults, including nine which worked only with adults. However, schemes which responded to the researchers' questionnaire seemed to have very varied procedures, with a minority of programmes not requiring an admission of guilt by the offender, nor necessarily being voluntary for offenders.

Umbreit *et al.* (1995) evaluated two programmes working primarily with adult offenders in Canada, one in Ottawa (the Criminal Pretrial Mediation Program of the Dispute Resolution Centre for Ottawa-Carleton, which started in 1987) and one in Winnipeg (the Victim Offender Mediation Program of Mediation Services, Winnipeg, which started in 1979). The Winnipeg programme was one of the largest in Canada, with 2,647 referrals between 1991 and 1993. There were multiple aims for both programmes, as for VOM in general:

> Victims of criminal behavior have been able to play an active role in the justice process, to receive direct information about the incident, to express their concerns about the impact of the criminal behavior and to negotiate a mutually agreeable resolution to the event and any losses incurred.

> Individuals involved in criminal behavior have been able to gain a far better understanding of the real human impact of their actions, to 'own up' to their behavior, and to have the opportunity for making amends directly to the person they affected. Both parties can gain a greater sense of closure and the ability to move on with their lives.
>
> (Umbreit *et al.* 1995: 1)

In both programmes, no formal admission of guilt was necessary. Mediation involved a direct meeting between 'accused' and 'complainant', with referrals from the Crown (prosecution) post-charge or pre-trial.

Compared to referred cases which did not proceed to mediation used as controls, victims who received mediation were significantly more satisfied in both sites and offenders significantly more satisfied in Winnipeg.[6] In both sites, significantly more mediation victims also felt they had been treated fairly by the justice system, and in Winnipeg significantly more mediated offenders felt the same. Generally, both victims and offenders were satisfied with the procedure and outcome agreement, but a small minority of victims (11–13 per cent) and offenders (12–13 per cent) felt their participation was not entirely voluntary. Important elements (which showed significant differences between mediated and non-mediated cases) were:

- the victim receiving answers from the offender about what happened;
- the offender being able to tell the victim what happened;
- the victim telling the offender the impact the offence had on them;
- the victim receiving an apology;
- the offender being able to make an apology; and in Winnipeg
- the victim and offender being able to negotiate restitution with each other.

Fear of revictimisation by the same offender was significantly reduced for victims who experienced mediation compared to those who did not. Mediation victims were also significantly less likely to say they remained upset about the offence.

Mediation services are still running in Winnipeg on a community basis, dealing with many different kinds of conflict (Mediation Services Winnipeg). In Ottawa, the Collaborative Justice Project took over restorative justice pre-trial work with adults, but recently funding has only been provided to do restorative work with young people.[7]

RISE: The Canberra Reintegrative Shaming Experiments

The Canberra Reintegrative Shaming Experiments (RISE), which mostly involved young offenders (see below), included one trial with a substantial proportion of adult offenders. This was, however, for an offence which has, often, no identifiable direct victim: drunk-driving, and the restorative justice experiment was diversionary – offenders who took part were not prosecuted. RISE was police-led and organised conferencing, but was evaluated independently by Sherman *et al.* (1998, 2000). Their final report, which focuses on reoffending, indicates that:

> the aim of the study has been to compare the effects of standard court processing with the effects of a restorative justice intervention known as diversionary conferencing for four kinds of offences … The key criteria for comparing court processing to conferences are these: perceptions of procedural fairness by victims and offenders; victim satisfaction with the process; costs to the public purse; patterns of repeat offending … A central hypothesis is that there will be less repeat offending after a conference than after court.
>
> (Sherman *et al.* 2000: 4–5)[8]

Repeat offending, it was argued, would be reduced partly because conventional criminal justice, according to Braithwaite's (1989) theory of reintegrative shaming, stigmatises offenders and so makes it difficult for them to lead conformist lives as normal members of society. The 'shame and mobilisation of a community of care engendered by a restorative intervention like conferencing should provide an opportunity for offenders to confront the consequences of their actions and allow the harm caused by the offence to be repaired' (p. 5). Partly it might be because conventional criminal justice may make offenders more defiant (Sherman 1993). Partly it might be because of the greater procedural justice involved in restorative justice, following Tyler's work which indicates that people who feel fairly treated by the justice system may be more likely to comply with the law in future (Tyler 1990). Clearly, the multiple aims of RISE are buttressed by drawing upon several streams of restorative justice theory.

Overall, RISE found that both victims and offenders found conferences to be procedurally fairer than conventional criminal justice (court) (Sherman *et al.* 1999). However, there were no direct victims for the drunk-driving experiment, so no victim interviews were conducted. Interviews with offenders showed that offenders in conference cases were significantly more likely than those who went to court to feel ashamed because of being criticised by participants at the conference.[9] They also, however, were significantly more likely to know what was going on and what their rights were, that their treatment was fair overall, that their rights were respected, that the police were fair in their own case and that the police were fair generally. Other significant results were that offenders were more likely to say that if the police had the facts wrong, they felt they were able to correct this, that if they felt the police had treated them unfairly they were able to complain, and that they did not feel too intimidated to speak. All of these are measures of procedural fairness and justice. Offenders were more likely to say they felt they had the opportunity to express their point of view – and indeed that all sides were able to present their views, that account was taken of what they said and that they were not pushed around. They were less likely to feel the outcome was too severe and more likely to feel that restorative justice allowed them to repay society for what they had done. They were far more likely to understand what it was like for potential victims, yet be able to make up for what they had done, and felt they had been forgiven. They were far more likely to feel respect for the justice system.

However, comparing before–after offending rates over one year as measured by crimes detected by the police for the drunk-driving offenders receiving restorative conferencing with their randomly assigned controls, it was found that those receiving restorative justice *increased* their offending rates by a small, but not significant amount (in relation to all offences and in relation to drunk-driving offences: $p = 0.10$) – though this difference vanished past one year post-conferencing. The difference is ascribed by the authors to the lack of ability of these conferences, because they were diversionary, to impose periods of suspension of driving licences, compared to the incapacitative effect at court (Sherman *et al.* 2000). Unfortunately, time at risk (in terms of being able to drive legally) was not factored into the analyses of reoffending, which would have been helpful.

Scottish pilots with adult offenders

Restorative justice services are available in five of Scotland's 32 local authorities, run by SACRO, a voluntary organisation (Kearney *et al.* 2005). Most restorative justice is for cases of minor crime, in which the service is available as a diversion from prosecution, but there are rare cases of pre-sentence and post-sentence work. The service is part of the Scottish government's provision for local authorities to offer diversion from prosecution services. The aim is primarily to offer alternatives where prosecution would not be in the public interest, though mediation is also intended to offer accused persons the opportunity to make amends to the victim for their actions.

In 2005, 630 referrals for restorative justice as a diversion by prosecutors resulted in 29 face-to-face meetings and 162 cases of 'shuttle' or indirect mediation. Both parties were willing to participate in 40 per cent of cases. Most cases resulted in both parties agreeing that the issue was resolved between them, with no wish for further formal legal action (32 per cent), with financial reparation (26 per cent), non-harassment agreements (26 per cent) and apologies (13 per cent) being other significant outcomes. Direct reparation in the form of work was rare (2 per cent).

Between 2003 and 2007, a total of 3,184 diversion referrals were made which were accepted by the SACRO service, resulting in 1,172 cases where the parties agreed to participate (150 of these were face-to-face meetings) and 969 which reached a satisfactory outcome (Kirkwood 2010).

The small number of post-sentencing cases, called 'Talk after Serious Crime', were primarily initiated by victims or relatives of victims in homicide or serious assault cases, who had questions about the offence for which they wished answers from the offender. A long period of preparation was necessary before any meeting. Case studies indicate that victims found the session, particularly the face-to-face meeting, very helpful in resolving issues which had bothered them for a considerable time (Kearney *et al.* 2005).

The aims and achievements of restorative justice with young offenders

Restorative justice has mostly been tried with young offenders rather than adult offenders. The scope of schemes has been wide, with some offering mediation or conferencing to individual victims and offenders, which is the equivalent of the schemes we have been evaluating. Others have used community panels, such as the referral panels in England and Wales (Crawford and Burden 2005; Crawford and Newburn 2003), though victims may not often be invited to or attend such events. The major evaluations of restorative justice offered directly to young offenders and victims are the RISE experiments in Australia, Kathleen Daly's work also in Australia, the evaluation of statutory youth justice in New Zealand and the evaluation of statutory youth conferencing in Northern Ireland. Because restorative justice with young offenders has considerably affected its development with adult offenders, the aims and overall results of these evaluations are described below.

The growth of the use of restorative justice with young people, whether in relation to criminal justice processes or in schools and community programmes, has, however, been far more widespread than these discrete programmes would suggest. We are also relatively lacking in evaluations of mediation with young people as opposed to conferencing, even though mediation is probably the most widespread technique being used internationally.[10]

RISE: The Canberra Reintegrative Shaming Experiments

RISE had three experiments with young offenders: in relation to youth violence, to shop theft as apprehended by store security officers and to property crime with personal victims. However, the age range of the offenders in the violent crime group, because of the need to increase the sample covered, can hardly be described as youthful: the experiment included people aged up to 30 years; the mean age of the 44 offenders in the conference group was 18.0 and that of the 41 offenders in the court group 17.3.[11] The shop theft experiment also involved the legal victim being a commercial company rather than an individual, though those staff of the company who had contact with the offender, such as security officers, may of course have been made fearful or even assaulted in some instances. The aims of RISE are described above.

The results in terms of victim views on procedural fairness and in terms of victim satisfaction have been reported for the youth violence and youth property experiments (Strang *et al.* 1999; Strang 2002). For these experiments, victims in the conference group were significantly more likely than victims in the control group to:

- be notified in good time about the proceedings;
- have attended proceedings;
- feel less vengeful towards the offender (youth violence only: seen as reconciliation of victim and offender);
- have received an apology from the the offender as part of the justice process, and have thought the apology to be sincere;
- have received some form of restitution from the offender;
- have increased respect for the justice system (youth property only) and feel less bitter about the way they were treated by the system (youth violence only).

There was a significant interaction effect in relation to what happened at the conference itself: when offenders stated after the conference that they understood how the victim felt, or when others had indicated in the conference that the offender had learned their lesson, the victim was more likely to feel the apology was sincere (Strang 2002). Positive emotions were said to have been 'transferred' between offender and victim, with the potential for emotional restoration for both. This shows the importance of the interaction between offender and victim at the conference. Strang concludes that conferences were particularly good at enabling such restoration – but that it is a relatively risky encounter for victims. Though many victims whose cases went to court were relatively indifferent about what happened, victims who attended conferences tended to feel strongly about their experiences – mostly positively, but for a few rather negatively.

The results in relation to reoffending show declines in reoffending for offenders taking part in conferences rather than increases, though none are significant at the conventional $p < 0.05$ level. Looking at offences detected by the police and comparing one year before the offence to one year afterwards, there was a decrease in frequency for the youth violence conferencing cases, compared to the randomly assigned controls (about one offence per offender per two years in terms of all offences, a reduction of 38 per cent). In the shop theft apprehended by store security officers and in the youth property offences with direct victims, it appears there was no significant effect on reoffending.

Youth conferencing in New Zealand

Family group conferences were introduced in New Zealand in 1989 as the main statutory way of dealing with youth offenders whose cases had reached court and who admitted responsibility for the offence. As Morris and Maxwell (1998) comment, restorative justice was not referred to in the debates leading to the passage of the Children, Young Persons and Their Families Act 1989. The Act and the general climate of discussion at that point, however, indicates that the aims included 'healing the damage that has been caused by youthful offending, to involve those most affected by the offending in determining appropriate responses to it and to "makes things better" [*sic*] both for young people who have committed offenses and for their victims'. The involvement of families and, for Maori, extended families of *whanau*, *hapu* and *iwi* (those descended from common grandparents, clan and tribe) was stressed. Families were to be given responsibility to deal constructively with their children's offending, with the role of professionals being reduced, but the state was to take responsibility for providing appropriate services. Either at the police level or through referral by courts, the Act has resulted in around 20 per cent of all young offenders known to the police receiving family group conferences, approximately 5,000 conferences per year.

The results of the evaluation found that around half the young offenders did feel actively involved in the conference (but the other half felt decisions had been made about them, not with them). Almost all conferences had family members present, and more than two-thirds who were interviewed felt they had been involved in the process and in deciding the outcome. Victims attended about half the conferences (victim attendance was not compulsory) – operational practice difficulties being the reason why most of the others were not able to attend (not contacted, not given sufficient time etc.). About 60 per cent of victims felt the conference was helpful, positive and rewarding, but a quarter said they felt worse for attending the conference, mainly because they did not feel the offender was really sorry.

Overall satisfaction measures are quite difficult to interpret because they depend upon people's expectations, but 84 per cent of young people, 85 per cent of parents and 49 per cent of victims said they were satisfied with the outcome of the conference. Dissatisfaction from victims was sometimes expressed because it was felt that the outcome was too lenient or too severe, but more frequently it was because the service arrangements did not materialise or they were never informed about the eventual outcome.

Because this is a statutory measure, it is not possible to find a satisfactory control group against which to measure reoffending. Morris and Maxwell (1998), looking at reconviction in the 12 months after the conference, found that 26 per cent had been reconvicted, with the likelihood of reconviction not only depending upon standard elements (age, offence etc.) but being reduced if victims were satisfied and increased if offenders failed to apologise. Factors differentiating the persistent reoffenders from those not reoffending (i.e. including frequency as well as likelihood of offending) included victims not being present at the conference (which is correlated with apologies). Maxwell and Morris (2001) looked at reoffending over a longer period of some six years after the conference and divided offenders into five groups, from not reconvicted at all to persistently reconvicted. Based on retrospective interviews with participants, it was found that three conference-related factors helped to differentiate the groups: feeling shamed at the conference, not being remorseful and parents feeling shamed.

SAJJ: South Australian Juvenile Justice conferencing

Stemming from perceptions of an increase in juvenile offending, Australian states all considered different forms of restorative processes for young offenders in the early 1990s, most of them passing legislation to create these possibilities. New South Wales decided to use the police-led RISE model (see above), but other states mostly adopted a conferencing model not led by the police (Daly and Hayes, 2001). Different states' schemes have different aims, though many stress diversion from criminal justice. The South Australian scheme ran 1,500 to 1,700 conferences a year in 2000/1. Here, the young offender and the police need to agree to conferencing before there can be a referral.

The evaluators of SAJJ were interested more in what elements of restorative justice might lead to lower reoffending, or to higher satisfaction, rather than in whether restorative justice was more likely to lead to these results than conventional criminal justice without participation in restorative justice (Hayes and Daly 2003) – i.e. whether 'better' conferences lead to greater positive benefits for victims and offenders (Daly 2003a). Given the statutory nature of the scheme, this is not surprising.

They found that both victims and the young offenders agreed there were high levels of procedural justice in the conferences and the restorative justice process (fairness, being treated with respect etc.). However, levels of 'restorativeness' were lower, in terms of the extent to which victims could see offenders in a positive light and accept apologies, or offenders' capacities to feel sorry for what they did and to be affected by victims' accounts of the incident. About half the conferences were 'high' on such measures. 'High' conferences were associated with positive outcomes, such as changed offender attitudes towards victims, very strong positive evaluations of conferences, increased respect for the legal system and police and reduced levels of offending.

Daly (2003a) reminds us that in South Australia, conferencing is routine for young offenders, even for serious offences. 'Success' on these measures may not be a result of how well the conference is run, but of the extent to which offenders and victims come to conferences with various degrees of readiness to make the conference work and varying attitudes towards others and offending. Daly (2003b) found that young offenders in South Australia were often not sure of the conference process and what was expected – nor were victims. The consequence will be, we suggest, that both offenders and victims will need to adjust to each other very quickly. This may be particularly difficult for young offenders dealing with adult victims. The effect of making conferencing routine and the resulting high case load is that preparation may be skimped.

In terms of reoffending specifically, Hayes and Daly (2003) looked at whether there had been any new 'official incident' to which the police responded by arrest or apprehension after the date of the conference for the 107 young offenders in the SAJJ sample in 1999, with a post-conference window of 8 to 12 months – a measure of likelihood of reoffending rather than frequency of reoffending. In this time, 40 per cent of the sample had police contact for a new offence. Conference-related variables which predicted less such contact were where the young person was observed to be remorseful and where they participated in conferences in which outcomes were decided by genuine consensus – very similar results, as Hayes and Daly comment, to those in New Zealand.

Youth conferencing in Northern Ireland

Statutory youth conferencing in Northern Ireland was introduced in the Justice (Northern Ireland) Act 2002, following the recommendations of the Review of the Criminal Justice System in Northern Ireland (2000). If the offender agrees, prosecutors may refer cases to a youth conference, run by the Youth Conference Service, with no further action following if the conference outcome agreement is undertaken. Courts have to refer cases prior to sentence to a youth conference if the offender agrees.[12] The evaluation of the initiative concerned the very large pilot (the whole of Greater Belfast, Fermanagh and Tyrone).

The Justice (Northern Ireland) Act 2002 defines a youth conference as 'a meeting, or series of meetings, for considering how the child ought to be dealt with for the offence' (s.57). The youth conference coordinator (facilitator – a civil servant), the young person, a police officer and an appropriate adult must attend. The victim, the offender's lawyer and, if the young person is already subject to supervision, their supervising officer are entitled to attend. The idea is for the conference to decide upon a 'youth conference plan' (outcome agreement), which then goes to the prosecutor/sentencer. The sentencer may incorporate it into the sentence or treat it as the whole sentence.

The Explanatory Notes to the Act state:

> The aim of the youth conference will be to devise a youth conference plan which will propose how the child should be dealt with (new Article 3C). The purpose of a youth conference plan is to require the child to carry out specified actions in order to make reparation for the offence, address the child's offending behaviour, and/or meet the needs of the victim. The content of the plan is for the youth conference to decide, from the various options listed in new Article 3C(1), such as apologising, making reparation, or participating in activities designed to address offending behaviour, offer education or assist with rehabilitation.[13]

The aims, therefore, concern both offender and victim and, particularly, that the meeting should be forward-focused and produce a youth conference plan, which could be aimed at victim needs and/or rehabilitation of the offender.

By the end of the pilot Campbell *et al.* (2005) report there had been 362 referrals, of which three-quarters resulted in a conference occurring. Conferences were more likely to occur in diversionary referrals (90 per cent), than in court referrals (69 per cent), with much of the shortfall being due to offenders subsequently withdrawing their consent. A victim was present in 69 per cent of conferences, with 40 per cent being personal victims and 60 per cent victim representatives (corporate victim etc.). Given these were young offenders, an 'appropriate adult' (parent or social worker etc.) was always present, but most conferences had a second offender supporter present as well. Victims only rarely brought supporters and lawyers rarely attended.

At conferences, both offenders and victims felt they were able to participate and that they were listened to (98 per cent of young offenders, all victims). In 87 per cent of conferences the young person apologised or agreed to apologise. Young people were observed to display some level of shame (77 per cent) and remorse (92 per cent) in most conferences. Almost all (95 per cent) of conferences reached agreement on a plan: 74 per cent of offenders and 87 per cent of victims were 'happy to agree' to the plan. Both offenders (93 per cent) and most victims (79 per cent) believed the plan to be either 'very fair' or 'fair' (Campbell *et al.* 2005).

The youth conference plans studied in the pilot were very varied and individualised, most being developed during the conference through discussion and negotiation. They might include apologies, mentoring, attendance at behaviour programmes, education sessions, offers of reparation, or community service/donations to charity. All conference plans returned to the prosecutor were agreed, while 63 per cent of plans were accepted by the court as they were.

The original evaluation was not able to undertake reconviction analysis. Subsequent work has indicated that youth conferencing compares favourably with other court disposals when the characteristics of the offender and offence are taken into account, though, as with other statutory large-scale initiatives, it is difficult to secure an adequate control group (Lyness 2008).

At the end of the evaluation, youth conferencing was rolled out to the whole of Northern Ireland. Although the Criminal Justice Review Group recommended that conferencing might in the future be extended to young adults and to adult offenders, this has not yet taken place.

Key aims and results from previous studies

We have seen that restorative justice initiatives with both adults and young offenders tend to have a number of different aims and so need to use a variety of evaluation measures in order to evaluate the extent to which the initiative is fulfilling its aims. The aims tend to fall into the following categories (we have deliberately sought to avoid the terms 'process' and 'outcome' because they have been defined differently by theorists):

Procedural aims

- Participants should feel they have been adequately prepared and that their participation is voluntary.
- The process should be experienced by all participants as allowing them to participate and communicate well with each other.
- Outcome agreements, where sought, should be achieved with the consent of everyone present and should be seen as fair.

Effects aims

- Participants should feel they have gained from their participation in restorative justice. (Often this is expressed as victims obtaining answers to questions, offenders and victims finding closure.)
- Problems between victims and offenders should be, at least to some extent, resolved (healing, resolution of conflict, feeling less angry, vengeful or frightened, restoration).
- (For some schemes) victims should receive reparation/offenders should pay reparation.
- Offenders should be enabled to address problems related to their offending.
- Fewer offenders should reoffend after restorative justice/offenders should reoffend less after restorative justice/restorative justice should lead to cost savings for criminal justice.
- (For some schemes) cases should be diverted out of criminal justice/fewer offenders should receive severe sentences (i.e. criminal justice priorities of the time).

It is important to note that, though some of these aims can be achieved by participants themselves, others require active work by outsiders – for example, in the provision of programmes for offenders to address particular problems or criminal justice practitioners, such as sentencers or prosecutors, changing their discretionary decision-making. These elements are likely not to be under the direct control of restorative justice practitioners.[14]

Most evaluations have compared those who participated in restorative justice with those who were not offered it. Normally these control groups were those who went through the standard criminal justice process for that type of offender and offence – though clearly the nature of that process varied considerably between countries and types of offender. The exception is where restorative justice was the normal process for that group, often where it is statutory for young offenders. Here large numbers of people experienced restorative justice and restorative justice was seen by practitioners as 'normal', but there could be no adequate control group and so evaluators have looked at which parameters have produced more of the desired effects. They have considered, as Daly (2003a) has suggested, variability between restorative justice processes and the ways in which they are experienced.

Reviewing the evaluations, the effect is that those initiatives with good control groups often had relatively small numbers of participants and restorative justice was 'new' or unusual, while we do not have studies where restorative justice is 'normal' but there are good control groups. This makes it particularly difficult to judge the effect on, for example, reconviction (which is very difficult with low sample sizes), though it is easier to look at participants' views on how they were treated and how they saw restorative justice.

The descriptions of earlier schemes working with adult offenders, above, also show strongly how funding (and therefore funders' priorities) has affected the scope and lifetime of schemes. Once beyond the pilot stage, often accompanied by an evaluation, schemes tend to wither if not then supported and funded by local or central government. Schemes may try to diversify (which makes it difficult to continue to evaluate results), but, almost by definition, restorative justice is a service which needs to be offered to victims and offenders – neither of whom, typically, have many funds – rather than paid for by them. The contrast between the experiences of the Leeds scheme (dropped by the government when it did not divert offenders from custody because sentencers did not change their sentencing patterns; dropped by probation following funding cuts) and those in New Zealand (supported by central government and by cities) is clear. There is also a contrast between schemes for young offenders – often continued and rolled out, as part of rehabilitative policies or 'responsibilisation' policies (Garland 1996) – and those for adult offenders, where criminal justice system priorities to do with offenders seem key (changing sentencing or prosecutorial practice; reducing numbers of cases at court; reducing reoffending). Encouraging desistance or aiding victims does not seem to be a priority for many governments in adult cases.

One way of amalgamating the results from the very different studies described above is a meta-analysis. This is, however, quite restrictive, in the sense that it can only deal with results which can be expressed in quantitative terms and for which an effect size can be calculated. It cannot easily take account of more nuanced views from victims or offenders.

Latimer *et al.* (2001, 2005) considered measures of victim satisfaction, offender satisfaction, the extent to which victims were more likely to receive financial restitution and reoffending (Latimer *et al.* 2001, 2005). Reviewing 22 studies examining the effectiveness of 35 schemes running in the last 25 years, which included meetings between victim and offender and had a control group, it was found that all four elements were significantly more likely to occur for those experiencing restorative justice than the control group.[15] The programmes tended to be for young offenders (26 for young offenders, 9 for adults) and to feature mediation (27 were mediation, 8 conferencing). Neither age, mediation/conferencing nor stage of criminal justice affected the results. However, the authors, correctly, point out that restorative justice, because it is a voluntary process, is self-selective – offenders wish to take part in restorative justice, whereas those in control groups may not choose the sentence or treatment they receive. Hence results against matched control groups where both have not previously agreed to take part in restorative justice may be suspect. The only real way round this is to use random assignment after agreement – which has been adopted by only a very few studies.

Sherman and Strang (2007), in a recent meta-analysis, were also constrained by the paucity of studies which met their criteria of methodological rigour. They included only studies which met at least the requirements of level 3 of the Maryland scale (Sherman *et al.* 1997), i.e. that there should be at least two similar groups (the treatment/intervention group and the control group), only one of which receives the treatment/intervention. They used, however, a broad definition of restorative justice, which included restitution or reparation payments ordered by courts or referral panels, as well as conferencing, direct mediation and indirect mediation. If we restrict the studies to those which might be included within Marshall's (1999) definition (see Chapter 1), then the studies they included which involved adult offenders were the RISE work, the Leeds and Coventry studies, the Brooklyn Dispute Resolution Center, the Winnipeg work, the New Zealand adult study (all described above) and the work of the Justice Research Consortium reported in this book. They concluded that restorative justice with adult offenders has, among other things:

- substantially reduced repeat offending for some offenders, but not all;
- reduced crime victims' post-traumatic stress symptoms and related costs;
- provided both victims and offenders with more satisfaction with justice than criminal justice;
- reduced crime victims' desire for violent revenge against their offenders;
- reduced recidivism more than prison.

It is clear that an evaluation of restorative justice needs to pay attention to measuring the effects of the aims of the schemes which are providing the service – and that it is likely that schemes will have a number of different aims. We have also seen, from previous experience with restorative justice, that sometimes schemes emphasise the rehabilitation of offenders, sometimes victim needs and sometimes criminal justice system goals (such as diversion or changing sentencing). What then were the aims of the schemes we were evaluating?

The aims of the schemes being evaluated

All three schemes being evaluated had responded to tenders from the Home Office to run restorative justice, primarily for adult offenders, in parallel with criminal justice processes. However, it was left up to the schemes exactly which stages of criminal justice would be addressed, the precise relationship between the scheme and criminal justice agencies, and the extent to which restorative justice processes and outcomes would be conveyed to criminal justice practitioners to aid their decisions.

The Home Office tender emphasised the definition of restorative justice formulated by Tony Marshall (1999: 5): 'Restorative justice is a process whereby parties with a stake in a specific offence collectively resolve how to deal with the aftermath of the offence and its implications for the future.' This definition was taken on board by all three schemes (and the evaluators). In our analysis, it includes the concepts of:

- inclusiveness ('parties with a stake');
- offence, rather than problem behaviour related discourse ('a specific offence');

- communication between the parties;
- concern with the effects of the offence on all parties ('the aftermath of the offence');
- looking to the future and what will happen now ('implications for the future').

The Home Office set out two key aims:

- to reduce offending;
- to 'retain a significant focus on the needs and rights of victims' (p. 43), so 'better representing the interests of the parties involved than the conventional criminal justice process is thought to do'.

(Home Office 2001: 39)

These two aims were originally considered as equal in priority, so that the schemes and the evaluation should concentrate upon both offenders and victims. As criminal justice priorities changed in England and Wales over the period 2001–8, so the first aim of reducing offending (or, rather, reconvictions) became more dominant for the government – a trend which was made very apparent to the evaluators. However, we have retained both original aims as equally important throughout our evaluation. For the evaluation of randomised controlled trials, it is crucial to have consistency over the time span of the project. For other schemes, we felt that the original aims, which governed the ways in which the processes of the schemes were set up, must continue to be the aims of the evaluation.

The schemes themselves needed to interpret the aims and definitions in the light of the culture and priorities of the agencies within which they were based and the stages of criminal justice with which they would be working. Their aims and definitions seemed also to be affected by managers' and workers' own professional backgrounds and what they saw as important about restorative justice.

Hence, as with other previous schemes described above, the aims of the three schemes, whether written or expressed in practice, were several and there were some crucial differences between schemes. We looked at schemes' written reports and publicity materials for what they themselves said about their aims. We also conducted two sets of interviews with scheme managers and facilitators, once after the initial set-up phase and once at the end of our evaluation.[16] Each time, we gave each interviewee a list of ten possible aims (see Table 2.1) and asked them to say, first, which they thought applied to their own scheme and, secondly, which three they would see as most important. The two key aims, as defined by the funders, are of course A and D. Additionally, we interviewed managers from key agencies who worked with the schemes.

Table 2.1 The ten possible aims

A	Meeting the needs of victims
B	Securing reparation for victims
C	Reintegrating offenders into their communities
D	Preventing or reducing the risk of further offending
E	Repairing relationships/reducing the likelihood of future conflicts between victims and offenders
F	Increasing the participation of victims and offenders in working out what to do about the offence
G	Meeting the needs of offenders/dealing with offenders' problems
H	Involving/strengthening families
I	Involving/strengthening communities
J	Providing a fair and just response and outcome in relation to the offence

Justice Research Consortium

JRC's original proposal to the funders contained three aims for all three JRC sites (London, Northumbria and Thames Valley), the first aim emphasising the randomised controlled trials (RCTs) aspects of their work and specifically the need to conduct RCTs which aimed at high levels of consistency between sites, within RCTs and between RCTs, so that the Consortium's work as a whole could be considered as a prospective meta-analysis. Their other two aims, which were specific to restorative justice, were:

- reducing reoffending; and
- providing benefits to victims, more specifically an opportunity for participation, fair and respectful treatment, the right to be kept informed and material and emotional restoration.

Managers and facilitators in all three sites consistently detailed these elements. So, for example, at the end of the evaluation, three-quarters of JRC staff interviewed, when asked first about their understanding of the aims of the scheme, responded it was to do research or test restorative justice (e.g. 'to test whether restorative justice works in different stages of the criminal justice system …', 'to do good scientific high-quality research …', 'to complete the trial …', 'to test whether restorative justice has an impact on offenders' reoffending rates and victims' satisfaction' and 'to finish the project in time'). Other answers related to preventing reoffending and meeting victim needs. Agency personnel interviewed gave similar responses, though slightly less prominence was given to the research.

Though the two main aims for restorative justice itself (A and D in Table 2.1) were the dominant ones throughout and there was little disparity between different kinds of staff or between sites, some other aims were mentioned. These included, at the first interviews, 'increasing the participation of victims and offenders in working out what to do about the offence' (F: 71 per cent), 'repairing relationships/reducing the likelihood of future conflicts between victims and offenders' (E: 65 per cent) and 'reintegrating offenders into their communities' (C: 59 per cent). By the end of the evaluation, 'increasing the participation of victims and offenders in working out what to do about the offence' received even more support (from 91 per cent of respondents), with 'providing a fair and just response and outcome in relation to the offence' (J) now being supported by 89 per cent of respondents and 'repairing relationships/reducing the likelihood of future conflicts between victims and offenders' by 80 per cent. All of our ten aims (A to J above) received some support. The view that restorative justice provided a fair and just response to offending clearly gained adherents as staff and agencies gained experience with running the scheme, with respondents, by the end, wishing to add to the aims that reform of the criminal justice system was necessary.

Almost all respondents thought that everyone in the scheme had been working towards the same aims. Were they achieved? There was general agreement between facilitators, managers and agencies that victim needs and victim satisfaction had generally been met and that some progress had occurred in preventing reoffending. Community-linked aims were the ones most likely to be cited as not having occurred (when respondents thought that this was an important aim of restorative justice at all). So 'involving/strengthening communities' (I) and 'reintegrating offenders into their communities' (C) were both likely to be cited as not relevant or not achievable on the model of restorative justice JRC adopted.

The picture in relation to JRC was therefore that, throughout the project, the two main aims (A and D) were consistently cited as the most important, with the aim of researching restorative justice also dominant. However, many other aims were seen as relevant and, increasingly, the need to incorporate restorative justice into mainstream criminal justice became important to staff.

CONNECT

CONNECT originally envisaged itself working at one magistrates' court in London, primarily with deferred sentence cases. Its original aims were:

- reducing reoffending;
- enabling the victim to ask questions and receive information from the offender;
- enabling the victim to receive reparation and/or an apology from the offender;
- increasing a sense of responsibility by the offender for the offence; and
- leaving the victim and offender with a greater sense of satisfaction about the criminal justice process.

As we shall see in the next chapter, CONNECT found it necessary to expand both the geographical scope of its operations and also to work with cases pre-sentence at the magistrates' courts and referred post-sentence from Probation Victim Liaison units. Its original aims encompass the two main aims of the funders, but spell out in more detail how these might be achieved.

CONNECT had a relatively small number of staff. None the less, at the first interviews, all ten aims on our list were mentioned by one or more staff members, with the following receiving the greatest support: 'meeting the needs of victims', 'preventing or reducing the risk of further offending' (though people commented they could not directly know if they were achieving this), 'repairing relationships/reducing the likelihood of future conflicts between victims and offenders', 'meeting the needs of offenders/dealing with offenders' problems', and 'providing a fair and just response and outcome in relation to the offence'.

At the end of the evaluation, there were also varied responses. Both offender- and victim-related elements were mentioned by all respondents, but there was an overall feeling about the need to involve the criminal justice system with restorative justice – a consciousness that restorative justice both affects and is affected by society, perhaps as represented by the criminal justice system. It was no longer being viewed as relating solely to the individual offender and victim, even though their 'relationship' might often only be through the criminal justice system. Unlike the JRC interview responses, there was no mention of research as an aim of CONNECT. CONNECT staff generally thought meeting victim needs had been achieved, but there was no consensus between staff on where the scheme had been less successful.

Though respondents thought everyone was working towards the same aims, there was clearly a wider range of aims being attempted at CONNECT than at JRC. There was, though, a similar awareness of the connections of the scheme with what criminal justice was doing, even though there was considerable variation between the two schemes in terms of the 'parent' agencies (police for JRC London and Northumbria; probation for JRC Thames Valley; the voluntary sector for CONNECT) and staff professional backgrounds (police, probation, prison, social work).

REMEDI

REMEDI was the only scheme of the three to have been established prior to the evaluation. Though it had links with the probation service from its foundation, it developed to provide mediation services in Sheffield, later expanding, at the time of the evaluation, out into the whole of South Yorkshire, but having a major emphasis on work with young offenders and young people generally, as well as adult offenders. It had always been, therefore, rather more removed from the adult criminal justice system, working post-sentence with probation-referred cases rather than pre-sentence at court, like CONNECT and JRC in London and Northumbria.

REMEDI's aims reflected this more plural remit, with its proposal to the funders being:

> REMEDI aims to assist in restoring and rebuilding communities throughout South Yorkshire by providing access for all offenders of crime and their victims in the area, and those who work with them, to a high quality, free and confidential mediation service. Such a service will provide a direct and constructive response to the effects of crime by enabling victims to express their needs and feelings and offenders to take responsibility for their actions. It provides a forum to discuss how to put right the effects of the offence, where possible, and aims to assist victims in recovering from the effects of crime and to help reintegrate offenders into the community. REMEDI believes that mediation may have a role to play, along with other interventions, in supporting offenders to cease or reduce their offending behaviour.

It is not surprising, therefore, that staff and agencies mentioned all the ten aims (A to J) as applicable to REMEDI at both sets of interviews. Though the two main aims of the funders, to meet victim needs and to prevent reoffending, were supported, there was far less emphasis on preventing reoffending at REMEDI than at the other two schemes, with it being seen as a desirable byproduct of what REMEDI was doing, rather than as a direct aim in itself. At the first interview, there was agreement on the main three aims from the list, which were: 'repairing relationships/reducing the likelihood of future conflicts between victims and offenders' (E); 'increasing the participation of victims and offenders in working out what to do about the offence' (F); and 'providing a fair and just response and outcome in relation to the offence' (J). At the second interview, the main aims supported were 'preventing or reducing the risk of further offending' (D); 'involving/strengthening communities' (I); 'meeting the needs of offenders/dealing with offenders' problems' (G) and 'involving/strengthening families' (H).

Though most staff felt everyone was working towards the same aims, some did not and there was continuing discussion in management meetings about where REMEDI's main focus should be. This reflected the need for REMEDI continually to raise funds to support its work and allow it to continue to take place throughout South Yorkshire – and the funds' differing priorities and target populations. Respondents were not always sure whether all the aims they mentioned had been achieved.

This plurality of aims reflects the different strands of REMEDI's work, not all of which were included in our evaluation. Few REMEDI staff had a criminal justice system background. As REMEDI's work developed over the three years of the evaluation, more funding came from youth work and local authorities/bids to community development sources. Much work was with young people and community or locality based. This is clearly reflected in staff priorities and aims. No REMEDI staff mentioned research as an aim for their work. We can see that, for REMEDI, restorative justice had a place not only in the lives of the individuals affected by the specific offences being dealt with, but also in the life of the wider local community, in working with other agencies, in the working of the courts and criminal justice system and in a changed cultural view of criminal justice, as well as in the moral and emotional education of people. In terms of restorative justice theoretical strands, REMEDI staff tended to focus upon reducing conflict and the effects of conflict between offenders and victims (through mediation), rather than on addressing offenders' offending-related problems.

Different aims, different goals for evaluation

JRC and CONNECT were strongly embedded in criminal justice, in most cases literally so. Some JRC offices were within or adjacent to police stations or in probation premises; CONNECT's offices were next to Victim Support. REMEDI's offices were either separate premises or within Youth Offending Team (YOT) offices. They saw themselves as providing a service to criminal justice, rather than being part of a criminal justice process (whereby, ideally, mainstream criminal justice would often encompass restorative justice).

The funders' aims were strongly crime-focused: to reduce reoffending – an aim which became more dominant over the course of the evaluation – and to meet victim needs (with the aim being to improve victim satisfaction and views of criminal justice). All three schemes contained a similar balance of aims to work with and meet needs of both victims and offenders and staff all supported this balance: no scheme seemed more offender- or victim-focused than any other; no scheme was biased towards one party. The trap which we would argue some previous restorative justice work has fallen into – to concentrate upon one party to the detriment of the other – and which has plagued youth restorative justice in England and Wales, did not apply to these schemes. Nor did the government's increasing emphasis (up to 2008) on reducing offending mean that schemes altered their priorities or their processes to the detriment of victim work.

None the less, the schemes did not all have the same emphasis on meeting crime reduction or system goals. JRC was highly focused on reducing reoffending, but definitely not at the expense of ignoring victim needs. CONNECT wanted to provide a more just criminal justice response. But REMEDI primarily wanted to work to reduce any continuing conflict between the two parties and help to reduce continuing effects of the offence, rather than to benefit the criminal justice system or society generally. We shall see, over the following chapters, the effects of these different aims and goals play out in the models of restorative justice they adopted, which worked through to the effects they had.

In terms of aims, JRC was very focused on research needs. Practitioners, though not as enamoured by the data and findings as research staff or evaluators, saw the need to keep records, meet quantitative targets and be accountable. CONNECT also saw accountability to the court as vital, but in relation to individual cases. Record keeping was more of a chore. REMEDI found developing systems for data capture and monitoring quite difficult, though the imperatives of the competitive bidding culture for funds for the voluntary sector made their administrators keen to have a system which provided good management information (though less detail on individual cases). Again, the priorities and aims affected the systems adopted and practitioners' day-to-day willingness to engage in monitoring.

3 Setting up and running restorative justice schemes

Evaluations of restorative justice have, naturally enough, tended to concentrate upon its effects and whether they match the aims of the schemes. For practitioners envisaging setting up new schemes or expanding existing ones, however, it is also important to know how the schemes were set up, what difficulties they faced and how they overcame them. The purpose of this chapter is to focus on the running of the three schemes we evaluated, to describe their experiences and to set out the challenges faced by their managers.

The lack of transparency in many published evaluations about setting up and running schemes is surprising, given that it is impossible for effects to happen and be measured unless sufficient people agree they wish to participate and unless restorative justice is delivered well and consistently over the period of the evaluation. Both those elements occurred in the three schemes we evaluated. But it is rare for this to happen: the history of restorative justice schemes worldwide is one of relatively low and often insufficient case flow. This was true in Miers *et al.*'s (2001) evaluation of youth and adult restorative justice in England and Wales, despite special resources being made available for piloting restorative justice there. It has even been true where restorative justice is statutory: Wozniakowska (2006) found that referral by judges to mediation in Poland was patchy and relatively scanty – and very dependent upon the views of individual members of the judiciary. Nergård (1993) found that in Norway rates of referral to the statutory Conflict Resolution Boards for diversionary mediation with young offenders were often low, with sometimes considerable delays before referral by the police to the Board (while Boards dealt with cases within two to three weeks). Whenever restorative justice has been linked with criminal justice, it has been found that the link can be problematic, with the priorities of referral to restorative justice tending not to be the key priorities of criminal justice practitioners and so forth.

This is not just the experience of restorative justice schemes. Problems in setting up new schemes related to criminal justice have been found whenever change has been desired in England and Wales – and in most other countries. Criminal justice, by its nature and remit, tends to be relatively slow changing and its processes tend to be conservative – so that citizens can know what the consequences are of breaking the criminal law. If one adds the workload of many criminal justice practitioners in their daily lives of processing routine cases (Sudnow 1964; Shapland 2003) to the work involved in creating protocols between agencies for multi-agency work (Shapland *et al.* 2006a), it is unsurprising, though sad, that it is very difficult for anything new to be created. If restorative justice is dependent upon project-based, fixed-term funding, or upon voluntary sector workers on insecure contracts, then the yearly ritual of bidding for funds, the competitive bidding culture and the uncertainty of future work also militate against consistency of delivery and a secure quality service (Vincent-Jones 1997). Miers *et al.* (2001: ix) comment: 'The schemes were also fragile, being vulnerable to funding cuts, and were often dependent on work "beyond the call of duty" by small numbers of exceptionally committed individuals.' We noted in the last chapter that changing funding priorities, where restorative justice is not part of a core criminal justice service, also mean a potentially changing service.

It was a considerable struggle for the three schemes we evaluated to set up the scheme, remain visible to criminal justice practitioners and develop a sufficient case flow. In this chapter we describe the solutions they found and the ways in which they needed to work to accomplish this. We hope they will prove useful for others who are faced with similar challenges.

Setting up the schemes

Two of the three schemes, JRC and CONNECT, were set up especially to take advantage of the funding provided by the Home Office under its Crime Reduction Programme. REMEDI used the funding to undertake a major expansion, opening offices throughout South Yorkshire. As is often the case with tendered projects, deadlines were relatively short: all the schemes had only a few months to respond to the tender and, when their bid was accepted, needed to start as soon as possible. Key initial tasks for all three schemes were therefore both internal (appointing staff, locating and renting offices, finding and equipping spaces in which to hold restorative justice events) and external (negotiating with key potential partners for referrals and information relevant to referred cases, meeting with funders re reporting, etc.).

Key initial appointments were a manager to coordinate the scheme on that site and, slightly later, an administrator to set up the office and systems and to help to produce publicity and answer queries. Managers were almost all previous or current criminal justice practitioners (from the police, from probation or from Victim Support). We think this was essential to help schemes to navigate the rather complex criminal justice system and also to provide credibility for the new scheme. The use of a full-time coordinator has been found by many criminal justice projects to be vital, even if other staff are part-time or volunteers – whether the project was an initiative in crime prevention, youth justice, victim support or rehabilitation (see, for example, Maguire and Corbett 1987; Crawford 1998).

All sites required a full-time administrator to keep track of cases, answer queries, undertake the monitoring tasks and run the office. In relation to employing staff and finance, those schemes which were part of statutory criminal justice agencies (police, probation) found it easier because they could utilise key administrative services provided by their host organisation (finance, human resources, ordering equipment, contracts with utilities and office suppliers), while voluntary sector agencies had to do everything themselves. Given the pressure to be operational quickly, this was important. However, there is no doubt that the demands of running restorative justice schemes posed some challenges for statutory processes and procedures, for example in relation to leasing suitable independent premises on the commercial market or providing financial data in suitable ways for undertaking cost-benefit analysis.

Though it was not clear that this was always a conscious process, most sites tried to acquire premises which were independent of statutory criminal justice agencies and so would not have possible negative connotations for either offenders or victims. They were all determined to be both inclusive and to appear neutral. JRC in London, for example, rented premises which were either renovated offices or in a separate building from a police station (even if it was once part of the same station). JRC in Thames Valley used probation-owned premises which were some way away from probation headquarters. CONNECT rented office space next to, but separate from, Victim Support in a building which housed several different projects. REMEDI offices were in various buildings, but only one was clearly in a building marked as part of a statutory body (the Youth Offending Team). Only in JRC Northumbria were the offices within operational police stations, primarily because the original intention of using just two police stations and two teams of facilitators had to be expanded to include eventually six urban areas, while funding did not allow for renting sufficient conference space everywhere to be independent.

Facilitators were all appointed a few months after the manager and administrator. All except REMEDI employed only paid facilitators/mediators: REMEDI used a mixture of paid mediators and volunteer mediators (the latter working in pairs). JRC Thames Valley, because of uncertainties about case flow and the geographical distances involved, employed a number of part-time, paid, community mediators to cope with any peaks in referrals, as well as using seconded probation officers, Victim Support workers and prison officers (the latter part-time). Teams tended to be relatively small. JRC, for example, had about four facilitators in each office (two offices in London, two in Northumbria, one in Thames Valley). REMEDI tended to operate with only two paid staff in each office. CONNECT had only two or three mediators as well as the manager and administrator.

Small teams promoted good team spirit and learning from each other. However, with just three people capable of undertaking mediation, CONNECT found there were difficulties in keeping up with case flow if staff left or were on holiday. The other schemes could, if necessary, bring in staff from other offices or use temporary secondments if major administrative tasks arose (keeping up with data entry to administrative systems, follow-up calls, letters, reports to courts, etc.). All schemes were, however, punctilious that only fully trained facilitators/mediators would be used in face-to-face work with participants or at restorative justice events. We would suggest that having a manager, administrator and three to five facilitators per office is probably optimal.

Restorative justice was to be delivered in parallel with criminal justice processes but was not a normal or statutory process in those areas. The schemes were hence creating something new and something which was outside the experience and knowledge of both potential participants and criminal justice practitioners and the sentencers. Considerable work, therefore, had to be put into inform criminal justice practitioners and sentencers about the scheme and in designing and producing material for potential participants. It is important for schemes to plan for a start-up phase in which facilitators are trained, details of the schemes are worked out and publicity materials prepared before moving to the higher, desired 'constant flow' rate of undertaking cases. Working out the right case flow is important before 'going live': both taking too many cases (with consequent delays in processing) and receiving too few cases can cause difficulties in terms of disappointed expectations of facilitators and partner agencies.

Environmental scanning and the numbers of cases involved

The initial plans of all three schemes proved, in practice, to be far too optimistic in terms of the numbers of cases they anticipated (Shapland *et al.* 2004a, 2006a). All three schemes had to expand the geographical areas they covered in order to attract sufficient cases. This need for 'enough cases' was partly due to research and evaluation demands: it is not possible to find out whether restorative justice meets victim needs or reduces reoffending if one is examining only a few cases. It was also, however, due to the wish to look at what it might be like to offer restorative justice as a mainstream option for adult offenders and how cost-effective this might be. In this evaluation, the practical aspects of running restorative justice were as important as its outcomes.

The initial experience of 'too few cases' is not one confined to these three schemes. As we described in Chapter 2, many restorative justice schemes have found the same – as have other innovative approaches in criminal justice. Limited case flow was found to be a problem for the evaluation of the dedicated drugs courts in England and Wales[1] (Matrix Knowledge Group 2008) and for programme evaluations of cognitive behavioural interventions in penal settings (Harper and Chitty 2005).

The key difficulty was not the case flow itself – it is clear that the three schemes were pulling in almost all suitable cases – but the surprise about the potential case flow. Essentially, new initiatives in criminal justice and the authorities setting them up tend to be poor at 'environmental scanning' – looking at how many suitable cases there might be for a given geographical area/stage of criminal justice as a routine part of planning and *before* the scheme is set up.

Suitable cases for restorative justice require, at a minimum, that there be an identifiable victim (and so, for example, will not include drugs offences). All three schemes wished to take only offences which involved an individual victim rather than a corporate victim (so not simple shop theft or credit card fraud). It was also necessary that the offender admitted the offence and that they were prepared to take responsibility for the offence. In terms of adult offenders in England and Wales, this means that the offender has pleaded guilty.[2] These three schemes also did not wish to include spousal abuse, child abuse or sexual offences,[3] though they did deal with cases where people knew each other, including as members of an extended family.

These necessary constraints mean that not all cases in which the offender has been convicted of a particular offence within the scheme's remit are suitable for restorative justice. The difficulty was that official statistics (in this case the annual *Criminal Statistics* published by the Ministry of Justice) do not indicate the type of victim nor whether there was a guilty plea. Estimates should have been made of all these factors before the schemes and evaluation started.[4] Unfortunately, that did not happen. The result was that schemes, quite soon after having acquired offices and recruited staff, needed to expand the geographical extent of their operations considerably.

The experience of JRC in London

JRC in London initially started in two police districts, looking at magistrates' court cases and youth court cases of assault, street crime and burglary (Shapland *et al*. 2004a). However, it became apparent that these areas would never produce sufficient cases at the magistrates' court and that running the pilot for youth cases, at a time when Youth Offending Teams were themselves setting up restorative measures for youth offending, would be confusing. Within four months, therefore, and with the support of the senior judiciary, JRC London changed radically, to take cases from the Crown Court, and undertake two RCTs – for burglary and street crime (robbery and theft from the person). It subsequently expanded the geographical areas involved so that, by the end of the period during which cases were taken for the evaluation, in 2004, all the Crown Court centres in Greater London were participating. Even so, it still proved difficult to attain the number of cases required for street crime and this RCT was granted a time extension by the Home Office to March 2004. In London, JRC accepted only cases where there was one offender, because the police were concerned that, should there be more than one offender and co-offenders were not caught or tried at the same time, then restorative justice conferences might imperil the trial of subsequent offenders.

JRC had always envisaged running a substantial pilot phase to train facilitators and make sure all the necessary protocols with the different courts and prisons involved were running smoothly before proceeding to random assignment. This was definitely a wise move. In fact 213 cases were referred during this initial phase ('Phase 1'). Facilitators started taking cases in the third quarter of 2001

(Shapland *et al.* 2004a) and random assignment (called 'Phase 2') commenced in summer 2002 at all JRC sites (Shapland *et al.* 2006a).

By the end of the evaluation period on 1 April 2004 and during the randomised phase, JRC London had dealt with 457 burglary offenders and 305 street crime offenders, and randomised 186 burglary cases and 106 street crime cases, in which both victim and offender had agreed to participate (Table 3.1[5]). This produced 98 burglary cases and 53 street crime cases in the restorative justice (experimental) group.[6]

JRC in Northumbria

The intention in Northumbria, where JRC was working with Northumbria Police, was to concentrate upon less serious cases. Initially there were plans for many different trials (Shapland *et al.* 2004a), but these coalesced, after the first few months of the setting-up phase, into a smaller number of trials: adult offenders charged with property and violent offences with individual victims being heard at the magistrates' court; adult offenders diverted from prosecution through being given a police caution; and young offenders diverted from prosecution being given a final warning. The adult magistrates' court cases were intended to be referred by the Probation Service, with all guilty plea cases which were not being remanded in custody prior to sentence being referred. Cautions and final warnings are administered by the police and it is a police decision whether the person will be charged (and go to court) or be diverted from prosecution – though the Crown Prosecution Service can recommend that a caution be considered. Both are formal processes, which require an admission of guilt from the offender and which are on the offender's police record, though they do not constitute an official criminal record. A final warning is intended for not very serious offences where the young offender has not previously been prosecuted but may have received a previous diversionary measure. It is accompanied by referral to the Youth Offending Team (YOT), who would normally provide a programme of activities designed to tackle the offending behaviour. In this instance, the YOT agreed to allow the JRC conference to constitute one element or the whole of the programme. For both cautions and final warnings, once the offender has been told officially by the police that he or she has been given the diversionary measure, the offender cannot be compelled to undertake a conference or any other activities.

Initially, JRC started with two teams of facilitators working on all three types of referral but at a small number of police stations/courts. As in London, however, the case flow proved to be smaller than expected and the scheme spread in geographical extent to more police stations and magistrates' courts in Northumberland. Youth final warnings proved in the end to be quite numerous, with 518 offenders being referred during the randomisation phase and up to 1 December 2003, resulting in 187 offenders being randomly assigned (Table 3.1) and 82 cases being in the restorative justice (experimental) group. There could be more than one offender per case in Northumbria.

Table 3.1 Attrition figures and resulting cases receiving restorative justice for JRC, CONNECT and REMEDI (number and percentage in brackets)

	JRC London		*JRC Northumbria*			*JRC Thames Valley*		*CONNECT*	*REMEDI*	
	Burglary	*Street crime*	*Court*	*Final warning*	*Adult caution*	*Community*	*Prison*		*Adult*	*Youth*
Total *offenders* referred to 1 December 2003	457 (100%)	305 (100%)	385 (100%)	518 (100%)	332 (100%)	568 (100%)	740 (100%)	146 (100%)	818 (100%)	426 (100%)
Out of scope of scheme	17 (4%)	14 (5%)	9 (2%)	21 (4%)	2 (1%)	131 (23%)	88 (12%)	3 (2%)	111 (14%)	5 (1%)
Unsuitable cases	60 (13%)	55 (18%)	43 (11%)	63 (12%)	42 (13%)	166 (29%)	86 (12%)	14 (10%)	261 (32%)	68 (16%)
Total suitable offenders	380 (83%)	236 (77%)	333 (86%)	434 (84%)	288 (87%)	271 (48%)	566 (76%)	129 (88%)	446 (55%)	353 (83%)
Hence cases to be approached	380 (100%)	236 (100%)	333 (100%)	434 (100%)	288 (100%)	271 (100%)	566 (100%)	129 (100%)	446 (100%)	353 (100%)
Offender uncontactable	23 (6%)	12 (5%)	69 (21%)	32 (7%)	3 (1%)	11 (4%)	0 (0%)	13 (10%)	69 (15%)	23 (7%)
Offender refuses	84 (22%)	37 (16%)	90 (27%)	136 (31%)	148 (51%)	88 (33%)	191 (34%)	22 (17%)	169 (38%)	112 (32%)
Victim uncontactable	15 (4%)	20 (8%)	10 (3%)	12 (3%)	4 (1%)	19 (7%)	84 (15%)	20 (16%)	37 (8%)	25 (7%)
Victim refuses	100 (26%)	75 (32%)	81 (24%)	64 (15%)	82 (29%)	97 (36%)	186 (33 %)	16 (12%)	106 (24%)	29 (8%)
Case finishes for other reason	5 (1%)	0 (0%)	0 (0%)	3 (1%)	6 (2%)	2 (1%)	3 (1%)	8 (6%)	7 (2%)	90 (25%)
Offenders randomly assigned/offenders for RJ	158 (42%)	92 (39%)	83 (25%)	187 (43%)	45 (16%)	54 (20%)	102 (18%)	50 (39%)	58 (13%)	74 (21%)
Major running phase: number of *cases*	186 (100%)	106 (100%)	105 (100%)	165 (100%)	45 (100%)	63 (100%)	103 (100%)	50 (100%)	58 (100%)	74 (100%)
Case placed in control group	88 (47%)	53 (50%)	52 (50%)	83 (50%)	–	33 (52%)	51 (50%)	–	–	–
Case proceeds to restorative justice	98 (100%)	53 (100%)	53 (100%)	82 (100%)	45 (100%)	30 (100%)	52 (100%)	50 (100%)	58 (100%)	74 (100%)
Offender drops out post-randomisation	2 (2%)	0 (0%)	3 (6%)	1 (1%)	0 (0%)	2 (7%)	5 (10%)	–	–	–
Victim–offender conference held	80 (82%)	45 (85%)	41 (77%)	75 (91%)	45 (100%)	26 (87%)	38 (73%)	2 (4%)	–	–
Victim drops out post-randomisation	11 (11%)	7 (13%)	4 (8%)	5 (6%)	–	1 (3%)	7 (13%)	–	–	–
Restorative justice event takes place*	92 (94%)	53 (100%)	47 (89%)	80 (98%)	45 (100%)	27 (90%)	43 (83%)	50 (100%)	58 (100%)	74 (100%)
Of which indirect mediation	–	–	–	–	–	–	–	37 (74%)	44 (76%)	53 (72%)
Of which direct mediation	–	–	–	–	–	–	–	11 (22%)	14 (24%)	21 (28%)

Notes: Unit is offenders for top half of table, cases for bottom half (in JRC London, CONNECT and REMEDI the case unit is also the offender unit).
*Restorative justice events include victim absent conferences
Source: Table compiled from data for Shapland *et al.* (2006a: Tables 3.1 and 3.2). Major running phase period is to randomisation by 1 April 2004 for JRC cases (except adult cautions), referral by 1 April 2003 for CONNECT and REMEDI and referral by 1 December 2003 for JRC adult cautions.

It was far more difficult to obtain sufficient case flow at the magistrates' court. Partly this was due to insufficient non-custodial cases with individual victims and guilty pleas existing at those courts.[7] Partly it was due to magistrates deciding to sentence people immediately rather than adjourning the case for probation reports (and the potential to be considered for restorative justice). Magistrates felt under pressure to dispose of cases quickly – as indeed they were being enjoined to do by national guidance on reducing delays at court. Despite considerable advice from the government department, and indeed ministers, that in this instance it would be helpful to adjourn relevant cases rather than sentence immediately, there was resistance to this course.[8] Eventually, however, 385 cases were referred during the randomisation phase up to 1 December 2003. Some 105 cases were randomised with offenders and victims agreeing to take part, and 53 were in the restorative justice group (Table 3.1).

The adult caution trial, though entirely under the control of the police, did not fare so well in terms of cases. It was concerned with offences of violence which had an individual victim (common assault and assault occasioning actual bodily harm). However, the ratio of such cases with an adult offender which were considered to be suitable for diversion from prosecution was very small.[9] As can be seen from Table 3.1, there was also a very high rate of offenders subsequently refusing to participate in restorative justice. This may have been because the caution had to be given first, with then no compulsion on the offender to participate in restorative justice. The flow rate was so weak that it was decided that it was not possible to move to randomisation after the initial phase and so this trial was never randomised. Though it continued, fewer resources tended to be devoted to it, given the pressure on the adult court trial. Overall, taking into account both the set-up phase and subsequent cases, 332 cases were referred, but this led to just 45 cases in which restorative justice was delivered (Table 3.1). We did observe conferences and interview some victims and offenders from adult caution cases, but it is not possible to provide reoffending results because there was no control group.

JRC in Thames Valley

JRC Thames Valley had always intended to run two trials from its probation base. One was for offenders sentenced to a community penalty for violent offences (the 'community' trial), who would be assessed for restorative justice prior to sentence, but the conference and any activity stemming from the outcome agreement would take place during the sentence. Attending the conference would be a mandatory part of the sentence. The second trial involved prisoners in Thames Valley prisons convicted of serious offences of violence (the 'prison' trial), who would be assessed and the restorative justice carried out during the 12 months before their predicted date of release from prison.

The community trial started in parts of Oxfordshire near the scheme's office. Case flow depended upon individual probation officers remembering to notify the scheme if they were doing pre-sentence reports on relevant offenders. Because of the relatively poor case flow, the trial was extended during the randomisation phase first to Buckinghamshire and then to Berkshire as well. Each time, it was necessary to try to inform all the officers writing reports about restorative justice. Eventually, a probation officer was seconded to write pre-sentence reports on relevant cases in Buckinghamshire, which improved the flow. Thames Valley has continued this trial since the end of the evaluation and it is clear that it has now been routinised into probation officers' work patterns. It demonstrates, however, that it is a major task to mount a new initiative which depends upon individual referral.

The prisons trial started in Bullingdon Prison, where four prison officers were trained as facilitators. It proved relatively easy to identify relevant cases from Bullingdon, though it was less easy for the prison officers to find time to do their restorative justice work after they had performed their required security duties, and one officer ended up doing much of the work. It was helpful to have prison staff acting as facilitators because they could visit prisoners in their cells and talk about the possibility of restorative justice without access difficulties. When the relevant initial batch of prisoners at Bullingdon was exhausted, other prisons in the Thames Valley area were approached. Eventually several other prisons and Young Offenders Institutions participated but it was time-consuming to obtain relevant data. An analysis of the extent to which relevant cases were referred shows that almost all cases from Bullingdon, where there were local staff involved, were acquired, but very few relevant cases were taken from the other custodial establishments (Shapland *et al.* 2006a).

CONNECT

CONNECT started its work in one magistrates' court in inner London, Camberwell Green, dealing only with offenders sentenced at the magistrates' court. Because of the particular offending and offender profile of the area, a considerable proportion of cases were sent to the Crown Court for sentence. After a while, CONNECT started to follow these through, working with the Crown Court centres as well. It also, after a year, expanded into a second magistrates' court nearby, Tower Bridge. Towards the end of the evaluation, CONNECT was asked by the Probation Victim Liaison Unit in London to take on a few serious cases where victims had requested a meeting with offenders who were serving long prison sentences. CONNECT's experience, like that of JRC London, was thus of geographical expansion and also moving to take on more serious cases from other referral sources.

REMEDI

REMEDI was the only scheme which did not expand geographically beyond its original intentions. Its aim was to use the funding to establish offices to serve the whole of the South Yorkshire area (Barnsley, Doncaster, Rotherham and Sheffield), moving out from its original base in Sheffield. This happened, but it was found that different referral paths needed to be established for the different offices. The reason was the separate identities and preferences of the four different Youth Offending Teams in those towns, which resulted in very different rates of referral of young offender cases, with a knock-on effect on resources available for adult cases. In Doncaster, for example, there was a very substantial number of young people referred for victim impact work from their programmes of final warnings. A number of these then agreed to mediation.[10] Further young offenders were referred for mediation work as part of referral orders made by referral panels as part of the young person's court sentence. This extent of referrals was encouraged by the REMEDI Doncaster young offenders' office being housed within the Youth Offending Team's premises. In contrast, very few young offenders were referred for mediation in Sheffield.

Over the time period of the evaluation, REMEDI, being a not-for-profit body, was constantly casting around for funding streams and adjusting its profile to fit potential funding. Some offices built up a considerable volume of work in schools in relation to dispute management, while others developed resettlement programmes in local prisons with adult offenders. Overall, six main referral streams took place which resulted in restorative justice events:

- referrals by YOT workers of young offenders from referral panels and final warning cases: 426 referrals produced 74 direct or indirect mediation cases;
- 'automatic' referral of cases from the Probation Service of adult offenders convicted of certain offences and sentenced to a community sentence. These cases produced a large number of referrals, but many were of unsuitable cases (no individual victim, etc.); it was difficult to obtain victim contact details; and many offenders, when approached, refused: 455 referrals before 1 April 2003 produced just five cases where mediation was completed;
- referral of specific cases by the Probation Service of adult offenders serving community sentences whose probation officers thought they might benefit: 135 referrals produced 23 mediation cases;
- self-referral by offenders on community sentences, which produced a small but consistent flow of cases, but where finding victim contact details might be problematic: 120 referrals produced 20 mediation cases;
- referrals as a result of REMEDI running resettlement classes and distributing literature in prisons: 91 referrals produced two mediation cases;
- victim-initiated cases, where victims approached REMEDI in relation to adult offenders, wishing to communicate with the offender: 17 referrals produced eight mediation cases.[11]

From referral to restorative justice event: the attrition process

As is clear from Table 3.1, there is considerable attrition between cases being referred to a scheme and eventually receiving restorative justice. For JRC in addition, because of the randomised trials nature of the research, approximately half the cases became the control group as a result of randomisation. However, for all schemes, prior to that, cases might fall out because they were outside the scope of the scheme (different offences charged to those taken by the scheme, no individual victim) or unsuitable (offender with very severe mental health problems, offender or victim abroad). The proportions of those outside the scope of the scheme or unsuitable very much depended upon the referral process and the assumptions those referring had about the scheme. If referrals were coming from practitioners from several courts or prisons or probation offices, it was much more difficult to keep all practitioners in touch with the scheme's characteristics and what was required (and to keep practitioners remembering about the scheme and the possibility of referral). REMEDI's experience with probation referrals on an 'automatic' basis and JRC Thames Valley's initial experiences with probation referrals particularly revealed this. Where scheme workers were themselves picking cases from lists created for other criminal justice purposes, as was the case for JRC London, then relatively few cases fell at this stage.

Overall, schemes put a lot of effort into making themselves visible to local practitioners and explaining the new initiative. Their success can be seen in the relatively low rate of attrition between referral and the case being deemed suitable (from 76 per cent to 87 per cent, apart from the particular problems encountered with REMEDI auto-referrals and JRC Thames Valley community cases: see Table 3.1). It was also clear that the schemes normally had sufficient staff to cope with occasional 'bulges' of referrals without dropping cases: this was only a real problem in CONNECT, with its small number of staff. The corollary was that staff did not 'cherry pick' cases – and so that we can see the attrition rates in Table 3.1 as representative of the populations of that stage of criminal justice in that area.

Participation in restorative justice was entirely voluntary for victims and offenders. Normally, offenders would be approached first, primarily for practical reasons (it took time to obtain victim contact details), but victims might self-refer (as at CONNECT and REMEDI) or both might be approached at about the same time. Facilitators were aware of the ethical debates around who to approach first – that victims might be distressed if offenders refused, but that if victims were not approached if offenders refused that might also disadvantage victims – and there was a continuing lively debate around the issue. In Table 3.1, refusals by victim or offender might occur at any stage prior to randomisation (for JRC randomised trials) or the event (for JRC adult cautions, CONNECT and REMEDI).

In general, offenders proving uncontactable was relatively rare – not surprisingly, given that offenders were still in the criminal justice process either pre- or post-sentence. Victims proving uncontactable was clearly not a problem for the police-run schemes (JRC London and Northumbria: low rates of attrition of between 1 and 8 per cent), but much more of a difficulty for schemes run by the Probation Service or voluntary sector agencies (JRC Thames Valley, CONNECT and REMEDI: rates between 7 per cent and 16 per cent). This ties up with the still ongoing issues regarding victim contact and data protection: issues which affect all victim services, not just participation in restorative justice. Schemes which did not incorporate police officers had to request victim contact details from the police, because criminal justice documentation often did not contain such information. The police obviously have many demands placed upon them, and providing victim contact details for a voluntary scheme was not always a high priority. We think it is important in future that these issues are explored at the beginning, so that victims are allowed to receive assistance or offers to participate in processes which may be beneficial to them – and to decide for themselves whether they would like to participate.

It is not possible directly to compare offender and victim refusal rates, because in most cases the offender was contacted first. If the offender refused, the victim was not contacted. Offender refusal rates can, however, be compared between different schemes and stages of criminal justice. We see from Table 3.1 that there were lower refusal rates when offenders were approached pre-sentence (JRC London, JRC Northumbria adult court trial, CONNECT: from 16 per cent to 27 per cent) than post-sentence (JRC Thames Valley, REMEDI: from 33 to 38 per cent). Facilitators commented that, pre-sentence, offenders tended to be thinking hard about the sentence and how they wanted to lead their lives in the future and so were relatively receptive to restorative justice, even though the courts had agreed it was not likely to affect the severity of their sentence in this experimental initiative.[12] Post-sentence, if on a community sentence, they tended to feel that they were already undertaking a number of requirements (e.g. reporting, offending behaviour programmes) – and one more thing was just too much. The refusal rates for diversionary schemes were particularly high (JRC Northumbria final warning, adult caution, at 31 and 51 per cent respectively; REMEDI youth, which was mostly final warning, at 32 per cent), possibly because, for legal reasons, there could be no compulsion to take part in any restorative (or other) activity once the decision to divert had been made.

For victims, this was an entirely new initiative and idea for almost all. The relatively low rates of victim refusal, for those victims who were approached about the possibility of restorative justice, are therefore very encouraging. Victims clearly felt there was a point in meeting or being in contact with the offender. The victim refusal rates were lower when the offender was a young offender (victim refusal produced attrition in 8 per cent of suitable cases for REMEDI youth and 15 per cent of JRC Northumbria youth final warnings). This is not surprising: a young offender may have been a less intimidating prospect; these tended to be less serious offences; and victims may have felt there was more point in trying to help young offenders stop offending. But victim refusal rates were not very high in even serious cases of adult offending: victim refusal accounted for between about a quarter and a third of attrition from suitable cases for JRC London burglary and street crime, JRC Northumbria adult cautions, JRC Thames Valley prison and REMEDI adult cases. These high rates for victim consent may be seen as surprising – but in fact several surveys in England and Wales have shown support among victims for compensation and non-punitive measures, particularly for young offenders (SmartJustice 2006; Hough and Roberts 1998).

It is also clear from Table 3.1 that, once victim and offender had agreed, it was rare for either to have second thoughts or the case not to proceed to restorative justice for some other reason (someone moves away, illness, another offence, etc.). Very few cases dropped out between agreement and the scheduled restorative justice event.

Once one adds up all these reasons for attrition, only a minority of suitable cases will remain to participate in restorative justice. The proportion of suitable cases which proceeded to randomisation (for JRC randomised trials) or straight to a restorative justice event (for other sites) varied from 13 per cent for REMEDI adult offender referrals to 43 per cent for JRC Northumbria final warnings. Overall, for all schemes, 955 out of a total of 3,436 suitable cases had everything in place to reach restorative justice events, which is just over a quarter (28 per cent) (Table 3.1).

It is interesting to compare the attrition rates for the three schemes with figures from the pilot of adult cases in New Zealand. In New Zealand, referrals from judges for restorative justice needed to be passed on to provider groups which were delivering the restorative justice events. This mostly happened, with 84 per cent being accepted by a provider and then 42 per cent of those reaching the provider having a restorative justice conference (Crime and Justice Research Centre, with Triggs 2005). This is a somewhat higher success rate than with the English schemes – but of course New Zealand has statutory youth conferencing, so victims, offenders and practitioners would have been very familiar with the concept. The main reason for referrals not proceeding to conferences in New Zealand was victim refusal (39 per cent), with offenders dropping out in 17 per cent of cases. Uncontactability and the case being unsuitable were only rarely a reason, but coordinators did make some judgments on what was unsuitable, primarily because the offender did not take responsibility or show much remorse. This selection effect was not very visible in the English schemes. The New Zealand evaluators question whether there should be this degree of discretion, arguing that remorse prior to the conference is not the only predictor of remorse at a conference – conferences can serve as a trigger to affect both offenders and victims in a positive direction. Coordinator prejudices about what may be appropriate cases may be incorrect, as Zehr (2002) has also argued.

To what extent did people want to participate in conferencing or in mediation?

Table 3.1 also allows us to compare the attrition rates for different restorative justice options. With JRC, offenders and victims could only choose to agree to conferencing or else would not receive restorative justice. With CONNECT and REMEDI, victims and offenders had a choice whether to have a direct meeting (direct mediation) or have the mediator pass information between them (indirect mediation).

Even though conferencing means that the victim and offender are agreeing to meet each other face-to-face, in fact the conferencing-or-nothing choice produced more cases reaching restorative justice than did the choice of direct or indirect mediation. The overall proportion of JRC cases with both victim and offender agreement, ready for randomisation/restorative justice, was 31 per cent (773 cases out of 2,508 suitable cases). The overall proportion of CONNECT and REMEDI cases reaching the same point was 20 per cent (182 out of 928 suitable cases). Offering just conferencing produced more cases for restorative justice than offering a choice between direct and indirect mediation.

Referral or extraction from criminal justice lists of cases?

One key decision for all initiatives within criminal justice is whether to rely on referrals of relevant cases from criminal justice practitioners or whether to expend scheme time in perusing criminal justice lists of cases so that the scheme identifies suitable cases itself. On a purely cost–benefit basis, the question comes down to whether the work involved in obtaining lists and going through them is more or less than the work involved in pursuing referrals to see if they are suitable, together with trying to train criminal justice practitioners about what is a suitable case. However, if the basis of the scheme is that restorative justice should be offered to all offenders and victims in suitable cases, ethically, the question is whether lists exist which are sufficiently comprehensive to permit almost all suitable cases to be extracted.

All three schemes started by using the referral route but ended up using lists – which we have called the 'extraction' route (Shapland *et al.* 2004a, 2006a). JRC London used lists of cases listed for hearing before the Crown Court, which gave details of cases likely to be heard in the following three weeks. They then contacted defence solicitors to see whether there was likely to be a guilty plea and to explain the scheme before contacting offenders and victims once the plea had been entered. JRC Northumbria used Probation Service lists of cases adjourned for pre-sentence reports for their adult court trial, and police databases for the final warnings and adult cautions. JRC Thames Valley used prison databases of all prisoners and their expected date of release for the prisons trial. CONNECT used Probation Service lists of cases adjourned for pre-sentence reports. REMEDI negotiated to have lists of those given community sentences from the Probation Service, though these post-sentence lists, as we have seen, proved to contain many unsuitable cases.

The pilot of adult restorative justice in New Zealand had similar findings. It was observed that needing to have judges to refer cases to restorative justice produced far fewer cases than automatic referral, despite the familiarity of restorative justice to judges (though 'automatic' referral still meant a coordinator assessing whether the case was suitable) (Crime and Justice Research Centre, with Triggs 2005). The pilot moved to the possibility of automatic referral where a pre-sentence report was requested and where the case met the scheme criteria, and found this did not create difficulties for the judiciary.

Pre-sentence, for the schemes we were evaluating, the use of court or probation lists of cases seemed to be far preferable to trying to rely on court clerks or probation officers to remember to refer suitable cases. The downside was that probation lists only contained those whose cases had been adjourned for reports – persuading sentencers that they might adjourn to permit restorative justice required additional continuing contact between the scheme and sentencers/clerks. Post-sentence, because lists tended to be offender-focused rather than offence-focused, they contained less information about the offence and so tended to have a higher proportion of unsuitable or eventually unprofitable cases (including those where offenders had not admitted responsibility but had been found guilty, cases without personal victims, etc.). For future schemes, we would strongly suggest that the potential of lists already being produced for other criminal justice purposes is explored early on in the scheme's development. Referrals (including self–referrals as the scheme becomes publicly known) and consultation with practitioners can then be supplementary sources of cases.

Training

As Van Ness (2003) and the Council of Europe's Recommendation on Mediation in Penal Matters (1999) have stressed, restorative justice facilitators need to undertake comprehensive training courses. The voluntary code of practice for restorative justice facilitators of the Restorative Justice Consortium (2007) in England and Wales, the umbrella body for restorative justice practitioners and academics, also stresses the need for good training. From the experience of the schemes we were evaluating, and like Van Ness, we would separate these needs for training into preparatory training (to be done before the facilitator runs a restorative justice event) and continuing on-the-job training.

JRC facilitators and managers were all trained initially by Transformative Justice Australia, using the TJA manual (2002), with practitioners from different sites being trained together. The training and manual set out the three-stage 'scripted' model adopted by JRC at all sites, which emphasised facilitators saying very little, but using silence and non-verbal prompts where necessary to encourage participants to speak. CONNECT staff were initially trained by NACRO, from their experience in youth restorative justice, supplemented later by two days' training from a restorative justice practitioner who had much experience of dealing with serious cases. REMEDI had an ongoing training programme for both staff and volunteers and staff recruited for the expansion into South Yorkshire took part in this. As a result of the expansion, REMEDI itself started to offer training to others, particularly in relation to the new markets in youth justice and schools.

All three schemes benefited considerably during the start-up and running phases of the work from regular meetings where staff would come together to discuss difficult cases and problems arising on a confidential basis. The range of work, the constant expansion into new criminal justice environments and the serious nature of many of the cases meant that new issues continued to arise. Between-site meetings for REMEDI (monthly managers' meetings) and for JRC allowed insights and solutions found in one place to be conveyed to others and also, we feel, increased the consistency of approach to restorative justice between the multi-site teams. On occasions, staff were brought together with external people (including feedback meetings with ourselves) and this also allowed queries to be discussed and solutions sought. We would strongly support this continuing exchange of views and learning between facilitators as a valuable training mechanism as restorative justice is developed.

Being and staying visible

Restorative justice has generally been set up outside the normal process of case progression through the criminal justice system. As a result, interactions with criminal justice agencies – for referrals, for accountability, to obtain information or to negotiate venues to hold restorative justice events – are often an ongoing process throughout the life of the scheme. The ever-expanding geographical remit of the three schemes and the constant turnover and numbers of criminal justice personnel meant that it was not possible to hold a series of initial events and then assume that criminal justice personnel would be aware of the scheme. Restorative justice was only a small part of their work – and a part which was unlikely to lead to serious problems for practitioners if referrals are not made.[13] It was unlikely to be at the forefront of their minds.

This constant need to be visible has been found by other schemes as well. In New Zealand, for example, even though practitioners were all very aware of what restorative justice was because of its statutory basis for young offenders, the facilitators for the pilot schemes for adults had constantly to bring eligible cases for referral to judges' attention. The four coordinators adopted different practices: some coordinators tagged or stamped the court papers of offenders who had committed offences eligible for referral to the pilot. Some coordinators sat in court for periods as visible reminders to the judge. All coordinators made a point of speaking with any new or visiting judge about the pilot (Crime and Justice Research Centre, with Triggs 2005: 81).

Similar tactics were used in the three schemes we evaluated. Where schemes still required court action (for example, sentencers to decide to adjourn prior to passing sentence, not to sentence immediately after a guilty plea), facilitators sat in court (CONNECT, JRC Northumbria), made sure they presented reports in person (JRC London, Northumbria) and stuck highly visible stickers on court files (JRC Northumbria). Facilitators proactively approached prisons where restorative justice was promoted in relation to resettlement (JRC Thames Valley, REMEDI). Schemes outside statutory criminal justice agencies constantly approached police to try to improve the flow and speed of provision of victim contact details (REMEDI). All, however, found that operating schemes outside the normal, routine flow of court business was difficult.

It also took considerable time to negotiate protocols with prisons to hold conferences and mediation in prison (where offenders were on remand in custody or on prison sentences) and to make arrangements in specific cases. Though prison staff, and particularly senior staff, were mostly very much in favour of helping to create opportunities for restorative justice where victims and offenders wished this, it remained the case that prison premises, systems and routines were not generally conducive to meetings involving outsiders. Suitable spaces for holding conferences were often hard to find and it was important for 'insiders' (usually probation officers based in prisons) to be prepared to give up time to escort victims and facilitators through the prison to the conference room.

Overall, managers needed to spend a considerable proportion of their time ensuring visibility to criminal justice agencies (police, courts, probation, prisons, Victim Support, agencies offering potentially useful programmes to offenders) and needed always to be aware of the need to remain visible throughout the course of the scheme. In England and Wales, the number of agencies and bodies involved in criminal justice is constantly increasing, as there is more outsourcing and more providers from the voluntary and commercial sectors are contracted to deliver services. This task of finding one's own space in the increasingly crowded system and of becoming and remaining visible to all within it is set to become more onerous. Should this be so? It can be questioned whether it should be for new schemes to have to jostle for their own place, or whether those statutory bodies in charge of particular stages of criminal justice (courts pre-sentence, probation service post-sentence) should themselves have the responsibility for making our multi-agency criminal justice system work. Until responsibility for multi-agency effectiveness is, however, taken up by one statutory agency, it will remain a major task for restorative justice to negotiate its way into criminal justice.

What should be the professional background of facilitators?

One key question has been from what professional background facilitators or mediators should come. This, we feel, is separate from the question of in which agency or body the delivery of restorative justice should be housed, though previous work has tended to elide the two questions. The most controversial aspect has been the use of police officers as facilitators, primarily in relation to conferencing and diversion from youth justice (McCold and Wachtel 1998; Hoyle *et al.* 2002; Daly 2003b). In several initiatives, it has been found that police officers acting as facilitators were lecturing or browbeating young offenders, essentially taking the conference away from the participants. However, it is less clear whether these tendencies, which are clearly not restorative, stemmed from inadequate training, inadequate supervision or inadequate quality control on the part of the scheme, difficulties with young offenders, or some intrinsic element of the police culture (Shapland 2009a).

On the other hand, some have argued that it is good for facilitators to be police officers, because policing, particularly community policing, is built upon keeping the peace and problem-solving and so police officers have both an interest in and skills for restorative justice (McCold and Wachtel 1998). They are likely also to be seen as authoritative figures and inspire victim confidence.

Indeed, victims in our own evaluation commented that they found the authority and security offered by police officer facilitators and conferences being held in police stations comforting in terms of reducing potential risks of intimidation by offenders. However, they did not feel the same about prisons, which were uniformly seen as negative places by victims.

One key finding, from all the schemes, was that it was important that it be the facilitator who approached the victim and the offender rather than depending on another agency or person (such as a police officer in the case) to do so (Shapland *et al.* 2006a). Facilitators said that it was necessary to introduce the idea of restorative justice gently (given it was a novel concept to almost all of those approached) and that a face-to-face meeting was best for the participants to gain trust in them and be able to ask questions about what would happen.

There has been little debate about other professional backgrounds for facilitators or mediators. Some have been civil servants working within a statutory agency, as in the Northern Ireland Youth Conferencing Service (located under the Youth Justice Board). Youth justice mediators within Youth Offending Teams in England and Wales come from a variety of professional backgrounds (seconded from social services, police, education, health, etc.), but Teams have also employed community mediators. There has been no comparison of the perceived effectiveness of personnel from different backgrounds in the Team when acting as mediators.

The three schemes we evaluated provide an opportunity to test out whether the professional background of facilitators matters and to see whether there is something intrinsic about police culture which makes it inimical to being a facilitator. In JRC London and Northumbria, all facilitators were police officers, dealing with adult cases as well as youth cases. In JRC Thames Valley, some were probation officers, some community mediators, some prison officers and some had originally been seconded from Victim Support. In both CONNECT and REMEDI, paid staff who acted as mediators came from a wide variety of professional backgrounds, including previously being police officers, but were employed as mediators by the agency. We therefore have facilitators from different backgrounds working within the same framework of restorative justice – and with both adult and young offenders.

We asked both victims and offenders how helpful they thought the restorative justice project staff were at the conference. Overall, 84 per cent of JRC victims and 75 per cent of offenders said they were very helpful or quite helpful.[14] Only 2 per cent of victims and 5 per cent of offenders said they were not very helpful. Similar results were found in the more qualitative interviews with CONNECT and REMEDI victims and offenders. There was no obvious difference for victims on whether facilitators were very helpful or quite helpful between JRC London and Northumbria (where facilitators were police officers) and JRC Thames Valley (where they were probation officers, prison officers, community mediators or seconded from Victim Support). However, the few offenders who gave negative reactions for JRC were concentrated in London and Northumbria and there tended to be lower ratings in London for offenders. When asked whether the facilitator was the right kind of person, all the victims and offenders said yes.[15]

JRC London, it will be recalled, dealt with much more serious offences at the Crown Court – so the slightly more negative reactions from some offenders were clearly not the result of police officers browbeating young offenders. Indeed, when we looked at the responses to questions about the extent to which facilitators were in control at the conference, overall, 88 per cent of victims and 84 per cent of offenders over all the JRC randomised trials thought the facilitator was in control – and not too much or too little in control. London victims and offenders were no different, nor were young offenders in Northumbria (80 per cent of young offenders in Northumbria thought the facilitator was in control, 9 per cent too much in control, 7 per cent only partially in control or not in control).

Clearly, our results for JRC show that police officer facilitators are able to run conferences fairly, helpfully and without dominating the conference. In fact victims and offenders at all sites commented upon the skill and abilities of the facilitators. This is not, however, to downplay the results in other evaluations where there were difficulties. The difference, we think, is the rigorous training, expectations of high quality, constant discussion about difficult cases and internalisation of restorative values that happened among facilitators at all JRC sites. Our findings are reminiscent of the work of Michael Lamb and his colleagues on training different professionals to interview child witnesses about child abuse (Lamb *et al.* 2008). They found that both police officers and social workers – in several countries – tended to fall back on their own, directive ideas of how to interview, unless given a strong model of non-directive questioning and rigorously trained to follow it. We think that similar factors underlie JRC's success, compared to the difficulties of other schemes in persuading police officers to facilitate well in restorative justice conferences. Police officers (and other professionals) need to be given a strong positive steer within a precisely defined model of restorative justice, so that they do not fall back on other, less appropriate, models of communication within their profession (such as interrogation).

In terms of other professional backgrounds, facilitators commented themselves that having knowledge of the criminal justice system was important, because these three schemes were intrinsically linked to the progress of criminal justice. There were indications that having a mix of facilitators from different professional backgrounds was helpful because some could bring particular expertise to the development of services in especially challenging cases. But the main elements to make a good facilitator were derived from selection of appropriate personnel, training and continuing supervision, and opportunities for discussion about cases between facilitators.

Where should restorative justice be housed?

Though police officers did facilitate conferences well, there were aspects of operational police culture which did impinge on the provision of restorative justice. Senior police officers might have demands in particular cases – to acquire intelligence on certain areas, to find offenders for associated offences – which led them to ask facilitators or managers to pose particular questions in restorative justice events. These pressures occurred in both police areas, but they were always resisted – though it was difficult for junior officers to do so. It was only possible because the police units delivering restorative conferencing were independent of the main operational units in those police areas. The need for independence from operational control of cases was potentially present for probation and prison-based work as well.

Hence, the question of where restorative justice schemes should be housed links to questions of independence, conflicts of interest and accountability. Restorative conferences which throw up additional offending or behaviour which might lead to breach of a community sentence create conflicts for facilitators if the facilitator is also the person who should be investigating the offending or starting breach proceedings. This is true not only for individuals but also in terms of agency and system responsibilities.

Should then restorative justice be housed in an entirely independent agency, separate from both criminal justice and social welfare agencies? In some ways this is an attractive idea, but there are practical and systemic constraints. A new independent agency would have to create its own culture and would not be able to rely on the authority or image attached to criminal justice (or social support).[16] When restorative justice is itself a novel idea to the general public, it would find it hard to strike the right cultural – and funding – balance. It would also find tensions in its interactions with criminal justice – and for offending by adults, unless very trivial, the criminal justice response will be the first response considered by victims and the general public. More practically, in England and Wales, there would be difficulties in terms of acquiring data if the agency housing restorative justice were not within the family of criminal justice agencies. It was the voluntary-sector independent schemes in our evaluation which had the most difficulties over victim contact and prison security clearance. Moreover, a small independent agency is likely to find it difficult to attract secondments from criminal justice practitioners. It will have problems providing the range of human resources, financial, monitoring and other ancilliary services which will be required.

An interesting model from England and Wales is the creation of the Youth Offending Teams from practitioners of different professional backgrounds seconded to YOTs to provide youth justice services. A similar model in Northern Ireland is the Youth Conferencing Service, which has appointed staff from different backgrounds, though these are not generally secondments.[17] Though a restorative justice agency could not be solely a youth agency, a similar model of agency to the YOT, housed under the umbrella of the courts, or another statutory agency (police or probation, for instance) would allow the opportunity to have a multi-professional team which nevertheless was seen as independent of particular operational responsibilities. There is no reason why volunteer, trained facilitators or mediators could not also supplement paid personnel,[18] as occurred in REMEDI.

Evaluation and monitoring

Another key practical aspect of running a restorative justice scheme is setting up adequate data systems and monitoring. The system required is more complex than those normally used in criminal justice agencies – because it has to keep details on the offence, offender and victim and also track the process of the cases both through criminal justice and restorative justice. Systems had to be specially written for all three schemes we evaluated.[19]

The data system needs to be able to provide accountability to lay participants – When is the conference? Has there been follow-up contact to update participants and to check on safety? What was the conference agreement? What has been the progress on each item of the agreement? It also needs to be able to provide accountability and management information for scheme managers, referrers and criminal justice agencies. If a case has been referred, there must be the means for that referrer to be updated as to what has happened in the case.

We would distinguish between evaluation and monitoring. Monitoring, we consider, is the duty of every scheme. It implies the routine keeping and production of information about the scheme itself, the number of cases referred, the stages they reach (in a similar way to the attrition data in Table 3.1), their outcomes and the time intervals taken for cases to get to each stage. It is important for the good running of the scheme and assessment of how it might develop in future, as well as for financial accountability and reports to other agencies (see Shapland forthcoming a).

However, evaluation – the results of which we are reporting in this book – we think is a more specialised business, requiring social research skills. There is still no accepted standard for effective evaluation (Balahur and Kilchling forthcoming), but, at a minimum, it would entail periodic research efforts to contact victims, offenders and other participants to find out their reactions (through postal or telephone surveys, or face-to-face interviews by independent evaluators). Conferences or direct mediation sessions would be observed using independent observers. The evaluation would also look at reoffending rates, acquiring criminal records data and constructing relevant control groups. All these are much more expensive than monitoring – but they do not need to be done continuously. They would of course need to draw from the data system of the scheme and any immediate feedback questionnaires or contacts the scheme has been using.

Cost elements and finance

Whether an initiative is value for money is determined by calculating whether the financial benefits it brings (for example, in decreased reoffending by offenders) outweigh the costs of running the scheme. In order to calculate value for money, it is necessary to work out the costs of running the scheme. Costs during the start-up phase are necessarily higher than when the scheme is up to steam and running cases consistently – both because office equipment, publicity material, etc. has to be purchased at the start, and because facilitators are being trained and working out the best ways of running cases. In JRC London, for example, the start-up phase costs were £6,217 per case where the offender had agreed to take part, which reduced to £2,333 in the running phase.[20]

It is quite difficult to obtain reliable cost figures for restorative justice schemes (or any other part of criminal justice), because agencies often work to different financial reporting points in the year and case figures may not mesh with finance figures. We had to interrogate finance officers closely to create the most accurate spreadsheets we could. Costs need to include: the employment costs of the staff; travel costs for staff in connection with restorative justice; payment of travel expenses to victims and offenders to attend restorative justice events; direct office costs of running the scheme (such as telephone, IT, photocopying); costs of holding restorative justice events (renting rooms, refreshments); staff training; building costs for the scheme's premises; and any indirect costs for finance, HR, auditing, etc. services. We have included the costs of inter-agency cooperation (the opportunity costs of personnel, including those from other agencies, attending events), but it was not possible to include opportunity or direct costs to victims or offenders because we did not have employment details.[21]

Working out how to present costs per case for each scheme is difficult for restorative justice, because there is no accepted standard or practice.[22] A cost per case can be calculated for each attrition stage in Table 3.1 – a cost per case referred (but this is greatly affected by referring agencies' practices), or a cost per suitable case, or a cost per case where a restorative justice event has occurred and so on. Because JRC was operating randomised controlled trials, this made it more difficult. The same facilitators were working on both experimental (restorative justice) and control cases at each site – and there were no accurate time measurements to allow for the extra costs of holding the conference and following up the outcome agreement in the experimental group. For JRC, therefore, we can only provide a cost per randomised case (where both victim and offender had agreed) and then try to estimate a cost per case where the conference had been held.

Table 3.2 shows the costs for each scheme during the running phase. The total cost per month was the expenditure of the whole site during that month and included all the different cases being worked on at that site. It was not possible to break down costs further to each trial or each type of case. The table points up both the larger size of the JRC sites and also the greater expense incurred by operating with professional criminal justice staff over a wide geographical area. REMEDI, though also operating over a large area, worked with volunteers as well as paid mediators.

The cost per case was very dependent upon the stage of restorative justice reached. So, in JRC London, for example, for which we have the most complete figures (including time estimates for reaching each stage) and for which there was little attrition due to referral errors, a cost per case referred of £1,343 became a cost per case in which the offender agreed of £2,027, and then a cost per case where both victim and offender agreed (and so was about to be randomised) of

Table 3.2 Costs for each scheme during the running phase

Costs	*CONNECT* £	*JRC London* £	*JRC Northumbria* £	*JRC Thames Valley* £	*REMEDI* £
Total cost per month	13,610	60,511	38,642	25,854	12,636
Average no. of cases referred per month	9	45	63	70	51
Cost per case referred	1,458	1,343	613	367	248
Average no. of cases per month where offender agreed	6	35	31	29	14
Cost per case where offender agreed	2,333	2,027	1,230	889	887
Average no. of cases per month where restorative justice was completed	3	9*	–	–	4
Cost per case where restorative justice was completed	4,666	5,457*	–	–	3,261
Average number of cases per month where cases were randomised	–	17	19	8	–
Cost per randomised case	–	4,173	2,088	3,120	

Notes: Table derived from Table 4.7, Shapland *et al.* (2007). Costs are all to a 2005/6 base. The running phase was during the randomisation phase for JRC and comprised a total of 12 months for CONNECT, 14 months for JRC and 8 months for REMEDI. JRC Northumbria does not include adult caution cases and appropriate adjustments were made to adjust for the work on these.
*Time estimates for work on conferences were only available for JRC London, thus permitting an estimated cost per case where restorative justice was completed there.

£4,173. The extra costs of holding the conference, doing brief follow-up checks, and following up on the outcome agreement then produced a final figure of the cost per case where a conference had occurred of £5,457. This, however, is not the cost of one conferenced case alone, but includes the cost of all the cases which fell during the attrition stage to produce one conferenced case.

JRC London was particularly expensive because it was working with such serious offences for which conferences often had to be held in prisons all round London and beyond with consequent time and travel costs. JRC Northumbria and Thames Valley produced much lower final costs per conferenced case (probably around £3,500 and £4,500 respectively[23]). These are very similar to the costs for CONNECT, which was a much smaller scheme operating in a much smaller geographical area.

It is also clear from the above that offering conferencing only was no more expensive than offering indirect or direct mediation, despite the greater number of lay participants involved in conferencing. The reason is that indirect mediation tends to include many more individual visits or contacts by the facilitator with victim or offender, passing information between the two. This is costly in staff time and tends to make cases take longer before closure. Offering conferencing for serious cases was no more costly than for less serious cases.

It is difficult to compare these costs with other interventions because these costs are not the cost of one individual case (except at the referral stage) but include all those which had some intervention but which dropped out on the way to a conference. They may seem high in comparison with some criminal justice costs, but, as we shall see in Chapter 11, JRC in fact was value for money, in that the costs of reoffending prevented were greater than the costs of running the scheme, at each site. Restorative justice, however, is not cheap – most costs were staffing costs, primarily of facilitators. The ease of operating restorative justice in conjunction with criminal justice, however, was an important determinant of lower attrition and so of lower costs per case. It is one reason why we have suggested above that it may be most helpful if restorative justice is set up under the umbrella of an existing criminal justice agency, but as an independent unit.

The figures quoted above must only be taken as a guide in relation to subsequent schemes or to mainstreaming restorative justice for adult offenders. They show, however, how the size of the scheme (beyond a minimum level) and the type of restorative justice offered are not important determinants of cost. What is far more important is the ease of obtaining cases and practical arrangements for cooperation with criminal justice – both of which affect staff time.

4 Accountability, regulation and risk

The intrinsic dangers of restorative justice

A key element of restorative justice is that it provides a forum for those affected by the offence to gather and communicate. Those affected are of course not a higher type of being or person who can create an idealised form of justice in which there are no selfish motives, no fear, no anger, no power imbalances, no problems. The point about restorative justice is that it is intended to bring together those affected, whoever they are. The people involved will reflect the hopes and fears of that society and those groups at that time and they will bring with them what they think justice means, which we have called their 'justice values' (Shapland *et al.* 2006b).

Some of the initial theoretical debates about the values and practices of restorative justice saw restorative justice being promoted from an unashamedly idealistic perspective – among other virtues, it is a means to wrestle conflict from an overweening state (Christie 1977); it promotes healing, forgiveness and apology (Zehr 1990); it both shames and reintegrates the offender (Braithwaite 1989); and it draws in the community, promotes solidarity and strengthens communities (Umbreit *et al.* 2000; Braithwaite 1998). These initial writers were relatively swiftly followed by a wave of others who warned of the dangers of restorative justice and the gap between theory and practice – restorative justice courts informality, but informal justice can lead to discrimination, domination and even lynchings (Crawford 2002; Roche 2003; Cook 2006); outcomes could be too severe or too minor (Roche 2003); there may be pressures towards participation, whether from professionals or family (Zernova 2007b); professionals can start to dominate (Daly 2003b; Christie 2009; Zernova 2007b);[1] one cannot necessarily expect healing, forgiveness or even apology (Shapland *et al.* 2006b; Roche 2003).

One of the major difficulties of assessing what is now a voluminous literature is that many of these claims are intrinsically either idealistic or comparative: either they describe an impossibly rosy world, or, as we saw in Chapter 1, they contain an implicit comparison with other forms of justice, but that comparator is not specified in detail. So, for example, is restorative justice being judged against the practice of criminal justice (or youth justice, or school justice, or whatever) in that country for those offenders at that time? Or is it being judged against a truly idealistic view of criminal justice, one in which human rights are always respected, the rule of law is entirely egalitarian and courts have unlimited time, resources and will to follow all legal procedures?

We think the debate about restorative justice needs to move from this stark comparison between its ideals and its possible downsides towards an appreciation that restorative justice necessarily always operates within the context of a particular society, with all its prejudices, views, structures and peoples. In a similar way, Pavlich (2002) has argued, from a postmodern perspective, that restorative justice is like hospitality, in that it should not be seen as ahistorical or acontextual, but will reflect the mores of that particular community.[2] Restorative justice is always to some extent 'bottom-up' (from the participants' input), but it always operates in a particular structural context of justice mechanisms in that society, which provide 'top-down' elements (whether through referrals, or simple comparative expectations in relation to criminal justice). Restorative justice hence needs to incorporate elements of regulation, which will assist in promoting best practice, trying to combat dangers, and allow accountability to relevant parties. It needs to develop practices, legislation and standards which will allow it to function within imperfect societies, with potentially damaged people, alongside the criminal justice system in that society, and still promote as far as possible its major values of inclusivity, communication, taking responsibility, problem-solving and healing.

Our own evaluation, because it included restorative justice within the ambit of criminal justice for adult offenders and serious offences, brought into focus a number of these issues. Youth justice has always been more innovative than adult justice. Aspects which are normal in youth justice, such as an emphasis on promoting rehabilitation and reintegration and consequent individualisation of outcomes or having a closed courtroom without media scrutiny, are seen to be more problematic if they are just taken across unchanged into adult justice – where ideals of consistency of outcome and open justice have traditionally held more sway. Similarly, operating restorative justice in parallel to criminal justice rather than as diversion from criminal justice meant that any discrepancies between restorative and criminal justice safeguards and values were highlighted. We therefore need to examine carefully both the potential dangers and downsides of restorative justice – and mechanisms to minimise these – and also the prerequisites for justice, in particular its accountabilities to many different people associated with the offence and to groups within society.

The first international attempts to create standards

We do not need to start from scratch in this task. Apart from very helpful academic treatises on standards and accountability,[3] the last fifteen years or so have seen the beginnings of an international collection of standards and rules. We need, however, to bear in mind that these standards are a first attempt and few have been subject to governmental and international publicity and discussion

– because they are not binding. They also reflect the pattern of restorative justice practice in force at that time, which was predominantly youth justice.[4]

In 1999, the Council of Europe published a Recommendation (No. R (99) 19) to member states concerning mediation in penal matters for the consideration of governments. The definition of mediation involved is wide: 'any process whereby the victim and the offender are enabled, if they freely consent, to participate actively in the resolution of matters arising from the crime through the help of an impartial third party (mediator)'. It would include conferencing, direct mediation, indirect mediation, community panels and other restorative processes. In 2002, the United Nations Economic and Social Council published Basic Principles on the use of restorative justice programmes in criminal matters (E/2002/INF/2/Add.2). Basic Principles provide general guidance to governments, but do not address in detail how the principles should be implemented (Van Ness 2003). Restorative justice was not defined in the document, which refers to 'any programme that uses restorative processes or aims to achieve restorative outcomes'.[5]

As well as international instruments, there have of course been many national statements of ethics in relation to restorative justice (including the American Bar Association's Victim-Offender Mediation/Dialogue Program Requirements in 1994 and the UK Restorative Justice Consortium's Standards for Restorative Justice in 1999), as well as statements emanating from meetings of academics and practitioners. There are also legislative provisions where restorative justice has been made statutory, in particular those from New Zealand and Northern Ireland.

Starting with the international (Council of Europe (CoE) and UN) and legislative documents from New Zealand[6] (NZ) and Northern Ireland (NI),[7] the provisions relating to regulation and accountability in these are:

1. Free consent by the parties (CoE, UN) / the offender (NI) in relation to participation, preceded by full information about rights, the nature of the process and possible consequences, and ability of any party to withdraw at any point (CoE, UN, NI). No inducement by unfair means to participate (CoE, UN).
2. The basic facts of a case should normally be acknowledged by both parties (CoE, UN). Restorative justice processes should be used only where there is sufficient evidence to charge the offender (UN) / where the offender admits the offence (NZ, NI).
3. Discussions in restorative justice should be confidential and may not be used subsequently, except with the agreement of the parties (CoE, NZ) / discussions in restorative justice not conducted in public should be confidential (UN). They should not be used as evidence of admission of guilt in subsequent legal proceedings (CoE, UN, NZ) / subsequent criminal proceedings (NI). However, information about serious imminent crimes should be conveyed to the appropriate authorities (CoE).

4. Restorative justice should be generally available, both geographically (CoE) and at all stages of criminal justice (CoE, UN).
5. The parties should have a right to legal assistance and translation/interpretation (CoE, UN) / the offender should have a right to legal assistance (NZ, NI). Young people should have the right to parental assistance (CoE, UN, NZ, NI).
6. The decision to refer a criminal case to restorative justice should be for the criminal justice authorities (CoE). Restorative justice should not proceed if any of the main parties involved cannot understand the meaning of the process (CoE). Obvious disparities in age, maturity, intellectual capacity, etc. (i.e. power imbalances) should be taken into consideration in referral (CoE, UN) and in conducting the case (UN).
7. Agreements as to outcomes should be arrived at voluntarily and should only contain reasonable and proportionate elements (CoE, UN).
8. Assessment of the outcome of the restorative justice process relating to a crime should be for the criminal justice authorities (CoE, UN), who should be informed about what has happened within a reasonable time frame (CoE, NZ) – but only about the outcome, not the content of restorative justice meetings (CoE, NZ). If there was no agreement between the parties, a decision as to how to proceed should be taken without delay (CoE, UN). If the case is discharged following a restorative justice agreement, then prosecution on the same facts is precluded (CoE, UN). Failure to reach or implement an agreement should not be used in subsequent criminal justice proceedings (UN).
9. Restorative justice processes should be governed by recognised standards, including in relation to competence and training (both initial training (CoE, UN) and subsequent in-service training (CoE) of facilitators, monitoring of the service (CoE), and research and evaluation) (CoE, UN).
10. During restorative justice, facilitators should receive all necessary information from criminal justice authorities, should act impartially (CoE, UN), should provide a safe environment for the parties (CoE, UN) and should work efficiently (CoE, NZ).

The documents vary in the amount of detail and specification they contain, but they all contain very similar elements and they all see accountability and regulation as relating to several parties:

- the participants themselves, in relation to how the case is dealt with;
- the human rights of the participants;
- the criminal justice system and, through this, the general public.

The Council of Europe (1999) Recommendation's explanatory memorandum specifically refers to article 6 of the European Convention on Human Rights on the right to a fair trial, thereby setting mediation in relation to crimes squarely within the ambit of criminal proceedings: 'Mediation, as an integral part of the criminal process, should therefore receive legal recognition and operate in conformity with the fundamental rights of the persons involved' (p. 25). However, it distinguishes the 'right to a court' from diversionary mediation, as long as the decision of the parties to proceed to mediation is well informed and strictly governed.[8]

The international instruments contain broadly drawn standards and may be seen to indicate those kinds of matters where it is necessary to lay down rules for good practice – where, in other words, potential dangers lurk for the running of restorative justice schemes in practice. The two examples of statutory legislation indicate matters where those countries have felt it necessary to have specific legislation: a much more restricted criterion and one which has primarily applied to matters of human rights and what happens after restorative justice.

To what extent did these potential dangers emerge for the three schemes we were evaluating? What kinds of solutions were adopted to provide good practice? What forms of accountability were used? The three schemes were not statutory schemes, nor were they subject to particular national standards – but they were closely monitored by the Home Office during the period of the funding and they were constantly being monitored (and fed back to) by ourselves. Their experiences may be helpful for those who are starting up restorative justice without a clear statutory framework.

Potential dangers and solutions: the use of regulation

Net-widening and the scope of referrals

Christie (2009) has drawn attention to the danger that restorative justice may start being used for offences which previously might have attracted no official attention or no official sanction: what has been called 'net-widening' (Cohen 1985). This is primarily a danger for diversionary schemes, which may come to occupy the territory previously inhabited by unofficial warnings or informal action. O'Mahony and Doak (2004) found that net-widening was occurring in police cautioning restorative justice for young offenders in Northern Ireland – but Maxwell and Morris (1993) specifically examined the possibility of net-widening and concluded that this was not happening in family group conferences in New Zealand. Where net-widening has been shown to have occurred, the culprits are normally those who are given the task of referring cases to schemes or scheme personnel selecting inappropriate cases. A related danger is that schemes may be sent cases in which criminal justice personnel have failed (and it is unlikely that schemes will be any more successful) or cases which are likely to be very unrewarding for criminal justice personnel to pursue: the 'dregs' – sent to restorative justice to get them off criminal justice backlogs of outstanding cases. These latter cases are likely to be those stemming from long-running disputes in which the parties know each other, which include neighbour disputes and domestic abuse.

The safeguard has to be to establish schemes at a particular intended point in criminal justice with clear criteria for the cases which will be accepted, and to police strictly referral criteria. Statutory schemes (as in New Zealand and youth conferencing in Northern Ireland) are likely to have both clearer criteria and more visibility as to what is being referred. If the scheme is not statutory, it is considerably easier if scheme personnel select their own cases, as was discussed in Chapter 3, rather than the scheme having to reject a considerable number of cases as unsuitable. Of the three schemes, JRC and CONNECT specified strictly the stage of criminal justice which each case had to reach to be part of a trial. Net-widening was therefore only likely to occur if criminal justice personnel themselves were giving disposals (for example, final warnings for young offenders) in cases which previously would not have reached that stage.[9] This essentially used the safeguard that the scheme could only receive cases already judged to be at the right point by criminal justice officials (referral through criminal justice, as in point 6 above). REMEDI took cases from many criminal justice stages, with the result that it was necessary for managers constantly to monitor the workload of each office, to ensure that there was an adequate flow of cases reaching mediation (rather than staff spending much time dealing with cases which were ultimately unfruitful or which ended in a non-restorative justice outcome, such as victim awareness training).

The question of the possible unsuitability of some cases which fell within the general criteria was one which caused considerable debate for all three schemes: if disputes were long-running, or people knew each other, or some participants had linguistic or other difficulties, should the case be accepted? Overall, all three schemes took a relatively open view of what might be suitable: more 'difficult' cases might well be more problematic to deal with, but criminal justice was clearly not doing well with them. Restorative justice, with its potential for communication and deliberation, might be more fruitful – but that was not a judgment to be made proactively by facilitators but by the participants themselves during the restorative justice process. Unless there were reasons why a case specifically and definitely would not fare well in restorative justice (which essentially revolved around the safety of participants: see below), then they would be accepted. The very low percentages of cases seen as unsuitable, as shown in Chapter 2, testify to this philosophy.

This is not, however, a view which has always prevailed in other restorative justice initiatives. The pilot of adult cases in New Zealand, for example, showed considerable selection by facilitators (Crime and Justice Research Centre, with Triggs 2005). To ensure that restorative justice is available as generally as possible (as in point 4 above), it is clearly important that there are sufficient facilitators available so that there is no temptation to 'cherry-pick' cases. Taking more difficult cases was found in the three schemes to require more preparation for participants, more detailed risk assessment and more work in persuading supporters to come so that there was support during the restorative justice event for all parties – generally more time. Schemes, though, also need to bear in mind that the responsibility for proceeding with restorative justice does not all fall on them: the parties themselves, if properly informed, are voluntary participants (point 1 above) and can withdraw at any point. The availability of legal advice also aids decision-making by the parties (point 5 above: Roche 2003; Morris 2002).

Facilitating communication and obviating power imbalances: accountability for deliberative justice within restorative justice

So are all cases suitable for restorative justice? The essence of restorative justice, Roche (2003) has argued, is 'deliberative justice': that the parties are able to communicate during the restorative justice event. It follows that if communication becomes impossible, then the processes of restorative justice cannot occur. In the three schemes, this happened – in a very few cases – in a number of ways. One was if the offender proved not to agree that he or she had committed the offence: the offender either denied responsibility or said that the offence happened in a very different way to that understood by the other parties. These restorative justice events caused considerable dissatisfaction and did not end in an agreement.

The reason is that they negated point 2 above and one of the essential prerequisites for restorative justice within a criminal justice setting: that parties acknowledge the roles already set for them by criminal justice as offender, victim, etc. (Shapland *et al.* 2006b). Some restorative justice theorists have indicated that restorative justice carries no roles and should assume no roles. This may be correct for community mediation and neighbour disputes, but it risks fatally undermining participants' expectations where people think an offence, and particularly a serious offence, has been committed. In such instances, whether in relation to divided societies, war or criminal offences, victims expect their status – and the effects of the offence on them – to be acknowledged.

There can, of course, be difficulties in communication because of linguistic difficulties (parties do not share a common language, disabilities). In almost all cases, the three schemes managed to surmount these difficulties and communication was able to occur (using interpreters, signing for the deaf, support workers, etc.). There were, however, one or two in which communication was difficult and here again parties showed dissatisfaction with the restorative justice process. The fact that dissatisfaction was confined to these few cases where there was denial of responsibility or communication difficulties (as we shall see in Chapter 8), shows how important deliberative justice is in restorative justice.

Can, however, restorative justice overcome intrinsic power imbalances between participants to allow free communication (point 6 above)? Cook (2006) argues that restorative justice processes may in fact not only duplicate power imbalances in society, but emphasise them. She suggests, from analysis of restorative justice in Australia, that the offender accounting to the victim, his or her supporters and professionals may rather accentuate dynamics around gender, race and social class. This is similar to Sherman and Strang's (2007) point that in societies where there has been historical repression, such as Australia, an Aboriginal young person may find any implicit requirement to apologise to white police or victims an extension of colonialism.

We would argue that the fundamental danger here is perceived pressure to act in a particular way (apologise, offer reparation, be angry, be fearful) on the part of offenders or victims, when that participant does not feel that way. It is impossible for restorative justice to remove all societal power imbalances from the restorative justice event: they are part of the cultural values participants bring with them. On the other hand, it is important not to exacerbate them (for example, by any inequality of treatment of participants by facilitators) and there seem to be some pointers to mitigating any fear and improving communication and safety.

Roche (2003) sees accountability as acting essentially as a check on the exercise of power. In relation to power imbalances within a restorative justice event, what check can accountability provide? One set of accountabilities which both Roche and Strang (2002) have argued is helpful is to maximise the number of participants to obviate power imbalances between one participant and another (typically between a young offender, for example, and an adult victim – Daly (2003b)). Having more people 'in the circle' means more people able to challenge any domination by one person and does not leave the facilitator having the major responsibility for apportioning conversation. This is a clear advantage of conferencing over mediation, because if one key participant is nervous, tongue-tied or otherwise finds it difficult to speak, their supporters can often help them out or elicit the things they want to say. Our observations of conferences showed that this could occur both with diffident victims, who were not sure about recalling the effect the offence had on them and with offenders.

Yet having more people present is not a guarantee of lack of domination or power imbalances. Some very large conferences, where there were multiple victims and victim supporters because the one offender had engaged in several incidents of disorder or crime incidents in the neighbourhood over time, could, if the facilitator was not able to keep control, look like the whole neighbourhood against one young offender (Shapland 2009a). Equally, there could be long-standing issues between groups of participants: one restorative justice event cannot hope to unravel years of abuse or hurt.

However, the restorative justice processes of deliberative accountability (challenging what other participants say), inclusivity (having everyone relevant there) and procedural justice (letting everyone have their say) have the potential both to quell over-domination by one participant and also to allow past issues to surface. They certainly have greater potential in this regard than traditional forms of criminal justice procedures between conviction and sentencing, which tend to be characterised by lack of inclusivity (only the offender, legal representatives and the judiciary are normally allowed to speak), lack of procedural justice (communication is by directed questions, other issues are discouraged) and general minimisation of communication (Strang 2002; Shapland 1981; Hall 2009). This raises the question of the comparator for restorative justice. Should we be considering the advantages and disadvantages of a restorative approach when compared to criminal justice (as does, for example, Strang 2002), or should we be setting an absolute standard – an ideal justice (as Roche 2003 and Daly

2003b seem to be doing)? In terms of power imbalances, it seems to us that we need to create safeguards which have the potential to minimise inappropriate domination within justice processes while recognising that power imbalances cannot be fully removed. In this sense, reaching the standard set by criminal justice needs to be a minimum.

Indeed we need to be aware that 'doing justice' itself can create or reinforce power imbalances, but that these change during the justice process. We have argued that undertaking restorative justice in the context of criminal justice processes has already normally set the role for each participant (victim or offender, victim supporter or offender supporter) (Shapland *et al.* 2006b).[10] However, though the victim clearly has less power at the time of the offence, the offender, while within criminal justice processes, is clearly subject to the power of the state and may come to the restorative justice event in a quite powerless position.

Another form of accountability for restorative justice associated with criminal justice may also help us to recognise and deal with over-domination. This is where the restorative justice event does not itself constitute the final stage, but the outcome of those deliberations are then reviewed by a criminal justice decision-maker (a judge passing sentence, a prosecutor or police officer in relation to diversion). This review allows any abuse of power within the restorative justice event potentially to become visible – in the same way as an appeals system is intended to function within criminal justice. Restorative justice events in which one participant was browbeaten, abused or forced to agree to outcomes could be set aside. Similarly, other legitimate interests (such as those of the 'community' or society itself) could be input.

Yet immediately one realises that other interests may surface, it also becomes clear that review by criminal justice personnel will necessarily take power away from the participants in the original restorative justice event. This is helpful, if there has been considerable abuse there, but it is potentially unhelpful if, routinely, criminal justice values and requirements were allowed to override the original outcome. Parker (1999: 74) cautions: 'While recourse to formal legal processes might help solve the tyranny of majority in community, it exposes citizens to the risk of tyranny by formalistic and professional procedures.' Roche (2003) is so concerned about the potential for dilution of restorative values by judicial review that he suggests that judges should only be able to refer the matter back to a further restorative event.

We do not think that there is one best answer to these dilemmas for all situations. If restorative justice is self-standing, then accountability through review by others, retrospectively, may be best minimised to cases where there are allegations of abuse within the restorative justice event – and the remedy may be a further restorative process. If restorative justice is encompassed within criminal justice (i.e. it is a non-diversionary process) then there are necessarily other interests involved beyond those of the participants present at the restorative justice event (including human rights needs, the need for judicially fair processes and the interests of wider society). In these instances, and for these reasons, review by criminal justice personnel may be important in its own right. It is why, for example, cases are passed back to the referrer in statutory youth justice in Northern Ireland and in court-referred cases in New Zealand.

Potential review by the state (the sentencer or prosecutor) is, however, only one element in accountability in relation to the state. The state has the duty that, in relation to proceedings connected with criminal justice, it should see that there has been a 'fair trial'. This, however, is quite a minimalist conception of the duty of the state in criminal proceedings: it would be quite possible for all the fair trial provisions to be in place, but citizens to have no confidence in criminal justice and to judge that criminal justice has little legitimacy. The state has the duty not just to provide criminal justice processes, but to ensure that, as far as possible, they are seen as legitimate by the public.[11]

Tyler (1990; Tyler and Huo 2002), in his findings on procedural justice, has shown that, for both criminal and civil processes, participants' confidence and perceptions of legitimacy are influenced as much or more by perceptions of the process than of the outcomes. Being treated fairly, with respect and allowing each person to have their say are important in how the police, courts, etc. are judged. The state's performance, therefore, is being judged by those members of the public who are participants in criminal cases in such ways. Procedural justice is not the same as deliberative justice: in deliberative justice, participants are holding each other to account, while in procedural justice, participants are holding the state to account. However, one could argue that unless the state is providing conditions for justice processes which satisfy procedural justice, deliberative justice cannot occur. In terms of restorative justice, this means ensuring the voluntariness of participation, equality of speech, respect, control of power imbalances, and neutrality of facilitators we discussed above.

There is one other sense in which the state may need to be held accountable which arises in restorative justice but less directly in criminal justice. This is the sense that it is normally the state which needs to provide the programmes or facilities which are encompassed within outcome agreements. It would be ludicrous, for example, if conferences were identifying the need for drug treatment programmes, offenders were volunteering to go on them but there were no such programmes available. Yet problems in the availability and geographical distribution of programmes for offenders have haunted restorative justice programmes, even statutory ones, since their beginning. As Morris (2002: 605) argues: 'Good programmes addressing the reasons underlying offending and effective support for victims need to accompany good restorative justice processes and practices, but providing (or at least funding) them is a state responsibility.'

Can participants hold the state accountable for deficiencies in the provision of programmes? Restorative justice participants do have a detailed specification of what should occur in outcome agreements. If it were a requirement not only that restorative justice events should occur, but that it should be reported back to victims and other participants whether offenders had completed the agreement, then victims would be able to complain if lack of progress was a result of the lack of availability of relevant provision. Unfortunately, as we shall see in Chapter 10, reporting back to victims was one area in which JRC fell down, while neither CONNECT nor REMEDI saw it as their remit necessarily to have outcome agreements, which were rare in mediation. Even with these deficiencies, however, restorative justice participants are far better equipped to hold the state to account for provision than criminal justice participants: the media and occasionally the judiciary may lambast the executive as to the lack of prison places or, sometimes, the inadequacies of provision for mentally disordered offenders, but neither victims nor offenders generally have the standing to do so.[12] We can see that the need for deliberative justice and communication within restorative justice implies accountability for participants to each other, but also accountability of the state to participants. In what ways, though, should what is said during restorative justice be recounted back to the state?

Inappropriate use of what is said during restorative justice

Restorative justice is all about communication between those gathered at a restorative justice event. However, to what extent should what is said be able to go beyond the participants? In one sense, the position in England and Wales is clear. If someone admits a (further) offence during a mediation or conference session, they are not doing so under caution (in relation to the Police and Criminal Evidence Act 1984). Their statement, thus, is not an admissible confession for subsequent criminal proceedings. However, should other participants be able to take that information and investigate it, or should it be reported to the authorities? The answer may be clearer if we take the situation a step further: should the police be able to encourage the facilitator or anyone else present at the event to undertake 'fishing expeditions' to glean criminal intelligence (including 'confessions' of further offences)? This is not a remote possibility: there were two occasions on which police officers running conferences which we evaluated were asked by other police officers to gain such information or it was indicated that restorative justice might be a good tool to use for police intelligence. In both instances, these approaches were rebuffed, because the police running the conferences felt it would undermine the trust participants were putting in the facilitators – and that it would be using a 'therapeutic' session for other, incompatible purposes.

These are dilemmas faced in other countries. In New Zealand, what is said in restorative justice events cannot be used as evidence in subsequent criminal or civil proceedings, and in Northern Ireland this is true for criminal proceedings (see above). In Belgium, police attend youth conferences (as opposed to penal mediation) and are obliged to report any admission of further offences to the public prosecutor (Vanfraechem 2009). However, this is in accordance with the general duty in Belgium to report criminal offences (a duty which does not exist in England and Wales) and the duty of care. It is recognised that it is in conflict with the overall principle of confidentiality in mediation. A similar specific reporting duty does exist in England and Wales with respect to offences of child abuse and, for conferences held in prison, in relation to prison security. The same (partial) remedy to the tension between public protection on the one hand and confidentiality facilitating trust and communication in restorative justice on the other has been adopted in all these countries: participants are warned beforehand that facilitators/police will have to report matters which appear to breach the specific reporting requirements.

Such a safeguard is insufficient, however, against pressure from police or prosecutors on facilitators to reveal details of what is said in restorative justice events for intelligence purposes. The only remedy here is to separate facilitators from such operational pressures – not necessarily by prohibiting police or prosecutors or probation officers or any other criminal justice personnel from acting as facilitators, but by ensuring that they do not come hierarchically under the control of operational authorities who want the intelligence. It is another instance of the doctrine of the separation of powers familiar in the criminal justice arena. Judges would be horrified if *in camera* discussion could be able to be requested by police. A similar position needs to apply to restorative justice: that events and facilitators are seen as within the judicial sphere.

The need for such boundaries for restorative justice is not only a matter of replicating criminal justice or human rights elements, but also because confidentiality, trust, communication and the impartiality of facilitators are intrinsic to restorative justice. They also are fundamental to empowering participants, who need to be aware when they agree to come to an event, what will happen as a result of what they say.

Restorative justice and adults: the tension of open justice

Another tension that arises among competing accountabilities is that of whether the proceedings of restorative justice should follow those of criminal justice with adult offenders – and be open to the public – or whether attendance should be restricted and the proceedings largely confidential. In all three schemes we evaluated, proceedings were private and limited to participants, facilitators, necessary criminal justice personnel, researchers and occasional observers (facilitators in training, criminal justice personnel who had an interest in what the scheme was doing). However, the presence of researchers and observers was dependent upon the agreement of the participants.

The tension has not often been considered in restorative practice to date because most restorative justice initiatives have been with young offenders for whom traditional criminal justice processes are normally private. However, the tradition and the expectations of the public, even more so of the media, are that proceedings for adults will be open. Were, for example, restorative justice for adults to become routine within criminal justice practice in England and Wales, there would certainly be media enquiries and, probably media pressure, to be able to report what went on.

We need to distinguish carefully the different reasons why there might be an expectation for the public to view proceedings. One is to know what the outcomes of justice are: accountability of criminal justice to the public. This, however, would imply that outcome agreements might be made public (and of course that they would be sent to criminal justice decision-makers sentencing, or deciding to prosecute, subsequent to restorative justice). It would not necessarily mean that the whole content of discussion during events would be made public. Another reason is to promote visibility to reduce abuses of power, as discussed above. We have argued elsewhere that there is good reason for a record to be made of restorative justice proceedings, both in the case of possible complaints about intimidation or assault, etc. and to ensure a record of what, after all, are proceedings connected with criminal justice (Dignan *et al.* 2007).

A third reason is for simple visibility: that justice should be open. This is an important general principle and is behind the basic human rights safeguards of habeas corpus and that those accused should know the charges against them, etc. However, it is a principle breached daily in the case of young people, in sensitive family proceedings and in relation to probation reports and medical reports to courts – in other words, where the potential dangers of revealing to the world private matters not necessarily connected with events of the offence are significant. Strangely, the principle of open justice pertains to adult criminal cases at court in England and Wales, but not to details of cases which are not prosecuted, are diverted, etc.

A countervailing difficulty, cited by Roche (2003: 16), is that public viewing of criminal justice can rapidly become public voyeurism: 'a form of popular theatre'. It might become rather like using the public gallery of courts as a place in which to stay dry out of the rain, but with additional entertainment possibilities. In the case of the courts, due to the routine nature of much court business, the entertainment value is limited. In the case of restorative justice, however, there would be the additional draw of potential conflict, confrontation, tears and drama: a real-life crime thriller. The question we are facing is whether it would be ethical to expose victims, offenders and their supporters to this gaze for the sake of the benefit it brings in keeping the local community informed about what is being done in the name of justice.

Roche (2003) himself reviews different attempts to restrict attendance: by numbers of people allowed, by restricting external attendance to 'less sensitive' elements, by adding a public element after the private session and so forth. Overall, he favours openness, if only because publicity is important to accountability – as Kant (1795) indicates: 'All actions affecting the rights of other human beings are wrong if their maxim is not compatible with their being made public.' We would agree that generally publicity is important: it is, for example, why victims of abuse of power and very serious offences seek publicity above all, because it means that their victim status is acknowledged and the state cannot bury the offence. However, we think that Roche does not take sufficiently into account in advocating open justice the likely unhappiness of all potential participants that everything they say may be reported in the media, and the resulting refusal to participate or a very conscious rehearsal and 'performance' for the perceived audience.

Instead, we think that what is most important is the perceived legitimacy of the event to participants. This implies safeguards against abuse of power (including a record of the proceedings) and accountability both to referrers (criminal justice) and participants, but it does not include potentially prurient reporting by the media. We think that participants may give their permission for the media to attend, but that it should be up to them and that it should be normal that the media do not attend. The corollary of this, however, would be that fairly full reporting would be sent to any criminal justice decision-maker, who would be able to cite, in general terms, reasons why it had affected the decision.[13]

Recreating criminal justice?

Several restorative justice theorists have seen restorative justice outcomes and criminal justice as antithetical: that criminal justice is about punishment and retribution, restorative justice about restoration and healing. They have warned that restorative justice which is close to criminal justice (as in many of the cases we evaluated) will merely start mimicking, or being taken over by, criminal justice – and stop being restorative.

We share some of these concerns – criminal justice is rather a dominant friend to have – but we do not think that this rather defensive reaction is the way forward. Though it is possible to advocate separation from criminal justice for much youth offending and for minor offences for adults, this becomes both impractical and illegitimate, we think, when adult offenders and serious offences are concerned. Victims will expect such offences to be reported to the police and dealt with finally, in terms of sentencing, by judges (but potentially after a restorative process – or with restorative processes during sentence) (Shapland and Vagg 1988). So are victims and offenders of serious offences to be denied access to restorative justice?

The discussion around punishment and restorative justice is a complex one and we cannot do it justice here. However, there is an accountability dimension to it: if restorative justice outcomes include duties which are onerous, then they necessarily include duties which might be seen as punishment – and this includes financial or other reparation to the victim. Duff (2002) would see restorative outcomes as potentially including forms of punishment. Zernova (2007b) has argued that in practice (young) offenders and victims often do not see these elements as punishment because they see them as reparation or as rehabilitation – and because facilitators are clever at disguising punishment elements. Offenders may agree to apologise or undertake other elements because they themselves think they want to. We consider there is no necessary incompatibility between voluntariness and accepting or even proposing punishment. None the less, it is important to consider what kinds of safeguards or regulation might need to be included within restorative justice processes which are likely to include onerous elements – though it is important to remember that state punishments, like imprisonment, can only be decided upon by state personnel, such as judges, not by participants in restorative justice events.

Overall, where restorative justice is a prelude to criminal justice decisions, then we would see it as important that criminal justice principles of proportionality (in sentencing or diversion: see above with regard to net-widening) predominate in the final decision – which will be made by the criminal justice personnel – for reasons of the need for legitimacy of criminal justice decision-making. That would be the position for most of the cases we have been evaluating, certainly those which were pre-sentence or pre-release from prison.

The position is not the same, necessarily, where restorative justice is free-standing. Roche (2003: 4) argues that consistency and proportionality are not necessary values for restorative justice:

> If restorative justice is to achieve its stated goals of empowering citizens and promoting reparation and reintegration, offenders should be entitled to pay more compensation or do more work than a judge would otherwise order, and victims should be allowed to decline compensation if they wish, or otherwise accept less than they would have received had the case gone to court.

We agree that 'outside' values cannot be imported into restorative justice: if it is to be democratic, then the justice values the participants bring should be the ones which shine out in the event. In other words, restorative justice which is separate from criminal justice cannot and should not be judged entirely by criminal justice values. Abuse of power needs to be prevented – overall human rights values, such as the proscription of cruel and unusual punishment, need to be respected. However, we must guard against trying to mould one form of justice into the image of another.

To what extent is there a need for legislation?

Much restorative justice practice has occurred in the voluntary sector and has not been accompanied by legislation or state guidance. Its very spontaneity and altruism, as well as the possibilities for links with the local community, have been seen as an advantage. Though standards have been developed for the training of mediators/facilitators and for mediation practice (for example, Restorative Justice Consortium 2007), these are normally voluntary and statutory guidance has only been developed for statutory schemes. In England and Wales, the delivery of services linked to criminal justice has developed so that providers may come from the statutory, voluntary and private sectors, with contracts being let by the government and criminal justice agencies for prisons, work with offenders during sentence, victim support and many other areas. Given this plethora of potential service providers, is there a need for placing mediation/conferencing services linked to criminal justice referral on a statutory basis or legislative regulation of any element? Or would statutory provisions fossilise the development of restorative justice?

In youth justice, those restorative provisions which are sentences of the court are necessarily statutory. (Referral orders, reparation orders, action plan orders and compensation orders are all restorative or may contain restorative elements.) However, England and Wales currently lack the possibility of taking an outcome agreement straight through to sentence through the imposition of a conference order (as can happen in Northern Ireland).

The procedure of undertaking restorative justice has not been regulated through legislation in England and Wales, though the Youth Justice Board has sought to steer provision and encourage direct work with victims/direct mediation or conferencing through targets and inspections (Youth Justice Board 2009). Though this has had some success, there is still divergent practice between local Youth Offending Teams, with some providing far more opportunities for victims to be involved than others (e.g. Joint Inspection Team 2004). If one wishes consistent provision, with the ability for victims and offenders to hold the state to account for any lack of provision geographically, then statutory backing for restorative justice provision is essential.

In terms of restorative procedures, some of the elements we have outlined above require legislation to compel regulation in individual cases. The clearest need – and the one which has been included in statutory provision in youth justice in other jurisdictions – is the prohibition on using what is said in restorative justice events as evidence in future criminal and civil proceedings. This is not currently in place for youth justice – but because youth proceedings are private, there has been less obvious need for it to occur. With adult criminal justice, where there may be far more media and police interest in cases, we would see such a provision as essential. Other similar matters would include specification of those who should receive copies of outcome agreements which would be used in relation to sentencing (the judiciary, defence legal representatives, the defendant and victim) and any further conditions regarding the privacy of restorative justice events.

Primary legislation is not the only way to encourage or regulate the practice of restorative justice. Braithwaite (2002a) has suggested that one should see the means of regulation as a pyramid, with a very small amount of primary legislation at the top and subsequent layers made up of state guidance through secondary legislation and good practice guides/protocols, professional practice guidelines and training standards. As he indicates, creating state standards does not necessarily impair the empowerment of participants: ‘State standards can enable the deliberative democracy of the people or it can disable it. It all depends on what the standards are and how they are implemented’ (Braithwaite 2002b: 564). So, we would argue, many of the forms of accountability to which we have alluded above need to find their home in guidance documents from the state or professional bodies. These would include the accountability to individual participants and criminal justice referrers of what restorative justice has done with their particular case (when it was referred, what happened when, what the outcome agreement was, when the case was closed), who can attend restorative justice events, the duties of facilitators, who is responsible for provision of programmes and admission of offenders onto programmes after restorative justice, feedback to victims, delay and time limits, and so forth.

Addressing risk

One of the key requirements for restorative justice events is that they should be safe places for those affected by an offence to meet. Risk assessments were made by facilitators for every case in the schemes we evaluated and this is obviously good practice. There are several means to ameliorate risk: (1) to consider what kinds of cases overall are suitable for restorative justice; (2) to consider whether specific cases or specific individuals should be taken on or invited; (3) to use more than one facilitator or member of staff for very big or potentially risky conferences, so that it is possible to have 'time out' in a separate room with someone there if the conference, or an individual, gets very heated.

Overall, all three schemes we evaluated were keen not to impose categorical limitations on the kinds of cases or individuals they would consider. They saw such limitations as potentially discriminatory and as not opening up restorative justice to every possible case (its democratic or republican function). All schemes, however, decided not to take offences involving spousal abuse (domestic violence) or sexual offences. The reasons were partly the potential for serious power imbalances and partly the need to gain experience on 'ordinary' cases before undertaking cases in which it was very likely there would be serious effects which the victim had suffered. For the same reason, no scheme initially undertook homicide cases, though, as we have described in Chapter 3, CONNECT staff then did have further training and undertook a few homicide cases at the request of the victim's relatives through the Probation Victim Liaison Service. In other countries, however, there has been some experience with sexual assault cases, including child abuse (in South Australia: Daly and Curtis-Fawley 2004; and by the Youth Conferencing Service in Northern Ireland), as well as with homicide cases.

We interviewed facilitators in the three schemes both after a few months of the scheme running on the Home Office funding and also at the end of the funding. The kinds of cases they saw as appropriate for restorative justice, not surprisingly, mirrored the cases that were being taken by the scheme. Inappropriate cases would be those without direct victims, homicide, serious drug cases, domestic violence (between partners/spouses), sexual offences against children and some rape cases. However, facilitators were far more prepared at the end of the funding to start to experiment with more difficult cases. Some facilitators said that it should be the victim, not categorical decisions by the scheme, which should indicate suitability. Assessment of risks was crucial, but facilitators should not have stereotypes about certain types of offences or make presumptions about victim views. In other words, facilitators were moving from the scheme having categories of cases which might be unsuitable because of risk to considering each case individually.

In that individual consideration of 'risky' cases, the potential for using support mechanisms (such as extra preparation or translators/supporters where there were communication difficulties), finding and inviting relevant supporters, and increasing the number of facilitators available for the event were key. At the suggestion of the researchers, schemes also adopted the practice of making an 'immediate feedback safety call' to both victims and offenders a few days after a direct meeting. This was to ask victims and offenders how they were doing, how they thought the meeting went and whether they had any concerns. It was to pick up both potential depression (because of the personal nature of the discussions about problems in events: particularly important for offenders in prison) and potential intimidation, as well as creating an opportunity to refer victims to victim support agencies should they not be in touch with these and require further support.

The success of these measures is shown in the very small number of 'unsuitable' cases which schemes decided to omit and the lack of physical violence in any direct meeting in the evaluation or intimidation thereafter. One conference was stopped because the offender was clearly intoxicated and several used the 'time out' with the meeting resuming after a pause. With large conferences – some had many more than ten participants – it was particularly important that more than one facilitator or scheme staff member was present in order to escort people to different facilities, cope with latecomers, provide refreshments afterwards, be present during time out, etc.

The multiple accountabilities of restorative justice

The above discussion emphasises that there is not one form of accountability or regulation for restorative justice. As Day and Klein (1987: 2) have shown in relation to several public services, there are multiple accountabilities: 'Accountability is all about the construction of an agreed language or currency of discourse about conduct and performance, and the criteria that should be used in assessing them.' It is about who should be able to demand an account of what is happening or has happened in restorative justice, on what terms. Day and Klein distinguish between:

- political accountability (to the people, to society – for restorative justice, this might primarily be accountability for outcomes);
- financial accountability (to funders – which might also be said to include accountability regarding time taken and personnel to referrers);
- managerial accountability (for staff, cases, having adequate data systems);
- legal accountability (acting according to the law and human rights norms);
- professional accountability (working according to professional norms regulated by a professional body or rules of good practice);
- accountability to citizens (in relation to restorative justice: participants) in terms of how their case is handled.

We think this is a very useful list to summarise the discussions above and to emphasise that there is no one accountability (and hence no one form of regulation) that will suffice for justice. Restorative justice has many masters to whom it must account in the different ways set out above. The regulation of restorative justice is primarily the setting out of means and mechanisms – and in particular the design of data and recording systems – to accomplish these forms of accountability. No one master can be dominant because of restorative justice's plural and inclusive ideology.

Experiencing restorative justice

5 Approaching restorative justice

At the time victims and offenders were approached to see if they would like to participate in restorative justice, almost none had previously heard of the concept. For REMEDI, for example, just five respondents to pre-mediation questionnaires (out of 207 returned questionnaires) had heard of 'mediation' before being asked to participate (Shapland *et al.* 2006a). The process of preparation is therefore key, so that participants are aware of what will happen during the restorative justice event itself and can give informed consent to participation. Preparation – facilitators talking with victims and offenders about what the scheme offers and what may happen – will also set up expectations about restorative justice. It is those expectations which will govern participants' subsequent reactions to what they experience. In this chapter, we explore the process of participation and participants' expectations.

Despite the mountain of literature on restorative justice, there has in fact been remarkably little research into participants' expectations measured prior to the restorative justice event. This may be because facilitators are nervous about researchers interviewing participants prior to the event in case the integrity of the process is impaired (particularly if participants are then to be randomly assigned), in case the participants are in some way 'put off' or in case they may rehearse what they are going to say (not under the watchful eye of the facilitator to correct any misapprehensions). Certainly, the three schemes we evaluated were very nervous about these possibilities. As a result, we only interviewed participants in the pre-randomisation phase undertaken by Justice Research Consortium (JRC) (one participant per conference to minimise delay before the conference caused by the interview) and asked mediators from CONNECT and REMEDI to give questionnaires after the preparation phase to participants, to be returned directly to ourselves. This indirect process for giving out and returning questionnaires was not wholly successful, resulting in 207 questionnaires being returned for REMEDI,[1] but only three from CONNECT. REMEDI questionnaires were given out whether or not the person subsequently agreed to participate in mediation or mediation went ahead. For JRC we have a total of 116 interviews, 54 with victims and 62 with offenders. Interviews were designed to be very quick, taking an average of 11 minutes, and took place immediately before the conference, so after participants had agreed to take part in restorative justice. Both interviews and questionnaires focused on expectations and reasons for participation, together with an evaluation of their contacts with the scheme during preparation. They deliberately did not look at what participants might say at the restorative justice event, or what they felt about the offence, in order not to pre-empt the event itself.

We can also compare these results with participants' memories of their expectations from the interviews done after the restorative justice event, though those interviews, for JRC, were done only for those who had experienced the main phase when randomisation was occurring – so we cannot compare results from the same person both pre-event and post-event. Both REMEDI and JRC interviews after the event were therefore with participants who had taken part in restorative justice.

What did participants say about why they wanted to attend the restorative justice event?

Because these JRC interviews needed to be completed quickly, before the restorative justice event could start, we provided interviewees with a list of possible reasons for participating and asked them to say whether they were, for them, 'not at all important', 'not very important', 'quite important' or 'very important'.[2] We can represent this as a score from 1 to 4, where 'not at all important' is scored 1 and 'very important' is scored 4. We also asked participants if they had any other reasons which were important to them, but few provided any other than those in Table 5.1.

The first point to make about participants' reasons for participating is that they often had several reasons for agreeing to participate and would rate more than one reason as very important to them. It is important that facilitators (or policy-makers) do not acquire stereotypes of why 'victims' or 'offenders' wish to participate in restorative justice. Each restorative justice event is unique and the participants bring different wishes and expectations to it.

A number of facets of the restorative justice process seemed to be attractive to potential participants. A key one was the opportunity to communicate with the other person. 'You wanted to express your feelings and speak directly to the other person' was one of the highest scoring statements for both victims and offenders. 'You would like some questions about the offence answered' was also a high scoring element for the REMEDI victims who were given this statement. Communication figured highly in interviewees' comments in JRC interviews:

> [You can] ask questions and be involved in the conversation.

> [It's] different to court, able to 'talk it out'.

Table 5.1 Participants' reasons for participating in restorative justice

Importance score	*JRC*				*REMEDI*			
	Offenders	*n*	*Victims*	*n*	*Offenders*	*n*	*Victims*	*n*
You wanted to express your feelings and speak directly to the other person	3.44	55	2.58	50	3.48	146	3.23	48
You wanted to help the other person	2.98	57	2.75	49	3.32	148	3.12	48
You were asked to attend/take part	2.69	60	2.29	44	3.16	138	2.97	44
You were told to attend/take part*	1.10	23	1.25	18	2.50	148	1.43	44
You felt a duty to attend/take part	2.74	55	2.35	54	3.15	145	2.64	44
You wanted to have a say in how the problem was resolved	3.33	56	2.86	46	3.16	131	2.96	45
You wanted to repay the harm (offenders) or be repaid for the harm you had experienced (victims)	3.24	56	2.00	50	3.61	142	2.49	47
You would like some questions about the offence answered	–	–	–	–	2.78	127	3.22	47
Taking part may affect what happens as a result of the case	–	–	–	–	2.77	129	2.83	41

*On this question, participants did not answer if they thought the question was irrelevant to them, interviewers noted.

> [The facilitator] did say that I could put my side of the story and listen to what the victim had to say: I'm glad that you can say what happened leading up to the incident.

Communication was desired both in relation to what had happened, and also in solving problems in the future: 'You wanted to have a say in how the problem was resolved' was important both for victims and offenders. As one JRC interviewee said, the conference would allow people to: 'Ask questions and sort it out so it doesn't happen again.' Conferencing (as with JRC) included a specific future-looking stage to the restorative justice conference. Mediation (as with CONNECT and REMEDI) did not have a future-oriented part specifically built into the mediation model, though it could be raised by participants.

Not surprisingly, some reasons for participating were linked to others. A principal components analysis suggested that, for JRC, there was a first, general group of linked reasons which brought together wanting to repay/being repaid for the harm done, wanting to express feelings and speak directly to the other person, attending because one feels a duty to attend and wanting to have a say in how the problem is resolved.[3] This accounted for as much as 24 per cent of the overall variance and is clearly being driven by the desire to communicate. It was common to both victims and offenders. For REMEDI, there was a similar first, general factor common to both victims and offenders, accounting for 32 per cent of the variance, which linked the reasons cited for JRC; the additional statements included for REMEDI of 'You would like some questions about the offence answered' and 'Taking part may affect what happens as a result of the case'; and also 'You wanted to help the other person', 'Being asked to take part', 'Feeling a duty to take part' and 'Being told to take part'. The last figured primarily for young offenders, with the person doing the telling being their parents. For REMEDI, the desire to communicate was linked with helping and feelings of duty towards the other person.

For offenders, we can see from Table 5.1 that a key reason why they wanted to take part in restorative justice was to be able to offer to repay the harm they had done to victims. For victims, however, obtaining repayment (by which they normally meant compensation) was only occasionally important to them. This is the main disjuncture between victims and offenders as to why they wanted to engage with restorative justice. Offenders felt they wanted not just to say sorry, but to offer recompense. That kind of financial recompense was not important to victims, but, as we shall see later, offenders taking action to change their lives and so not reoffend again – what we call symbolic reparation – was important to victims.

We suspect there will be cultural differences between countries in views about compensation and reparation in relation to restorative justice. We know that victims in England and Wales accord great importance at court to the offer of compensation and would like to see compensation orders play a larger role in sentencing compared to fines which go to the state (SmartJustice 2006; Hough and Roberts 1998). However, we also know that the offer of compensation is important to many victims, not because it means acquiring money (though that is vital to a few who have suffered very much financially as a result of the offence), but because it symbolises that they have been hurt and that the offender has recognised this (Shapland *et al.* 1985). At court, it may be that compensation orders are the only way of offering that symbolic reparation which is more directly addressed by offenders promising to change their lives towards desistance (reducing or stopping committing crime) in restorative justice.

Looking back on their feelings when they agreed to take part in restorative justice from a few months after the restorative justice event, as shown by the results of the post-restorative justice interviews, both victims and offenders gave very similar answers to those set out in Table 5.1 (Shapland *et al.* 2007). Expectations of restorative justice were multi-dimensional. JRC and REMEDI offenders found 'You wanted to express your feelings and speak directly to the other person', 'You wanted to have a say in how the problem was resolved', 'You wanted to repay the harm done' and 'You wanted to help the other person' to be the key reasons and expectations for them. Victims cited 'You wanted to have some questions about the offence answered', 'You wanted to express your feelings and speak directly to the other person' and 'You wanted to have a say in how the problem was resolved'.[4] Again, we see the importance of communication and problem-solving for the future.

These are also altruistic or other-directed reasons. Though respondents had things they themselves wanted to say or do, they also wished to help the other person. Post-restorative justice, half the JRC victims and three-quarters of the REMEDI victims said that wanting to help the other person was very or quite important to them. This is not a picture of grasping, self-absorbed, vindictive victims, as the stereotype of victims in the media is often portrayed and as the image of victims' interests as being solely concerned with their own compensation reinforces. Instead, most victims wanted to try to prevent reoffending, to stop what they had experienced happening to others in the future and to address the problems behind offenders' offending. This is very similar to the results from the Northern Ireland evaluation of youth conferencing (O'Mahony and Doak 2004).

The altruism and sense of duty of many participants was mirrored in what may appear, at first sight, to be surprising results from the post-restorative justice interviews. We asked, before the restorative justice event, whom participants thought the process was primarily for: themselves or the other person. Though 49 per cent of JRC victims and 55 per cent of JRC offenders thought it was for themselves (as indeed they should), 73 per cent of JRC victims and 71 per cent of JRC offenders thought it was for the other party as well (Shapland *et al.* 2007). Similarly, 44 per cent of REMEDI victims and 51 per cent of REMEDI offenders thought it was for themselves, but 83 per cent of REMEDI victims and 91 per cent of REMEDI offenders thought it was for the other party. Both victims and offenders were clearly going into the restorative justice process not just for themselves, but also for the other person.

But a minority of victims did want compensation – and interestingly this minority primarily came from the JRC control group who were not able to participate in a restorative justice event (because of the randomised nature of the experiment). In the JRC principal components analysis post-restorative justice, there were two much smaller factors which emphasised being a victim, being repaid for the harm caused, wanting to express one's feelings to the other person and having questions answered, one factor which related to youth cases and one which related to less serious offences committed by adults (Shapland *et al.* 2007). Both were clearly seeing restorative justice in a more instrumental way as a means of getting what they needed as victims. Agreeing and then not being able to participate seemed to be driving people towards more self-centred reasons.

An important part of the ethical and accountability framework around restorative justice is that participation should be voluntary. The statement 'You were told to attend' was designed to find out whether participants felt they had been over-pressurised by anyone to attend. As can be seen from Table 5.1, few participants indicated this had happened to them – indeed most simply did not answer that statement at all because they felt it was irrelevant. In the pre-restorative justice interviews, one JRC victim (but no offenders) said that this was a very important reason and two JRC offenders (but no victims) said that this was a quite important reason. For REMEDI, where, it will be remembered, questionnaires could be completed when the case did not go forward to mediation, 3 victims and 33 offenders said it was a very important reason, 3 victims and 28 offenders a quite important reason.

We followed this up – because being told to attend could be being told by relatives or supporters, not pressure from facilitators or criminal justice practitioners – and found that this was what had happened at JRC. Victims had been persuaded sometimes by supporters, offenders by their lawyers or their relatives. For REMEDI, however, there was an association between being told to attend and cases with young offenders and the case not going forward to mediation. Daly (2003b) found that in South Australia, only 30 per cent of young offenders said that being at the conference was their own choice and 22 per cent said they had some choice but were under pressure, while 47 per cent said it was not their own choice. The latter two groups felt pressured either by the police (who were referring participants to conferences) or their parents. Compulsion seemed to be a particular problem for young offenders, but compulsion may be ultimately unhelpful. Daly found that some young offenders were loathe to apologise to victims or take part fully in the conference. We found that cases where young people felt pressured into attending tended not to proceed further to mediation. Clearly feelings of compulsion are not linked to success in restorative justice, confirming the importance of the voluntariness principle.

Nervousness: will the other person agree?

In a climate of punitiveness, some members of the public and policy-makers may feel that restorative justice is a soft option compared to being at court.

The participants in the schemes we observed would not agree: there was a high degree of nervousness, particularly among offenders, about participating in a direct meeting, about whether one would find one's voice, about whether the other person would be there, about what they would be like.[5] For JRC, in pre-restorative justice interviews, as many as 36 per cent of offenders said they were very nervous and 33 per cent somewhat nervous, while 15 per cent of victims said they were very nervous and 37 per cent somewhat nervous. Greater nervousness from offenders was also characteristic of mediation at REMEDI, with 11 per cent saying they were very nervous and 35 per cent somewhat nervous, while 8 per cent of victims said they were very nervous and 24 per cent somewhat nervous.

What were people nervous about? Both parties said they were nervous about meeting each other and about this new, though interesting process – a fear of the unknown. Offenders worried that they would not be able to say what they wanted to say (typically apologies) because they would not be able to get it out in the right way and that the victim would not accept their apology. Sometimes they felt they did not have a sufficient explanation for the offence. Victims were nervous about seeing the offender and whether they might get emotional or not be able to say the right thing.

Even several months after the restorative justice event, participants – especially offenders – could still remember how nervous they were and how they worried as to whether the other person would come. Though 66 per cent of JRC offenders who had been to a conference thought the other party would be there, the others were not sure. Similarly, 71 per cent of victims thought the offender would turn up, but the rest were not sure. REMEDI offenders and victims were even less sure the other party would participate in mediation: only 29 per cent of offenders and 57 per cent of victims thought they would, while 38 per cent of offenders and 30 per cent of victims thought they definitely would not. Simply because it involves communication with the other person, restorative justice can be nerve-wracking in prospect, even though desired.

The importance of preparation

From the results above, it is clear that the preparation of participants by facilitators played a vital role in ensuring people had sufficient information about what would happen and were able to answer people's questions. Ethically, given the lack of awareness of restorative justice among the general public at that time, facilitators needed to provide potential participants with information about what restorative justice is, what the procedure would be, what would be expected of them and what might happen after restorative justice – and remain available to answer any continuing questions. Information about all of these areas was necessary to ensure there was informed consent.

Uniformly, participants in all three schemes praised facilitators for their preparation and for the way in which they answered any questions. However participants had initially been approached – by letter, telephone call, personal visit, at court or in a criminal justice setting – they felt that approach was fine. It seems that it does not matter how participants are initially approached as long as there is then sufficient time to have personal contact with the facilitator face to face, hear about the procedure and ask relevant questions.[6] This direct contact with the facilitator was very important to reassure participants as well as to inform them.

For JRC, once participants had indicated they might be sympathetic to participation, a further meeting between the participant (and their supporters if available) and the facilitator was arranged to discuss the conference itself. The vast majority of participants (87 per cent) had such a meeting, which went through the format of the conference, discussed practical arrangements (such as timing and transport) and considered any concerns the participant might have (Shapland *et al.* 2007). Practical difficulties could particularly occur if the conference was to be held in prison. Some prisons went to a great deal of trouble to organise conferences at times when all participants could be there, but others found it more difficult and there might be much less notice for participants than for conferences held in the community. Travelling to prisons could also be difficult for victims and supporters and JRC facilitators often gave them lifts.

How long did this whole process of preparation and meeting/transfer of information take? Overall, JRC cases which led to a conference took an average of 33 days from referral to the conference for burglary in London, 32 days for street crime in London, 21 days for Northumbria magistrates' court cases, 34 days for Northumbria youth final warning cases, 30 days for Northumbria adult caution cases, 111 days for Thames Valley community cases and 104 days for Thames Valley prison cases (Shapland *et al.* 2006a: Table A1.3).

For REMEDI and CONNECT, both indirect and direct mediation involved a series of meetings with victim and offender. For CONNECT, cases which led to direct mediation took an average of 60 days from referral to the meeting (Shapland *et al.* 2006a: Table A1.1). An indirect mediation case involved between 4 and 30 telephone calls, visits or letters, with an average of 14 such contacts (plus writing a report to the court and attending the court for sentence) and workers spent an average of six and a half hours on each case. Direct mediation cases took significantly longer, often because information was passed between participants before direct mediation was attempted. Overall, workers spent an average of 19 and a half hours (ranging from 7 to 37 hours) per case.

REMEDI's work was less time-constrained than that of CONNECT or JRC because it normally took place during sentence or after decisions had been made to refer a young person to a referral panel or for a final warning. Youth referral cases took an average of 38 days from referral to a direct meeting in relation to referral panel work and 59 days for YOT work, while adult cases varied very considerably depending on the type of referral (from 26 days for cases where the offender was close to release from prison to around 200 days for victim-initiated cases and offenders on community sentences) (Shapland *et al.* 2006a: Table A1.5). The time period seemed to be half taken up with obtaining the consent of both parties and half with preparing the parties and arranging the direct mediation. However, there was little difference between the time needed for indirect and direct mediation.

The time taken reflects the numbers of visits mediators made to each party (each visit was by two mediators). So, for direct mediation, on average there were 2.1 meetings with offenders, 2.4 with victims and the joint meeting. Indirect mediation, because it involves passing information in both directions, required on average 2.5 meetings with offenders and 1.6 meetings with victims – a similar workload. In addition, for both, there were numerous telephone calls, letters, etc.

Overall, there seems to be no simple relation between the work involved or the time each case lasted, and whether restorative justice was indirect mediation, direct mediation or conferencing. It might be thought that indirect mediation would be simpler and so shorter – but because it is the mediator who has to convey the information, rather than direct communication in a meeting between victim and offender, it can take longer and mean more work to arrange meetings, telephone calls, etc. Criminal justice constraints clearly imposed time limits when restorative justice was undertaken pre-sentence or pre-release, but it seemed to be more the culture of the scheme, rather than at which stage of criminal justice it was operating, which determined the length of cases. Restorative justice – whether mediation or conferencing – seemed to be able to operate within a time period of around 30–35 days on average, which was very similar to the period of time the Probation Service was taking to write pre-sentence reports at that time.

During the preparation, participants said that they felt they had been given sufficient information about the conference or mediation itself: over 75 per cent of JRC offenders, 86 per cent or more of JRC victims, 95 per cent of REMEDI offenders and 74 per cent of REMEDI victims said they definitely or probably had enough information. CONNECT participants also said they were provided with all the information they needed. We noticed that participants did not say they were always given written material about the scheme. This did not seem to matter, given that facilitators were prepared to spend considerable time, sometimes over several contacts, talking to potential participants. In mainstreamed practice, however, there may be more pressure on preparation time, and we think it is good practice to provide participants with a leaflet about the scheme and procedures for them to look at later (together with facilitators' contact details).

Participants were less clear, however, about what might happen at the end of the restorative justice process and any tie-up with criminal justice. This was true for all three schemes. For JRC, whose conferencing model involves an outcome agreement to be agreed by everyone at the conference, we asked participants both before and after the process whether they had been told about outcome agreements. Beforehand, few people specifically mentioned any outcome agreement (13 per cent of offenders, 17 per cent of victims). Afterwards, only 67 per cent of offenders and 64 per cent of victims who had attended a conference said outcome agreements had specifically been mentioned during preparation (Shapland *et al.* 2007).

Asked whether they were aware what might happen after the restorative process had occurred, participants seemed relatively unsure. In relation to pre-sentence conferencing (in London and Northumbria), only 40 per cent of offenders and 24 per cent of victims, asked before the conference occurred, said they had been told there would be a report to the court. CONNECT participants were not always aware, even after mediation, that CONNECT workers would be making a report to the court. In contrast, though REMEDI centrally did not see itself as influencing criminal justice outcomes, 5 per cent of REMEDI offenders and 44 per cent of victims thought it would help with the court case, sentence or release date (as appropriate). There was clearly some confusion about what might happen after restorative justice. In fact, REMEDI workers did write back to the Probation Service if they had received the referral from probation officers and REMEDI staff working with young offenders in Doncaster attended case conferences with YOT staff. These inputs were likely in some cases to have influenced the supervision planning.

Some of this uncertainty about what might happen afterwards may have been because staff themselves were not clear what effect the restorative justice might have – these were developmental projects, not designed to impact directly on sentencing, release or other outcomes in criminal justice. Where reports were made to criminal justice decision-makers (for pre-sentence or pre-release restorative justice), however, information from those reports may have been taken into account in criminal justice decisions. It is clearly important that participants do have information on how restorative justice may impact upon criminal justice and upon other outcomes. However, it may be information overload to provide all of this in the first encounter with potential participants. Outcome agreements, if they are part of the restorative justice model, do need to be mentioned – both because they are part of the main process and so that participants can be thinking beforehand about any key elements for such an outcome agreement. We wonder, though, whether what is happening after the restorative justice event needs to be covered in detail in a feedback session after that event (together with other issues such as the criminal justice outcome and safety, see Chapters 3 and 7). Wherever it is covered, though, it is important that it is covered: we found, as we shall see in Chapter 9, that where victims were not informed about what offenders had done, they tended to assume, wrongly, that nothing had happened.

Discussing indirect and direct mediation

For CONNECT and REMEDI, both indirect and direct mediation were offered – while JRC participants were only offered conferencing. Where participants were potentially offered both, far more cases ended up as indirect mediation than direct mediation (see Chapter 3). Why did this occur? It will be no surprise that participants were nervous about a direct meeting, for all the reasons outlined above. However, the result may not have been entirely due to participants' desires or nervousness. We have already seen that schemes were poor at outlining what might happen after restorative justice. For REMEDI, letters from offenders whose cases ended up with indirect mediation suggested that they would be happy to agree to whatever form of restorative justice the victim might want (including direct mediation). It is clear, however, that REMEDI did not in any way pressure or even suggest to victims that direct meetings might be helpful, nor point out the connection between direct meetings and talking about what might happen in the future. For adult cases, mediators saw themselves as entirely neutral, not suggesting ideas. During an adult direct mediation, REMEDI mediators did not point up the possibility of talking about the future or what might happen, but followed any lead the participants gave. For youth cases, however, REMEDI mediators had a more rehabilitative ethos, possibly derived from that of the YOT staff with whom they had considerable contact. In contrast, JRC's model included a third stage (after talking about the offence itself and the effects it had caused) in which participants were asked what they thought might help to solve problems or create solutions. This was a clearly future-oriented stage.

Looking back afterwards, we asked REMEDI victims and offenders whether they did want to meet the other party directly. Overall, 38 per cent of offenders said 'yes', 19 per cent 'possibly' and 38 per cent 'no' (the rest did not know). Victims actually were more positive about meeting: 52 per cent said 'yes', 17 per cent 'possibly' and 30 per cent 'no'. This does not entirely fit with most cases ending in indirect mediation. Looking back, all the REMEDI offenders and all but one of the REMEDI victims who did meet face to face said, 'yes', they did want to meet. However, 8 offenders (out of 21 interviewed) and 8 victims (out of 23 interviewed) whose cases ended in indirect mediation also said they would have liked to have met. We cannot know whether this desire to meet was there in the first place, but not encouraged by mediators, or arose because of disappointment with the indirect mediation process (see Chapters 7, 8 and 11). However, indirect mediation is often much less risky for mediators, especially volunteer mediators. Given the rather ambiguous tone of REMEDI literature, we suspect that some mediators were not advocating direct mediation. We need, therefore, to be careful in concluding that, because more cases end in indirect mediation, this is what participants themselves actively wanted. The culture of the restorative justice scheme may have a considerable impact on what forms of restorative justice result.

6 Through a different lens: examining restorative justice using case studies[1]

Why present restorative justice case studies?

The main results of major evaluations of restorative justice have to be couched primarily in quantitative terms, indicating what happened and how many victims and offenders said they found it helpful and so forth. We present these results in the following chapters. What these overall results cannot show, however, are the nuances of interaction in what is a complex process of preparation of participants, the event itself and further contacts. Though restorative justice writers give the impression of emotionally charged, rich events, is this actually so (Elonheimo 2003; Daly 2002)? Restorative justice also takes place over a period of time. Do participants change their views over time? Case studies allow us to show what the experience was like for real people and to analyse difference as well as similarity. Case studies of adult victim-offender conferences are relatively rare in the literature, though they can be particularly useful to allow both researchers and practitioners who have not observed conferences to learn what happens.[2] In the context of current discussions in many countries about the respective merits of mediation and conferencing, it seems to us particularly important to illustrate some cases in detail (though without compromising the anonymity of the participants), so that readers can have an idea of what actually happened.

In this chapter, we focus on the Justice Research Consortium (JRC) scheme which uses the Transformative Justice Australia (TJA) scripted method of conferencing. This is purely because we were able to observe JRC conferences and interview participants a number of times, whereas it proved not to be possible to observe many CONNECT and REMEDI direct mediations. According to the TJA manual, 'conferencing brings together everyone in a system of relationships affected by conflict. A certified TJA Facilitator prepares and convenes the TJA Conference. All those involved in the conflict hear what has happened, and how each of them has been affected. They then decide together how to make things better' (Transformative Justice Australia 2002). The conferencing observed normally involved a face-to-face meeting between the victim and offender, with supporters for both parties present. The evaluation included observation of 226 such conferences.

One difficulty in presenting case studies is that they can be chosen to illustrate particular points and may not be 'representative' of the particular scheme's work. We have attempted to minimise this problem by selecting cases solely on the basis of the amount of information that was available and without reference to any prior criteria, so that the cases could speak for themselves. The cases described in this chapter all involved adult offenders who participated in a conference which the victim(s) also attended. Cases were selected if they contained the following: contemporaneous notes from researchers directly observing the conference; interview notes from the brief post-conference interviews with victims and offenders carried out by facilitators; copies of outcome agreements; and the final post-conference interviews[3] by the researchers done with victims and offenders. What emerged was an indication of the richness, complexity, diversity and flexibility of RJ in practice. Every case was unique; there are insights to be gained from all the cases.

First, we shall briefly comment on some basic similarities and differences between five of the cases on which we had the fullest range of data, before turning to look at a number of major themes which emerged primarily from this case study method of analysis. They are:

- how victims and offenders viewed themselves and/or each other and how this might change over the course of the conference;
- how participants' problems emerged within the conference and how/whether these could be incorporated into the outcome agreement; and
- the role of supporters in the conference process.

Sameness and difference – is there such a thing as a 'typical' case?

Some elements were common to all cases. They included the initial voluntary agreement, by both victim and offender, to take part in the restorative justice experiment, the way the facilitator prepared for and conducted the conference, and the fact that participants were free to choose supporters to accompany them. As we saw in the last chapter, our quantitative data indicate a high degree of satisfaction by both victims and offenders in relation to the extent of preparation for the conference.

The conference locations were different from any courtroom, but wherever the conference took place, there were no 'props': no TV to watch, no iPods to play, no mobile phones to use to call a friend. Here, there were only people who had 'met' once before in unpleasant circumstances, now choosing to invest their time to meet again and engage in dialogue to try to 'make things better'. The facilitators did not talk about the other participants or give away details which might prejudice the conference in any way. They made sure everything was in place before people arrived – even to names on chairs to ensure 'face-to-face' interaction. In a sense, they kept themselves *hidden* in the *foreground*, 'being out of the way yet being acutely present' (cf. Umbreit *et al.* 1999).

The structure of the conference was the same in each of the cases, as the TJA script suggested it should be. After welcomes and introductions, the facilitator used the scripted open questions for the three stages of the conference proper. In stage one the offender was asked to give her/his account of what happened and to say what s/he was thinking at the time. That related to the past. The past and the present were then linked in stage two, as the facilitator asked the victim about the effects of the offence on her/himself. The facilitator moved from the present to the future in stage three: how to make things better. After everyone had an opportunity to speak, the offender was asked if s/he had anything to say to anyone. Then, at this point, the conference participants tried to formulate the 'outcome agreement', a non-legally binding document recording the wishes of the participants (the content of outcome agreements over all JRC cases is discussed in Chapter 9). The script seems to have been constructed in such a way that it follows the formula 'facts first then feelings' (Harris 2003: 127–8). In all of these ways, then, each case was similar and 'typical'. As the following accounts illustrate, however, each conferencing 'event' was nevertheless unique in terms of the parties' experiences on the day, and also with regard to their subsequent perceptions.

Conference cases

> It will be clear by now that what I find appealing about restorative justice is its openness to story telling and exploration of possibilities for creative and constructive responses to offences.
>
> (Hudson 2003: 192)

Summaries of five cases are presented below. The description of the first case is in some detail, because it illustrates the complexity of many of these more serious cases. All names are pseudonyms and places, etc. have been changed where necessary to preserve anonymity.

Case 1

Kevin was convicted of armed robbery and sent to prison for three years after confronting first Justin and then Val with a concealed weapon and demanding the contents of the till at their (separate) places of work. He did not know either victim but was desperate for money with which to obtain drugs.

The restorative justice conference took place in a prison several months before Kevin's release date and was facilitated by a probation officer. Kevin was accompanied by two trusted friends, Arthur and Ted, who were older men he had known for a long time. Justin brought his friend, Brian, and Val invited Jane, a friend, who had also been her employer at the time of the incident. After introducing everyone, the facilitator reminded them that they would hear what had happened, find out how everyone had been affected and see if there was anything to be done to make things better.

First, she invited Kevin to say, step by step, what had happened on the two occasions when he had committed these offences. Kevin told the circle he had been going through a bad time. His marriage and other relationships had broken down and, unable to deal with the resulting stresses, he had turned to drugs. In debt to dealers, he had robbed Justin and Val. Before this time, Kevin said he had always worked and had never been in debt. Kevin described the offences as 'opportunistic' since neither had been planned. All eyes were on Kevin as he gave his account of the incidents

The facilitator asked him to describe his thoughts and feelings at the time. Kevin said he became alarmed, after the second offence, at how easy it had been, as the victims did not resist him. Then he thought of his small daughter and how he had let her down. He said he did not want to continue down the criminal path, so he went to the police and handed himself in. When asked who he thought had been affected by the offences, Kevin replied that all of them had – himself and the victims though he didn't think at the time who might have been affected by what he was doing.

The facilitator then asked Justin how he had been affected by the incident at the time, what had happened since and how his friends and family had reacted. Justin replied that it had been his first week at work. When Kevin approached him with a weapon demanding money, Justin left the till open and did not press the alarm. He said he had not been terribly affected by the offence: 'It's not that big a deal in life. It happens: you can't make it not happen.' However, his parents and friends had been shocked and he had lost his job. Although his employers had said they felt he was not the right sort of person for the job, Justin felt it was because he had not resisted Kevin or pressed the alarm. Justin then asked Kevin if he would have used the weapon if necessary. Kevin did not know, but agreed that as he had been under the influence of drugs at the time, he might have used it if Justin had resisted him.

Justin had some other questions for Kevin but first the facilitator asked Justin's friend and supporter, Brian, how he had learned about the event and about its effects. Brian said he had been chatting with Justin only a short while before and was shocked when Justin phoned to tell him of this life-threatening incident. Brian wondered how Kevin's own family had reacted and was told they had disowned him. However, his friends were glad he had given himself in and Kevin said that he was now glad to be talking about it. Both Justin and Brian wanted Kevin to stay off drugs from now on.

The facilitator then asked Val how she had been affected by the robbery. Val was not sympathetic to Kevin to begin with and had already interjected, as he spoke, that her daughter had been badly affected. Kevin had then apologised, though Val's friend Jane had said that that did not mean anything. Val denied that the offences had been opportunistic, saying he must have known that she and Justin were alone in the shop(s). She had been traumatised by the incident, which had also affected her daughter, her husband and Jane, her employer, who had come to help her at the time. Nor did she have much sympathy with Kevin's excuse of not having any money. Kevin apologised again for what he had done. Val replied that she still did not feel safe and said it 'felt scary' to be on her own. Moreover, her colleague, her daughter and she herself were still wary of people who wore the distinctive clothing Kevin had worn. Val said she did not understand how Kevin had let things go so far. She asked if he still owed money and if so how he thought he would repay it.

While Kevin was replying to this question, Justin suddenly asked him if he had ever been so low as to contemplate suicide. When Kevin admitted he had, Val replied that someone she knew had also done so. Kevin suddenly said he had sent letters to Val and Justin just after the event. Val said she had not received one and probably would not have read it if she had, then. She again stressed that the episode had been hard also for Jane, who had installed CCTV since the event.

The facilitator then asked Jane the same questions. It had been very frightening, she said, and she had had more work to do in supporting Val, who could not be left on her own, and in installing the CCTV. Val was very upset as Jane spoke and the facilitator gave her tissues to dry her eyes. When asked how others might have been affected Jane replied that the press reports had not helped and Val's partner had time off work.

The facilitator next turned to Kevin's supporters. Ted had read about the incident in the press, not realising who the armed robber was until Kevin himself told him as he was about to hand himself in. Ted was very shocked. He saw that Kevin was 'in a mess' because of the drugs and life events but said his shock and dismay were now balanced by relief that Kevin was somewhere he could get help. Ted was picking up that the victims thought this meeting was solely for Kevin's benefit. He said it was good that they could come and discuss their feelings. Val agreed, saying that they were not benefiting from it but she had 'wanted to come to see Kevin's face'.

The facilitator gently directed the discussion to Arthur, who had not yet spoken. He had also heard directly from Kevin what had happened and shared Ted's shock. He was sad the letters had not reached Val and Justin: he had read them and said they were honest and frank. From his past knowledge of Kevin he said he must have been under the influence of drugs to do what he did. He too was glad that Kevin's problems were being addressed.

Justin now felt he could ask the other questions he had for Kevin, which were about the drugs culture and the effect of taking drugs. A lengthy discussion followed, with Val talking as well. Kevin said there was nothing he could say in his defence about the offences. He seriously promised not to be involved in crime again and apologised again – 'I am really sorry, really sorry' – to Justin and Val.

The facilitator asked the circle if there was anything they wanted Kevin to do. Both Justin and Val said they would like Kevin to stay off drugs and sort himself out. Justin said 'Everyone has a good and a bad side. If Kevin stays off drugs he should be all right'. Kevin said it wasn't so much the drugs but the underlying problems that were hardest to deal with but he was very determined. Kevin was somewhat upset and the facilitator offered him tissues.

The facilitator asked if it was realistic that they should ask that Kevin stay off drugs and suggested that perhaps they might like a 'progress report' on Kevin in a few months' time. Justin immediately agreed to this but Val had some reservations. The discussion in the circle opened up again and Val was now less dismissive of Kevin.

Brian said he could not imagine what the victims had gone through but felt now that Kevin had a future. Val suddenly asked Kevin if he would help others when he was released. Kevin wasn't sure – his first priority would be to find work then he could consider helping others. Everyone had a very positive attitude as the meeting had to be drawn to a close because of the time limit set by prison regulations. Kevin again said he was 'very, very sorry' and he hoped the meeting would be helpful and put their minds at rest.

The participants tried to formulate the 'outcome agreement' which would encapsulate what Kevin might do to make things better all round. The facilitator had explained that the agreement – that Kevin would stay off drugs and would supply a progress report after a while – was important but was not legally binding. She now asked everyone to sign it. Ted added that he knew it had not been easy for Kevin to come to the conference. The hope was that all could move on.

The conference had lasted one hour and twenty minutes. Usually conferences are followed by a time for refreshments: this time was very brief indeed, as the participants mingled amiably. Kevin felt it would be hard for him to go back to his prison cell alone while the others had an opportunity to talk about the meeting.

In subsequent interviews Kevin admitted the conference was tense at first but felt it went as well as could be expected. He had not expected it to be as emotional as it was for him. At the conference, seeing his victims face to face and hearing them speak of the effects on themselves and friends and family had made him feel even more ashamed and remorseful than before. The best thing for him had been that he could again say 'sorry' to his victims and reassure them that he was no longer a threat to them. Even so, it seemed to Kevin subsequently that 'sorry' was not a deep enough word. He had nothing but praise for the facilitator, who handled the conference very skilfully and was someone he felt he could trust. Kevin thought the restorative justice option a good one but that it should be used carefully so as not to be used as an 'escape' from punishment

Justin was also positive about the conference and its effects, both shortly afterwards and when contacted by researchers a few months later. He felt it was important for him to see Kevin and understand why he did what he did. He also felt he had benefited from seeing things from Val's perspective, too. He had not found the conference emotional for himself but knew that it was for Val. Justin acknowledged that while the conference might help to reinforce Kevin's commitment to address his problems, in reality his problems were bigger than could be addressed in the conference alone. Nevertheless, Justin was positive about RJ. He thought the CJS did not have a forum for victims to ask or answer questions nor for hearing the offender's side of the story, as RJ did. 'RJ helps people to see the offender not necessarily as a nasty person, out for all they can get. It helped me to see that – and the other victim as well, judging from what she said and did at the conference, her changed attitude.'

When interviewed soon after the conference, Val reported that she felt much better. She confessed that the meeting had been difficult at first, not helped by the wait outside the prison beforehand. She had not been able to say what she wanted at the beginning, and she thought Kevin was just making excuses, which made her angry. But as she learnt more she said she could see where he was coming from and that he genuinely regretted what he had done. She was particularly impressed by the fact that Kevin had admitted he had problems, which must have been difficult for him, and that he had handed himself in. As a result, she no longer had any concern over possible reprisals. Val was very glad she had not listened to her family telling her not to go to the conference, which they felt would only help the offender. By the end of the meeting she had felt able to say what she wanted to, was no longer worried about it and felt it was a good way of dealing with an offence of this kind.

The outcome agreement, that Kevin would send a progress report to the victims, was performed, and at the time of writing, more than a year after release, Kevin had not committed any further offences.

Case 2

Joan was assaulted and had her handbag stolen by a younger woman, Penny, while walking near her place of work. The offence involved considerable violence, and Joan needed medical treatment for head injuries. Penny was, at the time, coming down from drugs and was angry, following a quarrel with a friend.

Both women were supported by family members at the conference, which took place in a prison. Penny had three generations to support her, including her sister, her mother and her grandmother. Joan brought her partner and daughter. At the beginning of the conference, Joan appeared to be very upset and kept her face covered by her hands.

Penny seemed to find it hard to look at her family and Joan during her account of the offence, which she described as being 'spur of the moment'. She knew what she was doing was wrong but needed the money for drugs and discarded the handbag

When the facilitator asked how Joan had been affected by the incident, she spoke through tears, with difficulty. She did not altogether accept Penny's version of the incident, which made Penny defensive and somewhat angry. Joan described in detail the far-reaching effects the offence had had on her and her family, but explained that she had faith and believed this would eventually help her to come to terms with it. Joan's supporters confirmed the seriousness of the attack and the severe consequences for Joan. But after asking questions about Penny's drug-taking and hearing about her background problems, pity began to replace anger. However, both Joan and her daughter remained wary of being attacked in the street.

Penny clearly found it hard to hear what Joan and her supporters had to say about how the offence had affected them all: as they spoke she looked at the floor. However, she later acknowledged the violence used during the robbery and said she was both sorry and ashamed about what had happened. Penny stressed that she had been using her time in prison constructively, and was enrolled on training and education courses. She received a great deal of support from most of her family, who encouraged her, put their hands on her back, assured her of their love for her and apologised for her. They were able to give background information on her life and how she came to be involved in drugs. Tearfully, Penny's mother said she felt sorry for Joan and that Penny's actions made her feel like a bad parent. She intimated that Penny's problems were so great that she was not sure she would be immediately changed.

When the facilitator asked what could now be done to make things better, Penny offered Joan her hand, in an attempt to demonstrate how sorry she was. Despite appearing more relaxed than when she first came into the room, Joan was unable to take Penny's hand at that stage. After some discussion, Penny agreed to get help for her drug and anger problems in prison and Joan agreed that she would meet with Penny and her mother when Penny was released: both were included in the outcome agreement, which everyone signed.

During the refreshment period, Joan called Penny over to her, took her hand in hers and said a prayer for her. This was a very moving moment and among the tears there were also handshakes and hugs between some of the participants. Altogether, this was a very emotional conference, characterised by tears and apologies.

When Joan and Penny were interviewed some time after the conference, they both said that the hardest thing had been going over the details of the offence but the best thing was seeing the other person face to face. Penny said she had wanted to meet Joan and apologise to her, but she had been very nervous, fearing she would be met with violence and intimidation. In fact she had felt very safe.

Joan, on the other hand, said she had not been at all nervous about the conference. She had wanted to help Penny. She also wanted Penny to know how she felt. Joan said she was glad to see the reality of Penny, who was a young girl, 'not tall and strong' as she had been in her mind. When asked if Penny had apologised, Joan agreed that she had – and said she had accepted the apology. She said a proof that she was not so afraid of going out with a handbag again was that the very next day she had bought a replacement bag for the one that had been stolen.

Penny was given a prison sentence for this offence. Shortly after her release, she committed two more robberies and was sentenced to a further five years' imprisonment.

Case 3

Sam attempted to steal a mobile phone from Liz as she made her way home from work. She resisted him, which resulted in damage to her laptop.

The conference took place in a community centre before Sam was sentenced and the circle consisted of five people: the facilitator, Sam, his supporter (Joe, a youth worker who knew him well), Liz and Jack (her partner). Sam had refused to invite his family to support him, saying they had already asked him too many questions

Sam began by explaining that the offence had been opportunistic and unpremeditated. He wanted the phone to sell to buy something for his flat. Sam did not seem to find it easy to address the circle; he kept his eyes down and spoke briefly. The facilitator asked extra questions to draw out his story. Joe also helped Sam by giving a very positive account of Sam and his involvement at the youth centre. He said those who knew Sam had been shocked when they heard what he had done. Sam apologised that 'it had happened'.

Liz said she was glad to know these things: she had been tempted to judge Sam by his clothing and behaviour and to stereotype him as a typical offender. She had also thought of him as someone taller and more aggressive and was glad to see the reality: 'Now I see you,' she said. Both Liz and her partner had been shocked by the event. But although she was determined not to be afraid on the streets, Liz had become more aware and watchful since that time. She was not, however, looking for any repayment for the harm done.

As Liz and Jack learned more about Sam they agreed he would not be helped by going to prison – although, given the offence, this was a distinct possibility. Indeed, the outcome agreement included Liz's statement that Sam should be given work in the community, in educational or creative work; that the youth worker would help find Sam some appropriate tasks; and that Sam would write to Liz in three months' time to tell her of his progress. At the end, Sam apologised again.

The judge gave Sam a community sentence and ordered him to pay £60 compensation. He stayed out of trouble for a year then committed further offences, including robbery, for which he was sent to prison.

Case 4

Tariq set upon his victim in a busy city street in an opportunistic attempt to steal his mobile phone. George, who was on his way home from work, was shaken but not badly hurt.

At the conference, which was held in prison, Tariq brought a charity worker as his supporter while George chose to attend alone. An interpreter was also there if needed. Tariq was an illegal immigrant who was thus unable to find employment, lived on the streets and used alcohol and drugs to assuage his fear, loneliness and hunger. George wondered why Tariq had chosen him as a victim and why he had not attempted to steal the more valuable lap-top he was carrying.

Tariq's response was that George had not been specifically targeted, but his phone was obvious – in his shirt pocket – and Tariq knew he could sell it for cash to buy food or addictive substances. Tariq apologised several times to George, right from the beginning of the conference. Later, after hearing Tariq's story, George became sorry for him and said he would like to know how Tariq fared with the agreement they reached.

The charity worker expressed frustration at the lack of resources to help people like Tariq and the dangers and vulnerabilities of living on the streets. The facilitator reminded the participants of the consequent limited nature of any outcome agreements which could be made. They agreed that Tariq should continue to try to improve his English and that once out of custody he would stay off drugs and alcohol and again seek the help of the charity whose worker had supported him.

The judge sentenced Tariq to 14 months' imprisonment the next day. After his release he committed some minor offences, mostly related to his survival, and was in and out of custody for brief periods.

Interviewed some months later, George said he had been quite nervous on meeting his assailant and about being involved in a new process. He had not wanted compensation from Tariq but he did want an apology. He said he had not expected to receive one, but he was pleased he had and, like Tariq, he had found the conference satisfactory.

Case 5

While David lay asleep, Lee entered his home and stole some property. The offence took place in the dark so neither David nor Lee had seen each other.

The conference took place in prison (where Lee was being detained for a different offence, prior to being sentenced for the offence against David). The conference circle was small and comprised the facilitator, David, Lee and Lee's daughter, June, who was invited to attend by the facilitator as she seemed to be the only member of Lee's family in contact with him. The two men shook hands as soon as they met.

When Lee was interviewed some months later, he said he had been very nervous before the conference and was not sure if he would apologise to David, expecting him to be judgmental, 'would be more angry, would come down heavy on me'. Instead, David listened to him and treated him with respect so Lee did apologise to David. The judge took account of the conference and, interviewees said, gave Lee a sentence two years shorter than he might have given.

When David was interviewed, he said he had not been at all nervous and though at first he thought Lee was 'just going through the motions', he later thought he was taking it more seriously. David had been very pleased to receive a letter from Lee about his progress.

From the five cases above, we can see that the content of each restorative justice event varies considerably – following the details of the offence and the harm done, and the questions which the participants had. There are of course general similarities. People talked about the offence, about harm and about the future. These were the key areas on which JRC conferences focused and was what the preparation which people received had led them to expect. The overall ratings of each of those areas and how much people felt they could contribute and what they felt about the events and the outcome agreements are discussed in the next chapter. We identify below some themes which emerge from these five cases.

Case study theme 1: Changing perceptions during the restorative justice process

The case studies allow us to see that perceptions of 'the other party' sometimes changed during the event and even during the informal refreshments period after it. Face-to-face communication and interaction between offender and victim and their supporters allowed people present to adjust their image of the other and to gain a better understanding of what their lives were like. Their initial views seemed not just to be drawn from contact during the offence, but also from stereotypes of 'victims' or 'people who commit burglary', which would be influenced by cultural perceptions and media reports.

Drawing on Christie (1986), Dignan (2005: 15) lists the attributes of an 'ideal' or stereotypical victim. These include:

- being weak in relation to the offender (female, sick, very old, very young or a combination of some of these);
- going about their daily business;
- being blameless for what happened;
- being a stranger to the offender.

Victims, correspondingly, have expectations of the offender: they often expect the offender to be 'unambiguously big and bad'. Conversely, offenders frequently expect victims to be aggressive and judgmental – as we saw in the last chapter in relation to offenders' considerable nervousness about the conference. In the conferences, however, these stereotypes were not always confirmed and participants sometimes changed their view of each other.

In case 1, Val had many attributes of the stereotypical victim as a woman, alone at the time, a stranger to Kevin, going about her everyday work. She (and Jane) had initially seen Kevin as a 'lazy layabout' who only wanted to rob them, made excuses for himself and was not sincere. At the conference she was still afraid, but later admitted that as she learned more about Kevin she became more engaged with the conference, and was able to say what she wanted. Afterwards, she no longer had any fear of reprisals.

Justin, on the other hand, was not a 'typical' victim. Young, male and seemingly not much affected by the incident, he was quite philosophical: 'These things happen …' He also had negative thoughts about Kevin at first, but admitted that the conference had helped dispel these: 'It helps people to see the offender not necessarily as a nasty person, out for all he can get. It helped me to see that …'

Kevin did not see himself as a career criminal, only as someone with problems who had taken a wrong turn. He later admitted he was nervous about going to the conference, expecting that he would be 'like a lamb to the slaughter and have to sit while they hurled insults at me', but it had not been like that. The biggest change in perception for Kevin himself had been that he no longer saw the victims as 'targets' or obstacles to what he wanted but as human beings. Seeing them face to face and hearing them speak of the effects on themselves and their families had made him even more remorseful, he admitted. He was very moved by Justin's handshake as he was leaving.

In case 2, Joan came to the conference with an image of Penny as big and strong, yet found her 'a young girl'. Over the course of the conference, there was a marked transformation in Joan from being initially distressed and reluctant, to taking Penny's hands in hers and praying for her. Some months later her perception was that Penny had asked for forgiveness and she had forgiven her, despite their difference of opinion over what had happened, which remained. Most strikingly, however, the change in Joan was from a woman who initially hid her face and was extremely fearful to one who was able to go out the next day, buy a new handbag and walk with more confidence in the streets.

In case 3, Liz was at first tempted to stereotype Sam, judging him on his clothing and attitude and his reluctance to speak to her directly. But as he did open up she changed her opinion and viewed him in a more positive light. David, the victim in case 5, saw himself as somewhat atypical: he was quite philosophical about the offence and also felt some responsibility for it by leaving open a window at night. He had preconceptions of offenders, too, which Lee altered – at least in part. Lee himself expected David to be angry and judgmental but found him respectful and empathetic.

Case study theme 2: Offenders' problems and outcome agreeements

As was seen in cases 1 and 2, several offenders involved in restorative justice conferences had drug problems, which influenced their offending. Overall, 82 per cent of JRC offenders interviewed said there were problems behind their offending, while 28 per cent of outcome agreements included offenders attending drug programmes and 12 per cent trying to stay away from drugs or alcohol (Shapland *et al.* 2006a). Trying to understand why the offence happened and preventing reoffending through helping offenders deal with their problems were key reasons why victims wished to take part in conferences (see Chapter 5; Shapland *et al.* 2006a). But how could this occur? Unlike sentencers, victims and supporters were not given reports on offenders or their offending-related problems.

One of the facilitator's skills was to keep the conference focused on the offence and its aftermath while allowing the participants to take the dialogue where they wished. In the course of answering questions about the offence and its effects, other problems might emerge, sometimes connected with the offence (such as problems with drugs or alcohol), sometimes not. These often raised issues that victims hoped the conference would deal with and where they encouraged discussion of what could be done. However, the conference could need guidance in recognising which of these problems could appropriately be addressed and perhaps incorporated into the outcome agreement – and which were too intractable.

In case 1, it seemed on the surface that the offences had been committed because Kevin needed money for a drugs habit. During the conference, however, it became clear that his problems were more complex. Since Kevin had already taken steps to address them, the outcome agreement – already limited in scope because he was serving a prison sentence – could only reinforce this and allow for a 'progress report' to the victims. Both victims acknowledged the magnitude of Kevin's problems. Justin's question to Kevin about thoughts of suicide was a question which the facilitator might have deflected and one which, certainly, Kevin need not have answered. Yet it became the turning point of the conference.

In case 3 it became clear that Sam had problems relating to his attempts to live independently. Liz felt strongly that prison would not help him and her creative suggestion for a constructive community sentence was included in the outcome agreement, whereupon Sam was given a community order involving unpaid work and compensation to the victim.

Often, however, it would be unrealistic to imagine that a single conference lasting two hours at most could address all the underlying problems associated with an offence. Case 4 is a good illustration of the limited scope for any outcome agreement other than an apology, given that Tariq was in prison and would have few possibilities to repair the harm when back on the streets. Indeed, the conference was limited in other respects also, not least because of language difficulties (though there was an interpreter). Despite these frustrations, George found the conference useful in answering his key question ('why me?') and said he learned a lot more about Tariq, feeling empathy for him. These positive aspects were perhaps more useful than the actual outcome agreement itself.

The way the conference was structured – with a clear focus on why the offence came about, what effects it had on all participants and what might be done about it, seems to be powerful in both promoting communication and in allowing offenders to reveal problems which can then be considered and addressed in the outcome agreement. This forward-looking orientation was much less evident in the cases that were dealt with by the other schemes using victim-offender mediation.

Case study theme 3: The role of supporters

One of the differences between victim-offender mediation and conferencing is that participants in conferencing are encouraged to bring supporters with them. Braithwaite (1996) has suggested that, in line with his theory of reintegrative shaming, the rationale for inviting victim supporters to the conference is to inject 'shame' into the proceedings, while the rationale for inviting offender supporters is to facilitate reintegration within the ritual. What was the role of the supporters in the conferences we observed?

Participants were often family members (as in cases 2 and 3 above). Others preferred to bring friends or colleagues (case 1). Occasionally a professional person – for example, a probation officer or social or agency worker – attended (as in case 3). But some offenders and victims attended without any supporters at all (case 4). As with facilitators, the most important thing about supporters was that they were persons who could be trusted.[4]

In case 1, Kevin had not brought family members along because they had rejected him on account of his addiction and behaviour. He chose his mature and sensible supporters very carefully, and they were able to add detail to Kevin's story and suggest what was in his best interest. Justin invited the friend to whom he had turned immediately after the offence, thinking it might be 'boring' for his family. Val came to the conference in defiance of her family and brought instead a friend and colleague who was able to complement her account of the effects of the offence.

In case 2, all the supporters were family members. This was not altogether positive for Penny, however, as her sister visibly showed her disapproval at the conference by turning away from her. Penny later felt a less than successful aspect of the conference for her had been that her family were still judging and blaming her. At the conference, however, they appeared loving and supportive, though her mother made a realistic assessment of her chances of reform. Supporters essentially form a 'community of care' (Morris and Maxwell 2000) for the offender or victim. But this cannot always be sufficient to prevent offenders from making the same mistakes again. The stereotype is that victims may be judgmental (as Kevin initially feared). But offender supporters can also indicate their displeasure and show offenders the effects on them. Professional workers can help offenders to access resources and so create bridging capital (as in case 3: see McNeill and Whyte 2007).

Conferences can also be helpful in providing a sense of closure, which we shall discuss further in the next chapter. The conference sometimes helped in relation to supporters' anger and upset. One of Joan's supporters – her daughter – was initially very angry, to the point of wishing to do Penny harm (case 2). During the course of the conference her feelings changed from distress and anger to pity and empathy for Penny.

How did these processes occur (when they did occur – there was no compulsion on supporters to become so involved)? Where family members were present, they were fully incorporated into the dialogue. Offenders' family supporters could apologise or feel shame on behalf of the offender, as in the cases of Penny and Lee. Victim supporters were encouraged to talk about the effects on them, not only the victim. For offenders in prison, the presence of the family was not like just another visit in which the family might express assurances that all was well at home and they were coping and so on. In the conference, attention was focused on the future, on ways in which all the family might work together to solve the offender's problems and support his or her good intentions not to continue along a path of crime.

The results of looking at single case studies

The elements we have drawn out of the case studies stemmed primarily from the cases themselves. It cannot be assumed that similar processes will necessarily occur in other cases: as we have argued, restorative justice is created anew by each group of people brought together in mediation or conferencing (Shapland *et al.* 2006b). The cases do, however, reflect the real experience of a number of people and demonstrate how the conditions of the conference – who was there, what was said, how perceptions changed and so on – made a difference to each one. The cases we have illustrated show how different each case was in its circumstances and in the people involved – but also how similarly, in many ways, people often reacted.

Most of all, what is very clear is that it was the experience of meeting the 'other' face to face which had a noticeable impact on the participants. This affected views of the other, decisions about apologising and perceptions of what was possible for the future. It is clear that the image of the 'other' which participants brought to the conference, which often reflected stereotypes of offenders and victims, was deepened and became more complex as a result of the communication possibilities provided at the conference: cardboard 'cut-outs' became real people. We need to remember that many victims and offenders in cases involving adult offenders are strangers or slight acquaintances prior to the offence: few know each other well.

Realistic outcome agreements were not always easy to find, especially for offenders in prison where opportunities to attend courses such as drugs rehabilitation or anger management might be limited by prison resources or other restrictions. In adult prison pre-sentence cases this could be particularly difficult. The uncertainty of whether a prison sentence would be imposed – and if so how long this would be – could also affect the possible range of conference outcome agreements. In two of the cases (cases 3 and 5), the judge took some account of participation in a conference and reflected it in the sentence decision, but this might not occur.[5] When outcome agreements were not completed fully some participants (Liz in case 3, for example) expressed disappointment. But the disappointment was not with the experience of restorative justice per se, just with what happened (or did not happen) later. All the participants in these cases said they would take part in a conference again.[6]

The case studies show restorative justice cannot work miracles, not surprisingly since it only entails one meeting of a few hours at most. It is not a panacea for all ills. Deep-rooted personal habits of criminality, which incline offenders to adopt patterns of criminal behaviour, will not be uprooted by one meeting, as several participants in the cases noted (Bottoms 2003). But if the problems are aired then there is hope that they can be addressed: the outcome agreements point in specific directions for this. Family members, friends and colleagues could and did offer and give support in ways they might have found difficult to imagine and hard to achieve without the conference. The outcome agreements and expressions of future support are important, especially for those still in prison. This knowledge and other information gathered at a conference and not elsewhere becomes a kind of 'coinage': it has a value for participants.

The Finnish academic, Henrik Elonheimo (2003), summed up impressions previously given by some advocates of restorative justice thus:

> Restorative justice theory is ambitious and noble indeed. Furthermore, the international literature is rife with inspiring anecdotes of successful

> restorative ceremonies where the parties meet and experience a moving emotional shift from hostility to empathy and co-operation. Emotions are vent and the crime and its impact are lively [*sic*] discussed. Agreements reached are creative and satisfy all stakeholders. Family and friends are also involved in the conferences. Eventually, the parties may even hug, make friends and invite each other to a dinner, etc.

The cases we have presented do not convey such a uniformly inspiring story. But then they are real case studies, with real differences as well as similarities. Did any of the participants say they felt harmed by their experience of restorative justice? No. Did any wish they had not taken part? None said so in interview. Were all problems solved? No. Did all offenders desist from offending? No, but some did. Possibly we might sum up the views of the participants by suggesting that, on balance, for these participants, restorative justice conferencing – meeting the other face to face – was a better thing to do than not.

7 During restorative justice events

In the last chapter, we illustrated the process of restorative justice conferencing, as undertaken by JRC, using a small number of case studies. In this chapter we shall focus on restorative justice events and see how participants experienced them and what happened in them from our observations. For indirect mediation, we shall need to consider the flow of information between victim and offender as conveyed by the mediators. Restorative justice events, as we have seen, are complex. We shall be concentrating upon a number of areas which have been suggested to be key in making an event restorative: inclusiveness, participation and procedural justice; dealing with emotion and the effects of the offence; problem-solving for the future; building social and human capital; as well as bringing in community. All these stem from the original definition of restorative justice which all three schemes adopted: 'Restorative justice is a process whereby all parties with a stake in a particular offence come together to resolve collectively how to deal with the aftermath of the offence and its implications for the future' (Marshall 1999: 5).

Inclusiveness, participation and procedural justice

Clear objectives for restorative justice events are the attendance and participation of relevant parties and whether they are enabled to participate during the event itself. Events are not going to be very restorative if certain participants are routinely excluded, or one participant hogs the floor and no one else can speak, or someone is bullied or silenced.

Who was invited and who came?

In terms of who was present at restorative justice events, mediation is fundamentally different from conferencing, in that it only involves the offender and the victim. There are no supporters and no one from 'the community'. For all restorative justice, of course, all lay participants, including victims and offenders, can pull out at any point – so even if an event is arranged, not everyone may come.

In fact, the numbers of potential participants dropping out or not being able to make the event within the possible time frame, after agreeing to participate in restorative justice, was very low for all three schemes. For JRC, of the 413 cases which were randomised to restorative justice (Table 3.1), in just 13 offenders dropped out and in 35 victims dropped out. So 387 of the conferences involved offenders and 350 involved offenders and one or more victims.

This is a much higher rate of participation by victims than at court (Strang 2002) or in standard youth justice practice, such as referral panels/Youth Offender Panels (Holdaway *et al.* 2001; Zernova 2007a). So, for example, Zernova (2007a: 61–2), looking at one family group conferencing project in England which received referrals from YOTs, found that 80 referrals led to 40 conferences, with an estimate of 44 per cent of victims attending conferences in the first year and 64 per cent in the second year. This is a higher attendance than generic youth justice practice,[1] possibly because it was a specialist family group conferencing scheme, but it is still far lower than the 90 per cent in the JRC work. In addition, in youth justice practice in relation to referral panels, victims are typically not allowed to attend the whole event: after the victim is able to outline how the offence had affected them, ask questions and express their feelings (and the offender might apologise), the victim is asked to leave. The offender, his or her family and professionals then discuss what will happen as a result of the conference. After the conference, in Zernova's study, the facilitator was supposed to contact the victim and outline any reparation plans by the offender (but not necessarily the whole plan created by the event).

In our evaluation, CONNECT and REMEDI offered participants a choice of indirect and direct mediation. Most chose indirect mediation (Table 3.1), which did not involve any face-to-face meeting with the other party. Hence there were only 13 direct meetings (out of 50 where participants agreed to some form of restorative justice) for CONNECT and 35 for REMEDI (out of 132). The concept of victims or offenders 'dropping out' of direct mediation is not relevant here – because direct mediation was preceded by elements of indirect mediation, involving the exchange of information through the mediator(s) to each party, and so such cases were counted as indirect mediation. All the instances of direct mediation, however, had both parties present throughout the meeting. There was no separate discussion by the offender and their family or with professionals.

In JRC conferences, the number of people present tended normally to be relatively small. The average number of participants sitting in the circle and so able to speak (omitting observers, any second facilitator, researchers, etc. sitting outside the circle) was 6.3, with a range from 3 to 15 (Shapland *et al.* 2006a). Breaking this down into types of participants, the means were 1.1 offenders,[2] 1.2 victims, 1.7 offender supporters, 0.9 victim supporters and a facilitator. For REMEDI, the average number of participants was 4.0 (including a second mediator, who participated) and for CONNECT 5 people.[3]

How does this compare with youth justice work? Crawford and Newburn (2003) found that, at initial referral panel meetings they observed in England and Wales, the young offender attended with only one other person in 68 per cent of panels (normally a parent or responsible adult). In 15 per cent the young person was entirely alone. In Northern Ireland, an appropriate adult is required by statute to be present at youth conferences. This was normally the young person's mother (54 per cent) or someone from social services or their care home (21 per cent) (Campbell *et al.* 2005). A second supporter was present in 61 per cent of cases, a third in 17 per cent. Victims were present at 69 per cent of conferences, but only 40 per cent of victims were personal victims.[4] Victims only rarely brought a supporter (14 per cent, almost all personal victims, brought one or more). Partly this may have been because in Northern Ireland conferencing was only with young offenders, whereas victims may have felt they needed more support for the offences committed by adult offenders with JRC. We suspect, however, that whether victims bring supporters is mainly about the extent to which facilitators encourage them to do so.

Some JRC conferences, however, were much larger and this typically occurred in the adult caution conferences in Northumbria which were not part of the randomised experiments (see Chapter 1). The kinds of offences being dealt with here were often ones in which offenders and victims had some form of prior relationship, as neighbours, work colleagues, members of an extended family or acquaintances (Shapland 2009a). They were all for violent offences, but not very serious violence, typically common assault or assault occasioning actual bodily harm. The offence which led to the conference typically was part of a series of incidents, in not all of which the offender might be the initiator. Some of the offences were part of a pattern of behaviour by one person or a group of people which had affected many others: criminal damage, threats, general anti-social behaviour and nuisance. We observed 14 adult caution conferences out of the 57 cases running at any point since the start of the scheme and the 45 running during the main data-gathering period. The largest of these conferences had 26 people present in the room of whom 23 spoke, and the average was 9.0.

JRC facilitators tried hard to contact supporters for both victims and offenders. This was sometimes difficult, particularly when offenders had been in prison for a while (for previous offences, or where restorative justice conferences happened prior to release) and so had lost touch with their families. Yet, even where offenders were estranged from near relatives, there was often an aunt or uncle or someone from an older generation who was pleased that the offender was reaching out to them and who came. Where there were no close relatives or friends, offenders could turn to professionals (youth workers, probation officers), victims sometimes to Victim Support. When discussing the numbers of supporters, it is important to realise that what will be spoken about is often difficult (admitting offending, admitting substance abuse problems, talking about emotional reactions to offences). Both offenders and victims only invited those they felt were close to them and would support them. McCold and Wachtel (1998) have spoken about 'communities of care' for offenders, micro-communities which can continue to support offenders over an extended period. The JRC experience shows that it is possible to construct such communities where they are not obviously present – but it is difficult and it does take time to set up.

The value of inclusivity in relation to restorative justice emphasises the need for all those affected by the offence to be present and this has led to a debate about communities and community values which we take up below. As conferences progressed and all participants were encouraged to say how the offence had affected them, it became clear that many supporters present had been affected, as well as the offender and victim (see the case studies in Chapter 6 for some examples). The restorative tasks of working to acknowledge the effects of the offence and to restore what has been affected are not, as they are often portrayed, simply in relation to the direct victim. The victim's close relatives or friends can be affected both practically (in caring for the victim, taking her to hospital, etc.) and emotionally (in terms of guilt that the offence has happened, changes in relationships and shocked awareness that this has happened). Offenders' families and friends are also often impacted financially, practically and emotionally.[5] Research on how members of the public's attitudes to criminal justice and to crime are formed has shown how personal experience (directly *or* through friends, relatives and neighbours) is very important (Skogan 1994; Bradford *et al.* 2009). Though we were unfortunately unable to interview directly supporters who participated in restorative justice conferences, it is clear from our observations that the restorative work done in conferences was not just to and from offenders and victims, but also to and from their supporters. The element of the definition of restorative justice which speaks about restorative justice including 'all parties with a stake in a particular offence' (Marshall 1999: 5) clearly applied to the supporters in JRC conferences as well. In this sense, mediation is far less inclusive.

Who could – and did – speak?

At JRC conferences, it is only those sitting in the circle (victims, offenders and their supporters, together with the facilitator) who are allowed to speak during the conference. The model followed by JRC stressed that facilitators should say very little, merely introducing each part of the conference and then, in preference, using non-verbal communication to prompt. The mediation model followed by CONNECT and REMEDI tended to give mediators a more active speaking role during direct mediation meetings, with both mediators participating at REMEDI.

During observations of JRC conferences, which on average took 68 minutes (Shapland *et al.* 2006a), we were able to estimate the proportion of time that each participant spoke. Overall, the offender spoke an average of 55 times, taking up about 27 per cent of the conference time. Young offenders (in Northumbria final warning conferences) tended to speak less and for shorter periods, on average 49 times, taking 19 per cent of the conference time, but there was little difference at other sites. Victims tended to speak less often but for longer periods, so that on average the main victim spoke 36 times, taking up 21 per cent of conference time. The main offender supporter spoke an average of 22 times at conferences with an offender supporter taking up 12 per cent of conference time, while the main victim supporter spoke an average of 24 times (13 per cent). Overall, these figures suggest that victims and offenders (and their supporters) were all equally able to contribute to the conference – and that supporters played an important role in conferences.

We were only able to observe four REMEDI direct mediation sessions. REMEDI mediations tended to be shorter than JRC conferences. Though both victims and offenders were rated as being involved 'a lot', mediators were also talking for a greater proportion of the event time than in JRC conferences.[6] It is interesting in this respect that the Thames Valley JRC facilitators who had a background in community mediation said that they had found conferencing on the JRC model different from their previous experience:

> This model of [JRC restorative justice] is low intervention, we don't have to manage the conversation the way we do in mediation. In mediation you are very much thinking on your feet and responding to what's happening in front of you and how you're going to intervene, your mind is working constantly, whereas here we have a script we have to follow.
>
> (Final interview with facilitator)

Initial experience in Belgium with conferencing, which has been introduced recently to services which have previously worked with a model of direct and indirect mediation, suggests similarly that the greater numbers of participants in conferencing may lead to a less dominant role for the mediator/facilitator.[7] Belgian conferencing does not have a 'script' in the same way as JRC conferencing.

There has been concern about whether young people are able to contribute to restorative justice events. In referral panels in England, Crawford and Newburn (2003) found that most participants did contribute significantly to proceedings. Young offenders tended to speak less often and more briefly, but in only 11 per cent of panels observed did young offenders speak only in monosyllables or not at all. In JRC conferences, all the young offenders (in Northumbria final warning conferences) contributed to the conference and in 88 per cent of conferences, young offenders spoke directly to the victim. However, 22 per cent of conferences involving young offenders involved the offender speaking for less than 10 per cent of the time of the conference, while this was true of only 5 per cent of conferences with adult offenders. Young people clearly find it more difficult to speak during restorative justice events.

The extent to which young people might be rendered more silent, however, seems to vary considerably between different restorative justice (and criminal justice) processes. Hallett *et al.* (1998) found that 37 per cent of young offenders in Scottish children's hearings communicated only through monosyllabic and non-verbal responses. Daly (2003b) found that in South Australia, observers rated 4 per cent of restorative justice conferences with young offenders as resembling 'a powerless youth in a roomful of adults' to a high degree, while 41 per cent showed it to some or a fair degree. Doak and O'Mahony (2009) note that in one of their two sites in Northern Ireland, restorative justice cautions run by police officers continued to resemble normal cautions with little participation by young offenders (or victims), while in the other site, lay participants did manage to participate to a greater extent. Yet in Northern Ireland youth conferencing run by the independent Youth Conferencing Service, observers rated young people as generally engaging well when discussing the offence, with 93 per cent being given the opportunity to explain it from their perspective and 98 per cent feeling they were listened to when they did so (Campbell *et al.* 2005). We have seen above that in JRC conferences young offenders always contributed and the same was true of REMEDI direct mediation involving young offenders.[8] Enabling young offenders to participate seems to depend upon the structure of the restorative justice event, the skills of the facilitator and the extent to which it is expected by all participants that all will contribute. We ourselves observed that having offender supporters present (as in conferencing) can be helpful for this, particularly when they can encourage the young person to speak. Having a large number of unknown adults present (professionals or conferences which involve neighbour disputes and a large number of participants), however, will make it more difficult. Models of restorative justice events which emphasise non-verbal encouragement by the facilitator and which discourage over-dominance or talkativeness by facilitators seem also to be helpful.

Our observations of restorative justice events also covered whether participants contributed to each stage of the process. For JRC conferences, where there were the three distinct phases of talking about what had happened, talking about the effects of the offence and talking about the future and any conference agreement, the offender talked about what had happened in every case, while the victim talked about it in 98 per cent of cases.[9] The main offender supporter contributed to this phase in 58 per cent of cases, while the main victim supporter did in 87 per cent. Clearly, both the main parties and supporters were interested and had questions about the offence.

Similarly, people contributed when talking about the effects of the offence on them: 72 per cent of offenders, 98 per cent of victims, 73 per cent of offender supporters and 90 per cent of victim supporters talked about the effects on them. The third phase turned to discussing the future and what might be in a conference agreement. Here, 85 per cent of offenders, 85 per cent of victims, 76 per cent of offender supporters and 69 per cent of victim supporters contributed to this stage. Not all conferences led to a conference agreement (95 per cent of the conferences we observed led to such an agreement) – but it is clear that again most parties at the conference were actively involved in trying to think about what might be included. Indeed, victims, offender supporters and victim supporters were all involved in suggesting possibilities in several conferences and the offender's family was involved in elements of the agreement in 68 per cent of the cases. Overall, it is clear that in JRC conferences, supporters were strongly involved, not just in supporting the person for whom they were there, but also contributing to the conference process and the agreement.

Communication in indirect mediation

So far, we have been discussing what happened in face-to-face meetings between the parties. What kind of communication took place in indirect mediation? It would have been impossibly intrusive for us to have followed mediators from REMEDI or CONNECT around as they visited first one party and then the other, trying to obtain answers to the questions each had for the other. We had therefore to rely on the files kept by the mediators, which detailed what contacts were made and gave some of the content of what was conveyed (in order for other mediators, if necessary, to pick up the case). There was no doubt that mediators took pains to try to elicit what each party wanted to know from or to offer to the other. Communication, however, was quite a difficult business. Mediators preferred to visit each party – but timing difficulties meant that there could be weeks between a question being posed and the answer obtained.

There was no 'template' for either scheme as to what should be covered but, in both schemes, the emphasis tended to be on what happened at the initial encounter with each party. Once those queries were answered, the mediator might not 'continue the conversation' and try to elicit follow-up questions. This was particularly true of cases involving young offenders where, after the initial meeting, the offender might write a letter of apology (sometimes in a fairly predetermined format) and the mediator would finally send a letter back to the offender giving very brief details of the victim's reaction. Overall, REMEDI youth cases had just an average of 1.5 meetings with offenders and 0.8 meetings with victims (though the 'chain' was rather longer in adult cases, with an average of 2.5 meetings with offenders and 1.6 meetings with victims). CONNECT indirect mediation was very varied in scope – from a single meeting with offender and victim (followed by a report to the court) to much longer preparation and information exchange (Shapland *et al.* 2006a).

Indirect mediation is potentially more onerous on mediators, in terms of the overall time involved (primarily in making appointments). CONNECT cases took an average of 55 days from referral to the last contact with someone related to the case. A CONNECT indirect mediation case involved an average of 14 contacts (visits or telephone calls) and just under seven hours of worker time (though the range was wide: between one hour and 25 hours). REMEDI cases took an average of about 203 days from referral to last contact for adult offenders, with the time needed to obtain victim contact details being one of the chief reasons for the overall length of the case. Visits in adult cases were always made by two mediators and there was an average of 2.5 meetings with offenders plus 1.6 meetings with victims.[10] In REMEDI youth cases, referral panel cases which went to indirect mediation lasted on average 61 days, while YOT referrals were an average of 57 days from referral to last contact. There was an average of 1.5 meetings with offenders and 0.8 meetings with victims.[11] In contrast, JRC conferencing cases lasted an average from referral to closure of 20 days in Northumbria, 23 days in London and 51 days in Thames Valley, though they took up more worker time during this shorter period (17 hours, for example, for a case leading to a conference with both victim and offender present, held in London). Much of this time was involved in negotiating a venue and time for the conference (particularly since many conferences were held in prisons) and in ensuring all participants could get there. These elements (and the conference time itself) do not apply to indirect mediation.

Because of the nature of indirect mediation, much of the effort is spent by the mediator on shuttling between the parties and in arranging contacts. The time in direct contact with the parties is relatively small. Nor can parties easily engage in 'supplementary questions' or have an interactive session with the other party. Supporters can only be involved with their own 'side'. The result, as we shall see in the following chapters, is that communication in indirect mediation was clearly being felt to be more impoverished than with direct mediation or conferencing. In some instances, it led parties to question whether the mediator was really communicating what the other party had said.

Was everyone enabled to say what they needed to say?

We saw in Chapter 5 that for both offenders and victims, one of the key expectations of conferences was that they would be able to communicate with the other person. Did they feel that this had happened? Communication has several aspects: to be able to put one's own point of view, to feel that one is listened to, to understand what the other person is saying, to feel that, overall, everyone had a fair chance to speak. Contacted a few days after the conference, by the facilitator, one of the questions asked was: 'Were you able to say what you wanted to say?' A large majority of all JRC victims and offenders said they were: 99 per cent in London, 94 per cent in Northumbria and 96 per cent in Thames Valley. But these are views just immediately after the conference, as relayed to the facilitator. Given facilitators were highly regarded, it is possible that participants were just being kind. However, when we asked interviewees to look back at the conference a few months afterwards, the positive views remained: asked 'Did you feel you had the opportunity to express your point of view?', 84 per cent of offenders and 93 per cent of victims said they did (Shapland *et al.* 2007). Asked 'Did you think you had the opportunity to explain the consequences of the offence?', again 82 per cent of offenders and 89 per cent of victims said they did.

These very positive views about being able to participate and say what one wants to say are not unusual in evaluations of restorative justice. Crawford and Newburn (2003) found that 87 per cent of young offenders at initial referral panel meetings strongly agreed or agreed with the statement: 'You had an opportunity to explain your side of things'. With young offenders, this is not always so, however. Strang *et al.* (1999) found that, though 91 per cent of adult offenders in their RISE drink-driving trial felt they 'had an opportunity to express their views', that was so for only 69 per cent of young personal property trial offenders and 77 per cent of youth violence offenders. Victims, however, tended to produce higher praise: 91 per cent of victims in the RISE youth personal property and 85 per cent in the youth violence trials agreed they had an opportunity to express their views.

Young people being able to participate 'in a room full of adults' relates, we think, to the ways in which facilitators run conferences or mediation and their perceived dominance. Where facilitators have been perceived as more dominant, other evaluations have found lower rates of participation (and satisfaction) (Hoyle *et al.* 2002; Daly 2003b). In none of the three schemes we evaluated were facilitators seen as too dominant. Overall, for JRC, 88 per cent of offenders and 93 per cent of victims interviewed, looking back at the conference, said that the facilitator had let everyone have their say (another 4 per cent of offenders and 3 per cent of victims said they had done so 'to some extent') (Shapland *et al.* 2007). The vast majority found the facilitator in control of the conference (84 per cent of offenders and 88 per cent of victims), but not too much in control, nor too little. Similarly, for REMEDI direct mediation meetings, both offenders and victims generally felt facilitators let everyone have their say, were impartial and were in control of the meeting (but not too much or too little).

Over-dominance has been linked to the use of police officers as facilitators (Braithwaite 1994; McCold and Wachtel 1998), but we think that the association may have come about because schemes run by the police and using police facilitators have tended to adopt a more facilitator-dominant model. Our own evaluation is one of the first which allows comparison between professionals of different backgrounds using the same model of restorative justice, because JRC used police officer facilitators in London and Northumbria, but probation officer, prison officer, victim support worker and community mediator facilitators in Thames Valley. The results in terms of both observations of facilitators and participants' reactions were almost identical in all cases.[12] The JRC Northumbria youth final warning scheme is the closest to the conditions which proved difficult in Thames Valley (Hoyle *et al.* 2002) and the US (McCold and Wachtel 1998): police officers and young offenders. Yet we found that 87 per cent of young offenders responded 'yes' to the question of whether the facilitator had let everyone there have their say (only 4 per cent of young final warning offenders said 'not really' or 'no'; the others said 'to some extent').

Our findings are congruent with those of Lamb *et al.* (2008), who have been looking at different professionals' work in a slightly different setting: police officers and social workers interviewing child victims of abuse. They found that both professions tended to 'leap in' with directive questions, rather than let the child tell his or her own story freely (as the code of practice suggests), particularly when the professional interviewer felt more insecure or children's answers were shorter or more monosyllabic. It required considerable training – for both professions – to encourage interviewers to 'hold back' and use encouraging, non-directive prompts. We think the same is true in restorative justice, particularly with young offenders. What is key to good practice and allowing all participants to participate – and feel they have participated – is a non-directive model, backed up by rigorous training and feedback.

Procedural justice

Gehm (1998), considering victim-offender mediation, has posed the challenging question: 'Why would victims voluntarily reinvolve themselves in an emotionally charged setting that has the potential to restimulate all of the painful thoughts and feelings that the precipitating crime caused?' His answers revolve around the fact that victimisation involves feeling a loss of control over one's life, a shock to one's expectations of society (except in very high crime areas) and generally a loss of faith in a just and orderly world (see also Shapland and Hall 2007). Hence recovering from victimisation is partly a reordering or 'sense-making' process. This links well with the reasons victims gave for wanting to participate in the schemes we evaluated: communication (having questions answered, finding out more, expressing one's own point of view); and altruistic reasons revolving around preventing further victimisation (feeling a duty to attend, preventing reoffending) (see Chapter 5).

Both communication and preventing reoffending depend upon adequate process, which involves being able to participate and having adequate information with which to do so. Tyler (Lind and Tyler 1988; Tyler and Huo 2002; Blader and Tyler 2003; Tyler *et al.* 2007) has developed the theory of procedural justice – and tested it in criminal justice, civil justice and restorative justice contexts. The theory suggests that the process which justice adopts is extremely important to lay participants (both offenders and victims), to the extent that ratings of confidence in justice and associated ratings of fairness and legitimacy can depend more upon process than outcomes.

Procedural justice, in terms of judgments of 'fairness', involves people judging how fair the formal rules and procedures are, and how well justice professionals make decisions and treat them (Blader and Tyler 2003): in other words, the quality of decision-making and the quality of treatment. Restorative justice, compared to traditional criminal justice, tends to score far more highly, particularly on quality of treatment. Though Blader and Tyler's dimensions of decision-making and treatment are orthogonal, we might also postulate that where better treatment (participation, being able to get information and one's point of view across) leads to better information for the decision-maker (e.g. the sentencer) then the perceived quality of decision-making may also improve (see Shapland and Hall 2010).

Restorative justice has always prided itself on providing a higher quality of treatment (more respect for participants, more communication). So, for example, the RISE experiments in Australia, using conferencing with young offenders, found that 'Around 90 per cent of all victims responded that they had been treated fairly and respectfully. A further 92 per cent said that all sides got a fair chance to bring out the facts at the conference, and only 11 per cent said they had felt too intimidated to say what they felt' (Strang and Sherman 2003: 35). Victims were significantly more likely to know about the outcome of the case (a key aspect of good process) than if their case had gone to court. The complaint of victims that they are not kept informed by criminal justice of the sentence, etc. in their case has been a long-standing one in England and Wales (Shapland *et al.* 1985; Allen *et al.* 2006) and it is noteworthy that this remained a problem for victims in the schemes we evaluated – even though these were high-profile cases within criminal justice in the areas.[13] Indeed, one of the main elements about CONNECT's services which was appreciated by victims was that facilitators were happy to find out for victims what the *criminal* justice outcome of the case was and tell them.

Tyler *et al.* (2007) used data from the RISE drinking and driving trial, which involved conferencing with adult offenders, to look at the effect of procedural justice on respect for the law, comparing those who went to a conference with those in the control group who only experienced criminal justice. This is an atypical offence, with no direct personal victims, but they found that where the processes were found to be rated highly on procedural justice, there was increased respect for the law (and indeed decreased subsequent reoffending). However, this was true of both criminal justice and restorative justice processes – *if* they were rated highly on procedural justice.[14] They conclude that only effectively delivered programmes which gain respect from participants will be seen to produce procedural justice.

In our own evaluation, those victims who experienced restorative justice conferencing with JRC were significantly more likely to be satisfied overall with their *criminal* justice experience than were those who only received the standard criminal justice response.[15] Conference victims were also significantly more likely to rate the criminal justice process as fair (73 per cent thought it was very or somewhat fair compared to 61 per cent of control victims).[16] Similar effects occurred with offenders: 71 per cent of offenders in the conference group compared to 59 per cent of offenders in the control group said they were very or quite satisfied with the criminal justice response in their case: a significant difference.[17] Not only has participating in restorative justice resulted in views that the restorative justice process was fair (and legitimate), but, perhaps due to the close linkage between restorative and criminal justice processes in these schemes, the positive views spilled over into ratings of criminal justice overall.

Perceptions of procedural justice are clearly very important in relation to the perceived fairness and legitimacy of the law and of any processes, such as restorative justice, which seek to deal with criminal offences – particularly more serious criminal offences committed by adult offenders, where diversionary restorative outcomes are not a possibility. The idea of procedural justice is entirely compatible with – and indeed flows directly from – Marshall's (1999) definition of restorative justice, used by these three schemes, which emphasises processes of participation, inclusivity and fair treatment. In the schemes we evaluated, those perceptions and expectations were fulfilled.

Dealing with emotion and the effects of the offence

Victimisation, particularly violent victimisation, can produce serious and lasting emotional effects.[18] Talking about offending-related problems, such as substance abuse, (un)employment and family difficulties, is also potentially charged with emotion.[19] It is hardly surprising, therefore, that scheme managers, funders and ourselves were concerned, when the schemes started, that conferencing and direct mediation with adult offenders, particularly for serious offences, might produce not just emotion-filled meetings, but potentially aggressive meetings.

The results impressed us all. Emotion was indeed expressed during face-to-face meetings between offenders and victims, as we shall see, but it never boiled over into assault and there were very few threats: in only 5 conferences out of the 226 observed were any threats expressed. Four of these were verbal threats, one a violent gesture; two were made by offenders, two by offender supporters and one by a victim supporter. There was no physical assault in any conference or direct mediation in any of the three schemes. Sometimes, time out was used to calm down proceedings. In a very few cases, the conference was abandoned because of the lack of sobriety of one or more participants. But the effects of the preparation and room management by facilitators were such as to prevent any real problems – as shown also by the ratings on the control of the proceedings discussed above.

Indeed, emotion did not lead to feelings of insecurity or lack of safety among participants. Overall, in parallel with the views discussed above about facilitators being in control, participants overwhelmingly experienced the JRC conferences as safe experiences: 84 per cent of offenders and 85 per cent of victims said they felt very safe.[20] As a safety measure, victims and offenders who had taken part in conferences were interviewed by facilitators (or completed a questionnaire) a few days after the conference. Despite the seriousness of the offences and that many were violent offences, very few people said that they were worried the other party might find them or contact them (five people out of nearly 700 respondents). This can be compared with the greater fears of intimidation reported by victims and witnesses in traditional criminal justice procedures, where 8 per cent of all incidents revealed by the 1998 British Crime Survey led to intimidation of victims, rising to 15 per cent where the victim had some knowledge of the offender (Tarling *et al.* 2000).

To what extent were events emotion-filled? It is clear they varied considerably. Participants themselves were asked whether they found the event an emotional experience. For JRC, 35 per cent of offenders found the conference very emotional and 31 per cent emotional, but 15 per cent not at all emotional and 18 per cent not really emotional. Victims were similarly split: 31 per cent found it very emotional and 37 per cent emotional, but 15 per cent not at all emotional and 16 per cent not really emotional. There was little difference between different sites or, perhaps surprisingly, between victims of different kinds of offence. REMEDI participants' experiences of their direct mediation were equally varied.

In observations of JRC conferences, observers rated 14 per cent of conferences as being emotionally intense – but 41 per cent as not being emotionally intense at all. Observer judgments may not be a completely reliable guide to participants' own feelings, particularly because, as in this case, the conferences were being held in a country where overt expressions of emotion in a meeting with strangers are culturally rare. In fact, the participants most likely to break down or cry were offender supporters (23 per cent of observed conferences) rather than offenders (15 per cent), victims (15 per cent) or victim supporters (11 per cent). Overall, having considerable emotion in a conference was quite rare.

Harris *et al.* (2004) have suggested that emotion is a crucial element in the transformative processes that conferences can inspire. Considering offenders, reintegrative shaming theory, as set out by Braithwaite and Braithwaite (2001), indicates that restorative work depends upon the offender feeling shame emotionally before being restored. Harris *et al.* suggest that remorse or guilt (stemming from appreciating that harm has been done to others) may be as or more important than shame (emotion focused upon the self), but that emotion is still crucial. For the JRC conferences in England, the single case studies discussed in Chapter 6 show the relevance of such transformative processes, wherein the other party changes from becoming a stereotyped 'other' to a known person. However, in the JRC conferences we observed, though shame and remorse were present, it was difficult to judge emotion. This may be a particularly English cultural effect – or it may be, as Robinson and Shapland (2008) discuss – that offenders' emotional starting points are not always what restorative justice theorists have supposed. Harris *et al.* (2004) propose that the ideal-typical sequence of events in conferences would be, for the offender, embarassment/shame (possibly mixed with defiance) at the beginning of the conference which, through operation of empathy when the victim speaks of the effects of the offence, produces emotional shame in the offender, leading to apology and then the opportunity for acknowledgment of that apology and acceptance of reparation offered by the offender. Hence emotion and the expression of emotion are important. Certainly JRC facilitators trained in this tradition rated conferences as 'very good' or 'good' depending on how much emotional shame they believed was felt by the offender and how much emotion was expressed, particularly by the victim.

We are less convinced, from the observations and interviews, about this sequence always occurring or it being necessary for it to occur. In some cases, offenders could arrive at the conference already feeling shame and wishing to apologise. In others, expressions of emotional shame, remorse and hurt were more muted, though interviews after the conference showed that the victim had clearly picked this up. What does seem to be key is a growing sense of empathy and the way in which this turns defensiveness (on the part of both offender and victim) and hurt (on the part of the victim) into a wish to solve the situation. The process of recognising the hurt caused by the offence and its wrongness, but separating those from what the offender may be able to do in the future, seems part of the transformation from 'other' to 'a person' discussed in Chapter 6, in which growing empathy, rather than expressed emotion, may be the key element.

Apologies and the reaction to apologies

For some theorists, the apology is the key moment in restorative justice events. Indeed, in youth justice in England and Wales, bringing the young offender to make an apology is often seen as the outcome of restorative justice, whether or not the victim actually receives the apology, acknowledges it or accepts it. So, young offenders may be persuaded to write letters of apology, though these may not always be sent (Holdaway *et al.* 2001; Zernova 2007a). This occurred in some REMEDI cases in our own evaluation, but because a letter of apology not sent to the victim cannot count as two-way communication between victim and offender, we have not included them within cases in which restorative justice occurred.

Apologies, however, are very complex speech acts (Shapland *et al.* 2006b). In relation to criminal acts, it can be argued that an apology ought really to be made not only to the individual victim, but also to the state (because the criminal law has been breached) and sometimes to the local community as well (because the act has caused local anxiety, fear or disruption). Though this state/communal apology is a routine part of mitigation speeches by legal representatives (Shapland 1981), apology does not seem to be so pressing for offenders when the victim is not present. So Crawford and Newburn (2003) found that in initial referral panel meetings attended by victims, 77 per cent of offenders apologised – but where they were not attended by victims (the vast majority), only 30 per cent of young offenders apologised to anyone. 'However, a larger proportion of young offenders expressed remorse in initial panels in some way other than by apologising. Four fifths did this verbally' (2003: 127).

Having the victim present, particularly in a face-to-face meeting in which everyone speaks, seems definitely to be a major element in the offender working through embarassment and nervousness (and sometimes defiance or not taking responsibility for the offence) to remorse, expressed in an apology. It seems to be a reaction to hearing the effects of the offence from the victim and victim supporters. Indeed, offenders often apologised in JRC conferences multiple times (up to twelve in one JRC burglary conference: Shapland *et al.* 2006a). Overall, offenders apologised clearly in 88 per cent of the JRC conferences, with another 9 per cent giving a partial apology and 18 per cent not apologising at all. The JRC 'script' did contain a pause which presented the offender with an opportunity to apologise, but offenders might well apologise earlier when discussing how the offence came about. Offender supporters could also offer apologies: 'I apologise for my son and what he's done to you' (mother, London robbery case).

Multiple apologies can seem over the top, along the lines of 'methinks he doth protest too much'. For a serious offence, what seemed to carry much more weight was if the offender was, while apologising, also saying that they were intending to turn round their life in practical, realistic ways. By doing this, they were indicating they were aware of the seriousness of what they had done, taking responsibility for it, and producing means by which they would not do so again.

As we shall see in Chapter 9, concrete reparation (financial or work-based) only rarely figured in outcome agreements – but we have suggested that apologies which are linked to these promises to lead a different, non-offending life can be seen as 'symbolic reparation' (Shapland *et al.* 2006b).

Apologies are of course dyadic structures whereby the offender apologises, but the victim is supposed to acknowledge, even accept the apology (Tavuchis 1991). For more serious offences, however, we need to distinguish between acknowledgment, acceptance and forgiveness. Just as it is almost patronising to expect victims of serious offences to be 'healed' of the effects of the offence after one restorative justice event (Shapland *et al.* 2006b), so it is wrong to expect forgiveness. Forgiveness has to be something freely offered. Some victims and victim supporters wished to do this; others felt the offence was still too raw for them to be at this stage (and might doubt they would ever be). Yet some victims, as we saw in the single case studies in Chapter 6, still wished to acknowledge that the offender had come to the meeting and was prepared to take responsibility for the offence and apologise for the hurt they had caused.

Given the severity of some offences which resulted in direct mediation or conferencing in these schemes, some victims found it hard to reconcile the offence with the apology being offered by the offender. They doubted the sincerity of the offender's apology. Overall, 90 per cent of JRC victims interviewed said the offender had apologised, while 91 per cent of those who said they had received an apology said they had accepted the apology (Shapland *et al.* 2007). Asked overall, however, whether they thought the offender was sincere, 45 per cent of victims said they did think the offender was sincere, but 21 per cent did not. We cannot know whether these judgments of insincerity were about the way the offender described the offence, or offenders' expressions of remorse, or apologies, or what offenders said they would do in the future. It is interesting though that Strang (2002), evaluating a similar model of conferencing in Australia, the RISE project, found that 77 per cent of victims of young offenders there thought that the apology they heard was sincere – but 23 per cent did not – a similar percentage.

Strang (2002), however, compares the likelihood of victims thinking the apology was sincere between those who attended a conference (which was a diversionary conference) and those whose cases went to court in the normal way. The difference was considerable – only 41 per cent of victims at court thought the apology was sincere.[21] The difference was primarily because victims thought apologies at conferences were less likely to have been 'coerced' from the offender (by relatives or legal representatives) than those received as part of the criminal justice process. Strang also points out that the likelihood of a victim receiving an apology at all in the normal criminal justice process is much smaller. We found the same: in the control group (criminal justice only), only 19 per cent of victims said that the offender had apologised at some point to them (compared to the 90 per cent of victims in the conference group who said the offender had apologised). If apologies are important to victims as acknowledging the hurt that has been done to them so that they can move on (see Chapter 8), then conferencing or direct mediation provides that opportunity while criminal justice in England and Wales currently does not.

Problem-solving for the future

We saw in Chapter 5 that the key reasons for both offenders and victims to wish to attend a restorative justice event were communication and trying to prevent reoffending in the future. To what extent did the different models of mediation and conferencing allow this problem-solving for the future – and did participants take advantage of it?

The JRC model of conferencing had a third stage built in, in which participants were invited to think about what would happen after the conference and in what ways problems could be solved. How did participants respond? We found a little initial hesitation but after that considerable participation in problem-solving. Very few offenders (10 per cent) did not contribute to this stage of the conference (note that conference agreements were made in 96 per cent of conferences) – observers rated offenders as contributing 'a lot' or 'quite a lot' in 39 per cent of conferences. Similarly, 8 per cent of victims did not contribute, but 42 per cent contributed 'a lot' or 'quite a lot'. As we saw in the single case studies, supporters were also important. In 80 per cent of conferences, offenders were prompted at this stage by someone suggesting something they might do. However, this was not a professional or facilitator 'taking over' at this point – the prompter was either an offender supporter or the victim. The offender's family was involved 'a lot' or 'quite a lot' in sorting out the outcome agreement in 27 per cent of conferences. Everyone present showed 'a lot' or 'quite a lot' of agreement about the eventual outcome agreement in 93 per cent of conferences observed. Clearly, when the framework of the meeting facilitates all the participants contributing to what should happen next, they are well able to do so.

It is not surprising that there was sometimes some hesitation when participants were invited to discuss what would happen next. These restorative justice events were run in close connection with criminal justice, with four of the six JRC trials being pre-sentence or immediately post-sentence. Participants were therefore having to bear in mind what sentence the offender was likely to get and what kinds of programmes or support might be available for that sentence – which in a number of cases was going to be a prison sentence. Just like youth conferencing in Northern Ireland, they were essentially feeding into sentencing. Historically, discussion of what is likely to happen during sentences has been confined to professionals in England and Wales and there has been little discussion with offenders, let alone victims.[22] Enfranchising offenders, victims and their supporters to discuss potential solutions to offending-related problems is potentially very effective – because it is they who are likely to see innovative and individually suitable solutions – but it is also new – and participants seemed to need 'permission' to undertake the task. We discuss the results – the outcome agreements and whether they were successfully completed – in Chapter 9.

The JRC model deliberately built in discussion of the future – and so met participants' expectations and wishes for the events. Mediation does not necessarily have such a future-oriented stage, though nor does it prohibit it. There is a paradox about mediation. Mediators say that they will follow what victims and offenders wish to talk about and bring up – and certainly both REMEDI and CONNECT mediators would have discussed whatever victims and offenders wished to raise. CONNECT's work in finding out about what had happened in criminal justice for victims and offenders illustrates that. However, mediators have clear ideas of what it is appropriate for victims and offenders to discuss – and it is these subjects, informed by mediator culture, which form the basis of what mediators say when victims and offenders ask what mediation is.[23] Given that few victims and offenders knew about mediation before being approached, they are likely to have taken the clues offered by mediators. These emphasised communication about the offence and the effects of the offence, both of which look backwards in time. Given the theoretical basis of mediation, they should also have mentioned and emphasised reparation and restorative solutions to deal with the effects. However, perhaps because youth offenders were subject to criminal justice proceedings such as referral orders while adult offenders were generally at the stage of resettlement, concrete reparation (money or work) seemed inappropriate and mediators fell back upon suggestions of letters of apology.

Theoretical strands in victim-offender mediation have tended not to emphasise a future orientation in terms of practical steps addressed by the participants or addressing reoffending by offenders. So, Gehm (1998) refers to the main framing theories for mediation as participative justice which emphasises process, equity theory emphasising peacemaking and saying what the hurt has been, and narrative theory, which suggests reduction of anxiety may come through discourse. Umbreit *et al.* (1995: see Chapter 2) saw key outcomes as participation, agreeing an acceptable resolution to the dispute and arranging reparation. Mediation in Belgium stresses the process and arranging payment of restitution (Vanfraechem 2009). Mediation in Finland 'provides the opportunity to discuss the mental and material harm caused to the victim by the crime and to agree on measures to redress the harm' (Iivari *et al.* 2009: 9). This emphasis on process and restitution/reparation rather than upon preventing reoffending may be partly due to the fact that mediators in both mainland Europe and Scandinavia are generally independent, working for mediation associations, rather than being criminal justice practitioners, who would be more infused with criminal justice priorities such as rehabilitating offenders.

REMEDI is an independent voluntary-sector organisation providing mediation services over a range of contexts while CONNECT was created and managed by a criminal justice voluntary sector body, NACRO, together with the Probation Service. Though CONNECT, which worked pre-sentence, clearly discussed with both offenders and victims what might be possible in relation to sentence provisions – and subsequently wrote a report to the court – their model did not include outcome agreements and suggestions for detailed practical arrangements from victims and offenders were not normally part of CONNECT's model.

REMEDI only worked post-sentence or post-disposal. Some direct mediations finished with informal outcome agreements, but written agreements with all parties signing them were generally not part of the model (see Chapter 9 for details of outcome agreements). In common with other countries, mediation did not seem to have such a future orientation as conferencing in the schemes we evaluated.

Building social capital: bringing in community

A key value for restorative justice is that offenders, having taken responsibility for their wrongdoing, should then be reintegrated into the community. For Braithwaite (1989) it is this reintegrative aspect which distinguishes the reintegrative shaming of restorative justice from the shaming of traditional criminal justice. The question arises, however, into which community or what kind of community should the offender be reintegrated? In order for the outcomes of restorative justice to flow seamlessly from its process, if reintegration into the community is to occur, it would seem also important that members of the 'community' be present during the restorative justice event.

Some restorative justice projects have sited themselves deliberately within a particular geographical and cultural community, seeking to build on communitarian values already emphasised within that group. This was true, for example, of the New Zealand adult pilot restorative projects discussed in Chapter 2 (Maxwell and Morris 2001). The roots of restorative justice in some countries have deliberately reached back into previous cultural traditions, as for example the Maori in New Zealand and First Nations projects in Canada. More common now, however, is the situation where projects are geographically limited – to a town or a region – but there are no obvious community cultural links. Projects may build on local traditions developed by voluntary-sector organisations – as with the John Howard Society in Canada or REMEDI in South Yorkshire – but links with criminal justice practitioners, other voluntary-sector agencies and local authorities remain to be made and strengthened. Indeed, as we saw in Chapter 3, the business of creating and maintaining links in a busy multi-agency environment is a major task for restorative justice schemes.

To what extent, therefore, was 'community' represented in the restorative justice schemes we evaluated and to what extent were community links important in restorative justice processes? None of the three schemes explicitly invited participants on the basis of them being community representatives. Victim-offender mediation for REMEDI and CONNECT only involved individual victims and offenders. Victims and offenders in JRC conferencing were asked who might be their supporters among people who were important to them. Though occasionally a victim or offender might ask a community leader (such as a faith group leader) as a supporter, this was primarily on the basis of their individual relationship with that person. The only exception was for Northumbria adult caution conferences, which involved violent offences and, normally, offences which had been committed in the course of the parties knowing each other. Where the result was a neighbourhood dispute, often involving patterns of conflict over a considerable period of time, then some participants might be community police officers or other well-known persons in the community (Shapland 2009a). However, if the context was a work dispute or an extended family dispute, they would not be there. In terms of the process of restorative justice, therefore, there was no obvious 'community' presence.

When JRC conferences turned to consider what might happen in the future, however, they did quite often call upon community resources. There was mention of the local community or community resources in 42 per cent of the outcome agreements in observed conferences, of which 11 per cent made considerable mention of such resources. This was not simply in youth offender cases, but was as likely to occur in cases with adult offenders of burglary or street crime. Drawing upon programmes running in the local community, or local expertise, is not uncommon in restorative justice conferencing with young offenders in other countries. In Northern Ireland youth conferencing, for example, conference plans (outcome agreements) normally feature assistance for the young person, which might include mentoring, reparation, substance abuse programmes and voluntary work, all linked to the local community (Campbell *et al.* 2005). Difficulties with the initial stages of New Zealand youth conferencing focused around the lack of fit with local community facilities and resources (Maxwell and Morris 1993). It is important to recognise that, even for adult offenders, there is a need to link with local opportunities and programmes.

Because restorative justice was initially associated with strong local communities drawing upon previous cultural traditions, there has been concern as to whether it can succeed in modern localities where there is little community spirit or action and, though there may be considerable affinity to the local area for individuals, the bonds between individuals are weak, so that there is little capacity for dealing with problems of conflict and disorder (Bottoms 2003). This is a similar argument to that which bemoans that community crime prevention initiatives tend to succeed in middle-class areas (with more social resources), but not in the working-class areas where there are more crime problems (but fewer social resources) (Bennett 1990).

Putnam (2000) has usefully distinguished between different forms of social capital.[24] So, 'bonding social capital' refers to ties between people in similar circumstances, such as family or neighbours. These are often strong, affective ties and may be drawn upon by individuals for help. In the context of restorative justice conferencing, participants typically drew upon those with whom they had strong bonding social capital as supporters. However, to problem solve for the future, participants may need 'bridging social capital' – often more distant, weaker ties (acquaintances, workmates, bosses, criminal justice practitioners), but with people who can control opportunities and resources.

McCold (2000) has suggested that deficiencies in modern communities are relatively immaterial to restorative justice, because what matters is the 'communities of care' for the victim and offender: those who know them well and can support them through the restorative justice process and help them achieve the outcomes. We would agree that these communities of care are indeed those who victims and offenders choose as their supporters during conferencing, who are typically drawn from those with whom participants have strong bonding social capital. It is also very clear from our observations and interviews that it is these micro-communities who are the most suitable as supporters – restorative justice, particularly for serious offences and with adult offenders, involves people talking about very sensitive matters which are often inappropriate for any wider community.

However, supporters, though they did contribute much to outcome agreements and agreed to support participants after the restorative justice event, do not have access normally to the bridging social capital necessary to access the kinds of programmes, support and opportunities which can encourage desistance and reintegrate offenders into the wider community (see Chapter 9). McNeill and Whyte (2007) argue that this is a key role for probation officers and social workers – working with offenders and their families to create such social capital and such practical opportunities to facilitate desistance. A very similar role may need to be placed upon facilitators to suggest relevant possibilities during the future-oriented stage of conferences, when participants themselves know what kind of opportunity is needed but not where to find it. In modern communities, reintegration may need to be a much more active and knowledge-driven process than when it was possible to rely on self-contained localities where everyone knew everyone and where to obtain necessary contacts.

Looking back at restorative justice: what do people think it achieved?

8 The victims' views: satisfaction and closure

Restorative justice events cannot provide victims with all the support and action they would wish to see following victimisation: many of those tasks must fall to victim support and assistance organisations, and to criminal justice practitioners and the criminal justice system. Restorative justice theorists, however, have argued that restorative justice can add to the possibilities of victims being able to communicate effectively with the offender if they wish to do so; to a more victim-oriented criminal justice response; and to recovery from the effects of victimisation. Some of these possibilities stem from the inadequacies of criminal justice in relation to victims: that criminal justice agencies do not meet the proper expectations of victims for information about their case, support and having their needs taken into consideration in sentencing, etc. (JUSTICE 1998). Others, such as possibilities for reparation and for a reduction in fear or feelings of revenge, have been more intrinsically linked with restorative justice (Zehr 1990; Strang 2002).

In this chapter, we shall look at victims' reactions to restorative justice, as delivered by the three schemes we evaluated, when they looked back at their experiences some months after the events. We consider overall victim satisfaction and its determinants, whether what victims experienced was what they expected, and how restorative justice was seen in the light of the effects of the offence on victims.

Looking back at restorative justice: overall judgments of satisfaction

Satisfaction is a complex concept and depends upon people's expectations of what they think should occur. In the final interviews with victims, we asked a considerable number of different questions which were aimed at tapping into different elements of satisfaction: whether the process was useful for victims; how satisfied victims were with the outcome of the conference/mediation; to what extent the restorative justice event had solved any problems caused by the offence; whether victims thought restorative justice was a good way to deal with the offence committed; and whether victims would recommend restorative justice to others for a similar offence (Shapland *et al.* 2007). The answers to these questions are shown in Table 8.1 for JRC and REMEDI.[1]

In fact there was very substantial inter-correlation between victims' views on these different measures – perceptions of the process related to perceptions of the outcome, perceptions of the usefulness of the process related to whether victims thought it was a good way to deal with the offence, and so forth. For JRC, these four questions, when analysed statistically, produced one overall general factor, on which all four questions loaded at levels of 0.76 or above.[2] For REMEDI, all the satisfaction questions were included. There was a similar general factor,[3] but also a second factor associated primarily with indirect mediation and related to doubts about the principle of mediation but independent of views about the process itself. It seemed as though concerns about the idea of mediation then led victims to choose indirect mediation, but this choice did not then relate to subsequent experiences of mediation or the likelihood of being satisfied or not satisfied with what happened.

The ratings of satisfaction for JRC and REMEDI are clearly high: 70 per cent or more victims were satisfied with what they had experienced. These positive reactions were in relation to both the process of restorative justice and its outcomes. They culminated in generally positive views as to whether victims would recommend restorative justice to others. The views of CONNECT victims, though we can only analyse them qualitatively due to the small number of interviews conducted, were very much in the same vein (Shapland *et al.* 2007). As we saw in the last chapter, victims in all three schemes primarily valued communication, the positive ways in which they were treated and being part of problem-solving on what would happen next.

Though few reported any negative experiences, where they did, these were related to difficulties in communication and confounded expectations. The communication problems tended to be quite different in different restorative justice events: difficulties in hearing other parties; difficulties in one party concentrating on the proceedings related to diagnosed psychological problems; some 'hogging' of the proceedings by one participant. In indirect mediation, they were, as discussed in Chapter 7, a result of the necessarily delayed and mediated process of communication: if one party did not receive the kind of answer they were expecting, there was little opportunity to question or challenge it. Where expectations were confounded, this tended to be where offenders did not admit responsibility for the offence – blaming co-offenders or refuting others' views of it. Restorative justice cannot function, within criminal proceedings, as a trial. It is important that offenders are prepared to admit they were responsible for the offence. These rare cases where there was dissatisfaction underline the importance of this element.

These results are similar to the positive reactions victims have given to restorative justice in other schemes and in other countries (Umbreit *et al.* 1995, 2000; Strang *et al.* 1999). However, the victims in the three English schemes were almost entirely adult victims of often serious offences committed by adult offenders. Restorative justice internationally has primarily been developed for

Table 8.1 Victims' satisfaction with restorative justice events

	JRC (%)	REMEDI (%)
Overall, how useful did you feel the process was for you?		
Very useful	43	35
Somewhat useful	30	35
Not very useful	10	17
Not at all useful	9	13
Don't know	3	0
(n)	(216)	(23)
How satisfied or not are you now with the outcome of the [conference/indirect mediation] process?		
Very satisfied	36	53
Fairly satisfied	40	27
Not very satisfied	11	13
Not at all satisfied	7	7
Don't know/can't remember	0	0
(n)	(216)	(15)
To what extent has [the conference/mediation] solved any problems caused by the offence?		
Very much so	13	9
To some extent	23	27
No effect	28	41
Made the problems worse	4	5
No problems caused by the offence	14	18
Don't know	14	0
(n)	(216)	(22)
Do you think that having the [conference/mediation] is a good way to deal with the offence which was committed against you?		
A very good way	36	44
A good way	28	35
It is OK	21	4
A bad way	7	17
A very bad way	2	0
Don't know	2	0
(n)	(216)	(23)
Would you recommend restorative justice to others?		
Definitely	57	65
Probably	21	4
Not sure	9	13
Probably not	5	9
Definitely not	5	9
(n)	(216)	(23)

Note: JRC data in table derived from Tables 4.1 and 4.2 Shapland *et al.* (2007). REMEDI data include both direct and indirect mediation, except where specified.

young offenders (see Chapter 2). Prior to this evaluation, victim responses to restorative justice with adult offenders were perhaps not so easily predicted. It needs to be remembered that, in many instances, these were the kinds of offences for which the criminal justice system is seen as the key forum and on which society judges criminal justice – serious violence, robbery, burglary. However, victims' reactions to the normal criminal justice response are not always favourable (Shapland forthcoming b; Hall 2009): they find that they are not kept informed, do not always know whether their input (such as victim personal statements) will be used, and can be kept waiting to give their evidence, etc. (Allen *et al.* 2005; Hoyle *et al.* 1998). These restorative justice processes – run in parallel with normal criminal justice responses – were able to provide victims with a more adequate overall package.

Expectations fulfilled?

The level of satisfaction among JRC victims with both the process and the outcome was so high as to make it difficult to analyse whether victims of particular types of offence were more or less satisfied. However, we know that victims, as well as offenders, have a number of different reasons for agreeing to restorative justice (Chapter 5) and we can look at whether victims with particular reasons were more likely to be satisfied.

The main reasons victims gave for deciding to take part were that they wanted to express their feelings about the offence to the other person, that they wanted to help the other person, that they felt a duty to take part, that they wanted to have a say in how the problem was resolved, that they wanted to have some questions about the offence answered, that they wanted to be repaid for the harm they had experienced, and that taking part might affect what would happen as a result of the case. For each, they said whether this reason was very important to them, quite important, not very important or not at all important.

Victims who said that wanting to help the other person was a very important reason for them were significantly more likely to be very satisfied with the conference itself[4] and with the process,[5] though there was no relation with what they felt about the outcome. Whether victims wanted to express their feelings to the other person approached significance in relation to how useful they felt the process was for them, with those who saw this as very important being more likely to be satisfied.[6] Communicative and problem-solving expectations hence seemed particularly likely to be satisfied by the conference format. There was no relation between any of the other reasons and satisfaction with the process and outcome – with all effectively being equally satisfied.

As we shall see in Chapter 9, outcome agreements for JRC only occasionally included the payment of financial compensation to the victim or others (7 per cent) or reparation (work) for the victim or community (11 per cent). Yet this clearly did not affect victims' satisfaction with the agreement or the outcome of the process – even for those victims who had said they wanted to be repaid for the harm they had experienced. This is perhaps surprising given that obtaining reparation (financial or otherwise) has a high profile in youth restorative justice (Campbell *et al.* 2006; van Dijk and de Waard 2009).

We do not know exactly why there was this relative lack of importance for reparation. For JRC, it was only an outcome occasionally (Chapter 9), it occupied a relatively low place in the scale of wishes and expectations of victims (Chapter 5) and we have now found that, even for victims for whom it was important, there was no significant association with satisfaction. We think that this is one of the effects of undertaking restorative justice with adult offenders and with more serious offences. Financial reparation for serious offences would have been well outside the financial means of the majority of offenders, particularly if the offender were to be sentenced to prison or was about to be released from prison. Victims of serious violent offences, robberies or burglaries may not be particularly keen on having much more contact with offenders (as would occur if they were to do reparative work for them). This is quite different from the attitudes of Dutch shopkeepers to having young shoplifters working in their stores – which they saw as an opportunity to educate the young people into the problems which shop theft was causing the stores and their staff (Kruissink and Verwers 1989). Instead, the JRC victims put much greater stress on the symbolic reparation of offenders taking control of their lives and deciding to change their life patterns away from offending (desist) through tackling the problems leading to offending.

The process of recovery from victimisation: hurt, the need for recognition, fear, anger and closure

The restorative justice process, which might occur a few weeks, months or even years after the offence, was just one event related to the offence which victims experienced. Because these restorative justice events were run in parallel with criminal justice processes, they might also have made statements to the police, written victim personal statements about the effects of the offence on them, attended court, dealt with insurance matters and/or applied to the Criminal Injuries Compensation Authority for compensation (if it was a violent offence). In addition, they will have talked about the offence to their friends and relations and may have used the services of Victim Support.[7] The restorative justice process is only one small part of all this activity and it would be wrong to expect that it would be the sole or even a major means for victims to use as part of their recovery from the effects of the offence.

Secondary victimisation and the 'right point' for restorative justice

There has been some debate as to when restorative justice should be offered to victims: do they need to 'get over' the offence before they could consider meeting the offender? Would discussing the offence and its effects shortly after the offence be secondary victimisation? We asked victims and offenders at the final interviews whether, looking back on the process, they thought the restorative justice event was held at the right time after the offence. For JRC, 72 per cent of victims thought it was held at about the right time, but 22 per cent thought it was held too long after the offence (Shapland *et al.* 2007: Table 4.1). Almost no one said it was too soon after the offence (which is the response one might expect if there were feelings of revictimisation). There was very little difference between JRC trials, so those who were experiencing restorative justice prior to the release of the offender from prison (Thames Valley prison trial), which was necessarily many months or years after the offence, were as likely to say it was at the right time or too long after as those who experienced restorative justice pre-sentence. Mediation for REMEDI and CONNECT victims was primarily indirect mediation, so time frames for starting it were less clear. Though, as we have seen, some victims felt the process of indirect mediation itself took too long (too long to obtain answers to questions, etc. – see Chapter 7), there were few comments as to whether the mediation started too soon or too late.

Wemmers and Cyr (2005) examined whether victims participating in a victim-offender mediation programme for young offenders in Canada said they suffered any revictimisation. However, they were only able to examine victim views as expressed post-restorative justice, so could not look at the longitudinal impact of the process on the effects of the offence. They researched victims' perceptions of their feelings of safety when contacted by the programme, whether meeting the offender increased or reduced fear, and whether or not participation helped victims to put the offence behind them (what we have called 'closure'). As in our own evaluation, very few victims felt fear or did not feel safe. Those who did feel more fearful associated it with the offender failing to take responsibility for the offence (and so victims were afraid they might be offended against again). Similarly, those who felt worse after a direct meeting with the offender said it was because the offender did not take responsibility for their actions.

Our evaluation suggests that victims were not being revictimised by the restorative justice process – there was no evidence for secondary victimisation – and that they were not being 'pushed' into accepting restorative justice at an inappropriate time. Secondary victimisation can also be broken down into likely pressure points, such as whether victims feel afraid that being contacted about restorative justice might lead to a further offence against them by the offender, whether victims fear revictimisation and whether victims felt safe at any direct meeting with the offender. We examined these separate aspects in previous chapters (Chapters 5–7) and found that, providing the process was well managed and victims were told what would happen, none of these occurred.

Does restorative justice reduce the harmful emotional effects associated with victimisation?

Strang (2002) considered the level of emotional effects suffered by victims who participated in the RISE conferencing trials (see Chapter 2). She found that 60 per cent of victims in those cases which were diverted to conferencing experienced a significant reduction in their level of fear and anger. The RISE studies (Sherman *et al.* 1998; Strang *et al.* 1999) found that those who had been to a conference dealing with youth violence offences were significantly less likely to say they would do some harm to the offender themselves (revenge, anger) than those victims whose cases had been to court.

Strang *et al.* (2005) used data from both RISE and the JRC trials reported in this book to look at reported psychological effects, comparing victims before they went to a conference with their feelings afterwards. They found that victims reported significantly less fear of the offender afterwards, substantially less anger, were less anxious about why they themselves had been victimised (the 'why me?' question) and tended to be more sympathetic towards the offender. They see the last as a potential precursor to forgiveness.

Restorative justice commentators have cited findings such as these to suggest that restorative justice has a positive effect in reducing harmful consequences of the offence on victims. However, methodologically, it is very difficult to prove this has occurred. The problem is, as we indicated above, that the 'natural' process of recovery from an offence tends to result in reduced levels of negative affect over time. People become less fearful, less angry, less depressed, less fearful of going out, less worried about meeting someone looking like the offender. Reactions to victimisation are individual so that, though it is true that more serious and more violent offences produce, on average, greater and more long-lasting emotional effects, individuals may be devastated by apparently minor offences and may react only slightly to very serious offences (Shapland and Hall 2007; Shapland *et al.* 1985; Allen *et al.* 2005). When thinking about the effect of restorative justice, therefore, what one would need to prove, in order to show that it has an overall positive effect, is not only that victims report less negative effects afterwards, but that they report less negative effects compared to those who have not experienced restorative justice.

There are very few studies which meet this methodological challenge. The ideal would be to undertake a longitudinal study, with measurements at several points in time, of victims' perceptions and psychological observations of their emotional state, so that one could see what happens before and after they experience restorative justice – whether the decreasing slope of negative effects over time sharpens after the restorative justice event. There are no such studies. The next best, perhaps, is to compare similar cases for those who experience restorative justice and those who do not.

Caroline Angel (2005) reinterviewed victims from the JRC London trials (robbery and burglary victims) after they had experienced conferencing, using a post-traumatic stress scale measure. These data were then combined with the RISE results (where victims were also interviewed using a similar measure) to compare, using the randomised controlled trial methodology set up for both studies, victims who had been to a conference with those who had only experienced criminal justice (Sherman *et al.* 2005). The results showed that victims who had experienced conferencing were significantly less likely to have feelings of revenge towards the offender,[8] though there were no significant differences on self-blame,[9] which is a key element of post-traumatic stress syndrome.

We asked JRC victims about the extent to which they felt depressed, felt angry, were upset and were afraid of the offender immediately after the offence – and then about the extent to which they felt each of these at the time of the interview (which was some weeks after the conference). For each trial, most victims – but not all – said they felt each of these emotions. So, for example, 24 per cent of robbery victims from London assigned to the conference group said they felt very depressed immediately after the offence and 22 per cent depressed, but 55 per cent said they did not feel depressed. By the time of the interview, 2 per cent said they were very depressed, 13 per cent depressed, but 85 per cent not depressed. There were similar reductions over time for the other trials and for anger, upset and feeling afraid of the offender.

To see the effect of participating in restorative justice, we can compare those who were randomised to the conference group and those who were randomised to the control group (criminal justice only). We looked at the data collected by Angel in London during the follow-up interviews a few days after the offence. This showed some positive effects immediately after the conference which related to aspects of post-traumatic stress (Shapland *et al.* 2007). So, victims in the conference group were significantly less likely to say they felt like retaliating against the offender than victims in the control group (paralleling the RISE results reported above (Sherman *et al.* 1998; Strang *et al.* 1999). They were significantly less likely to say they were thinking about the offence when they did not mean to (burglary victims), other things made them think about the offence when they did not wish to (robbery victims), they tried not to talk about the offence (robbery victims) and they stayed away from reminders of the offence (robbery victims). However, the results for other trials and measures were not significant.

In the longer term, we can see whether the experience of restorative justice reduced the numbers who feel depressed, angry, upset or were afraid of the offender, comparing the numbers of victims who initially felt that emotion with those who still felt it by the time of the final interview weeks later.[10] The results for each question showed that the numbers in the conference group who were experiencing each negative emotion decreased more than did the numbers in the control group, but the difference was not significant.[11] There are hence suggestions that the restorative justice conference did have a positive effect on reducing the negative emotions associated with victimisation, but we cannot reject the null hypothesis.

Closure and security

If, however, one asks victims whether they themselves think that restorative justice has made them feel better, the answer is predominantly positive: 15 per cent of JRC victims said it made them feel very much better, 49 per cent better to some extent, 30 per cent said it had had no effect and just 2 per cent (five people) said it made them feel worse. In relation to feeling secure, 39 per cent of victims said it had made them feel more secure, 46 per cent said there was no effect and 9 per cent said they felt less secure (Shapland *et al.* 2007).

Both conference and control JRC groups experienced criminal justice procedures,[12] but the addition of restorative justice seemed to make the JRC conference victims feel more secure – though 31 per cent of control group victims said the criminal justice system had made them feel more secure, 45 per cent said it had no effect and 20 per cent said it made them feel less secure. If we look purely at those who felt more or less secure (omitting those who said there was no effect), then the difference is significant, with the restorative justice group feeling more secure.[13]

REMEDI victims, all interviewed in relation to cases with adult offenders, were also asked whether mediation had made them feel more secure and whether it had made them feel better in any way. In terms of security, indirect mediation generally did not seem to affect victims' feelings of security – 71 per cent said it had made no difference, while 14 per cent said they felt more secure and 14 per cent less secure (n = 14). They were more positive, however, about feeling better: 50 per cent said mediation had made them feel very much better or better to some extent, while 43 per cent said it had had no effect and one person said they felt worse (primarily because of lack of communication from the offender). The results for direct mediation were very similar.

Victims themselves, therefore, usually derive positive benefit from restorative justice in terms of it lessening the negative effects of the offence (making them feel better) and making them feel more secure (lessening fears of revictimisation). The JRC model of conferencing appeared to be slightly more successful at this than mediation (direct or indirect), possibly because it allows victims to engage offenders in conversation and work out what the offender is like and what was behind the offence.

Lessening negative effects and feeling more secure are aspects of closure: the extent to which the victim feels they are able to put the offence behind them. Victims who took part in JRC conferencing were asked 'Has the conference and the process provided you with any sense of closure in relation to the offence?' Of the 216 victims interviewed, 52 per cent said it had provided closure, 20 per cent said it had to some extent, 7 per cent said 'not really' and 15 per cent said it had not (Shapland *et al.* 2007). Victims in trials with, generally, more serious offences which are likely to give rise to more serious and long-lasting effects (London burglary, London robbery, Thames Valley prison trials) were as likely as those in trials with generally less serious offences (Northumbria magistrates' court, Northumbria youth final warning, Thames Valley community trials) to say that restorative justice had resulted in closure for them.

Closure cannot mean that the victim would be able immediately after the restorative justice event to return to the same psychological position as before. As Norris and Kaniasty (1994) have shown, victimisation may have long-term effects which means that victims will remain affected over substantial periods of time – and may never regain their previous physical or emotional state.[14] Closure is a complex concept and an intensely personal one. There are psychological and emotional elements related to the effects of the offence: whether memories fade, whether there are still flashbacks. Wemmers and Cyr (2005) have suggested that the experience of being able to talk about the offence and its effects – a key feature of restorative justice – is therapeutic in itself and can result in it being easier to feel that one is able to put the offence behind one. Kenney (2004) has stressed the importance of agency for victims in their coping with the effects of very serious crime: that victims need to be enabled to take action themselves and not remain powerless while social agencies take all the decisions. We suspect that achieving closure equally contains elements of being able to turn a very unpleasant experience to some good: to add to a process which is likely to prevent reoffending; to be able to help the offender take responsibility for the offence; to receive an apology and be able to indicate that it is accepted, even though the hurt of the offence remains. It is interesting that, for JRC victims, closure was significantly related to whether victims felt that restorative justice had helped to solve problems caused by the offence.[15] Conferencing is an active process in which victims can engage and themselves take action to help to resolve what the offence has caused. Through this, it may help victims to move towards closure.

9 Outcome agreements and their progress

Introduction

One of the key debates in restorative justice concerns the relative importance of processes and outcomes. In this chapter we turn our attention to the latter, and in particular the written outcome agreements which were produced in the context of restorative justice events. As we noted in Chapter 5, the three schemes which were subject to evaluation differed in regard to the importance they placed upon reaching and recording specific outcomes as part of the restorative justice process and this reflected their use of different models of restorative justice: mediation or conferencing. For JRC, which only used conferencing, discussion of outcomes formed the final part of all restorative justice events and a written outcome agreement was produced in the vast majority (98 per cent) of cases. The other two schemes, REMEDI and CONNECT, did not view a formal agreement as a necessary outcome of mediation, preferring to allow the participants to set and pursue their own agendas. REMEDI cases produced 11 outcome agreements from 35 mediations (4 adult and 7 youth cases), while the CONNECT scheme did not produce any written agreements.

In this chapter our principal focus will be the outcome agreements which were routinely produced in the context of JRC conferences, although we shall refer to REMEDI's outcome agreements where relevant. We present an analysis of the content of those agreements which were available for analysis (in excess of 300 for JRC) and consider some of the likely influences on those agreements. In the final part of the chapter we consider the extent to which outcome agreements were monitored or followed up by scheme staff, as well as what we were able to glean – from scheme databases and from interviews with participants – about compliance and completion. We also explore victims' and offenders' reactions to the outcome agreements when they looked back at them at the time of the interviews we undertook a few months later.

Outcome agreements: the JRC scheme

As already noted, JRC conferences almost always ended with an outcome agreement being reached, because a focus on outcomes and the future was the final 'scripted' part of the conference process adopted by the scheme. However, this part of the script was non-directive in that it did not include suggestions made by facilitators or by criminal justice personnel as to possible or desirable outcomes: agreements were thus intended to be flexible to accommodate the particular circumstances and wishes of participants. These agreements could be understood as an informal 'contract' or 'compact' (Crawford 2003) in that they included undertakings from participants to do things – or sometimes refrain from doing things – in the future, but they were non-enforceable, in the sense that there were no sanctions built into the schemes concerning non-compliance.

Agreements were usually written up by a facilitator during or after the final phase of the conference and they generally consisted of a list of numbered items with details of the relevant parties (i.e. who would be responsible for ensuring that the item was completed). Outcome agreements were usually signed by participants (83 per cent of conferences with an agreement),[1] and in some cases, in addition, there was a specific indication of whether the victim had agreed with the outcomes listed. There were also examples of outcome agreements which specified that a named person could at a future date agree to a modification of the proposed outcome(s), in special circumstances. Some agreements also gave details of the range of recipients of the agreement, which included (for example, for London pre-sentence cases) JRC researchers, the sentencing court, the Crown Prosecution Service, the Probation Service and the offender's legal representative. The content of outcome agreements was entered onto a database in all JRC sites with a view to monitoring progress toward objectives in due course.

One of the findings of our analysis of outcome agreements and our observations of JRC conferences was that the content of agreements evolved as experience grew, so that items became more precise, specific and (in theory at least) achievable.[2] This stemmed in part from a growing realisation that offenders might not always be able to deliver the sorts of life-changing (and rather 'woolly') aspirations they sometimes voiced (e.g. 'to avoid trouble from now on'), but the move toward greater precision was also reinforced by the practice of following up progress in respect of outcome agreements, which started relatively slowly but eventually became a more standardised and routine part of the process (Shapland *et al.* 2006a). Once facilitators began to monitor progress toward objectives, it became clear that realistic targets with straightforward milestones were both more amenable to measurement and easier to feed back to other participants. The monitoring of outcome agreements by scheme staff is discussed further below.

Examining the content of outcome agreements

In Table 9.1 below we present our analysis of the content of the 346 outcome agreements[3] produced by JRC in the main experimental phase of the project (Phase 2). Our analysis revealed that the number of items included in outcome agreements varied from one to eight, with the mean number of items (for Phase

2 conferences) ranging from a low of 2.7 for Northumbria adult court cases to a high of 3.6 for Thames Valley community cases. The timescales for items to be completed ranged from the day of the conference itself (e.g. an offender's apology voiced during the conference) through to over 12 months after the conference; however, for most items with specified timescales, completion was expected within six months (83 per cent of items). Reflecting the move toward more measurable objectives (as noted above), there was a distinct increase in items which had specified deadlines for accomplishment between Phase 1 and Phase 2 of the JRC scheme's work (from 48 per cent to 70 per cent).

As Table 9.1 shows, the most common item was the expression of an apology by the offender (in 62 per cent of agreements), which normally took place in the context of the conference itself. Although outcome agreements did not always specify the recipients of apologies, our observations indicated that they were in the vast majority of cases victims, but could also include others, such as the offender's own supporters or those of the victim.

Symbolic reparation, in the form of apologies, was then a common element in outcome agreements.[4] In contrast, material reparation, in the form of financial compensation (which could be court-ordered or voluntary) or other material offers of 'help' (either directly to victims or, indirectly, to 'the community'), was relatively rare, with less than one in five agreements including such an item. Other items in agreements which centred on or in some way implicated victims concerned how participants said they would behave if they met in the future, or undertakings on the part of offenders to avoid future communication with victims.

What is very clear from Table 9.1 is that JRC outcome agreements were dominated by items relating to offenders' future behaviour. These items tended to flow from earlier discussions in conferences which centred on the reasons behind offending behaviour which other participants commonly learned about for the first time in the restorative justice arena. As can be seen from the table, they included both general undertakings to 'stay out of trouble' or 'avoid reoffending' and also to participate in various therapeutic or otherwise 'positive' activities, with an emphasis on tackling criminogenic problems or needs (Bonta 1996). These more specific undertakings were quite varied, and a number of different programmes and interventions were referred to in agreements. The most commonly mentioned category of interventions, however, related to substance misuse problems. These were concentrated in London, where the two RCTs focused on serious acquisitive offences (domestic burglary and street robbery) known to be commonly related to substance misuse. So, 63 per cent of London burglary conference agreements contained a specific item about attending or applying to attend a drug programme, as did 55 per cent of London street crime conferences (compared with only 7 per cent of Northumbria adult magistrates' court conferences). Pursuing education, employment and, to a lesser extent, constructive leisure activities and suitable accommodation were other items which featured on a number of outcome agreements and which constituted attempts to tackle offenders' identified criminogenic problems or needs.

Table 9.1 Items included in 349 outcome agreements produced in JRC conferences during the randomised phase (Phase 2)

Outcome agreement item	Percentage of agreements including this item
Any apology,* of which:	62
verbal apology	53
written apology	10
offender accepting responsibility for offence/behaviour	1
To pay compensation (including court-ordered compensation)	11
Other reparation to victim or work for community	7
Victim expressing hope offender will not do it again	4
Other specific victim-related item	9
Offender promising to stay out of trouble or prison/not do it again	16
Offender promising to avoid previous peers/not mix with the wrong crowd	5
To apply to or attend drug programme, of which:	28
CARAT** specified	7
Narcotics Anonymous specified	1
To stay away from/abstain from drugs/alcohol	12
To apply to or attend alcohol programme	7
Other specific drug/alcohol-related item	7
To attend anger management/aggression replacement programme	5
To attend counselling	8
To attend Enhanced Thinking Skills programme	2
To engage in education, of which:	15
while in prison	9
when released from prison	2
while in the community	4
To seek or maintain employment, of which:	14
while in prison	3
when released from prison	6
while in the community	5
To get involved with a sport/social activities	3
To move away from area or sort out problematic housing	5
Offender's family agreeing to support offender/maintain family relationships	6
Other specific family-related item	8
Participants promising to get on with/acknowledge each other	5
Participants agreeing to ignore each other if/when they meet	2
Praise for offender/acknowledgment of offender's worth	4
Other specific item	17
Total number of outcome agreements	349

* An outcome agreement might contain both verbal and written apologies.

** CARAT stands for Counselling, Assessment, Referral, Advice and Throughcare (May 2005).

Source: Shapland *et al.* (2006a: Table 4.1).

Our observational data help to make sense of the finding that outcome agreements tended to focus much less on victims' needs than on the needs of offenders. We found that this was not because victims or their wishes were ignored but rather because victims, in common with other participants, actively wished to focus on addressing the offender's problems, with a view to minimising the chance of reoffending. This reflected the finding that in pre-conference interviews about why they wanted to participate in the conference, 72 per cent of victims said it was very or quite important to them to help the offender, and 'wanting to be repaid for the harm experienced' was not rated particularly highly (Shapland *et al.* 2006a; see also Chapter 5). Our observations revealed that this marked concern with seeking ways to help offenders was linked to an explicit desire to prevent future victimisation. Thus it was not necessarily simply the case that victims wanted to 'win the battle for the offender's soul', as Clifford Shearing put it after observing two Australian conferences in the early 1990s (see Braithwaite and Mugford 1994: 149): rather, victims' (and other conference participants') aspirations for offenders were often expressed as a desire to help or 'save' others (i.e. potential future victims) from the harm they themselves had suffered at the hands of the offender. Indeed, we observed that for many victims, an offender's stated intention to 'do something' about their offending behaviour constituted a form of symbolic reparation: it was for many victims a valuable addition to a verbal apology (Shapland *et al.* 2007). The majority of victims appeared then to regard the rehabilitation of the offender as a legitimate aim of 'their' conference, and did not regard the pursuit of such an aim as incompatible with their own needs.[5] Interestingly, very similar results have been obtained in the evaluation of statutory youth conferencing in Northern Ireland: victims were not found to be vindictive, but rather to want to help offenders not to reoffend, both to decrease the likelihood of others becoming victims in the future and to help offenders to put their lives on a more useful footing (Doak and O'Mahony 2006).

While quantitative disparity makes it difficult to directly compare outcome agreements produced by JRC and REMEDI, we can say that for the small number of REMEDI cases which produced some form of outcome agreement (n = 11), there tended to be relatively few items: the range was 1 to 4 and the mean was 1.9. As previously noted, the emphasis in REMEDI mediations was on the victim and offender setting the agenda themselves and answering questions each had of the other rather than specifically thinking about the future. There was, then, no standard format for outcome agreements, and items tended to focus upon resolving any continuing difficulties between victim and offender which had arisen during mediation. Other items tended to centre on the offender and included the offender writing to a relative of the victim, avoiding the victim's house, being able to contact the victim, direct reparation, leading a drug-free lifestyle and not getting into the circumstances which led to the offence.

Immediate responses to outcomes

Restorative justice events can involve strong emotions and be very challenging for participants. Given that these schemes were involving serious offences, with adult offenders, with some events taking place in prison, JRC decided that it would be important for facilitators to contact participants (both offenders and victims) a few days after the event, to see how they were feeling and whether they had any concerns. Concerns might have been about intimidation, or about the conference, or about depression (particularly in relation to offenders who might just be returned to their cells after the event and who would be recalling what had been said and how they felt about themselves).

Overall, these follow-up interviews (or questionnaires where it was impossible to meet face-to-face or make a telephone call to participants) took place for 216 victims and 282 offenders for JRC who had experienced a conference (and for 252 victims and 125 offenders who were in the control group). Very little intimidation had taken place – just three offenders and four victims from the conference group said they had been revictimised or harassed in some way since the event (all in Northumbria), with all such subsequent harassment being verbal. Yet 78 victims and 60 offenders had seen the other party since the event – mostly because they had had an existing relationship prior to the offence which gave rise to the conference. There is clearly a potential for harassment following restorative justice, but these figures are actually considerably lower than the incidence of harassment of witnesses who attend court (Tarling *et al.* 2000). A minority of participants remained slightly worried that the other party might know more about them, for example the area in which they lived. So, for example, 9 per cent of JRC London victims and offenders had some residual worries that they might meet the other party again. However, since we were not able to talk to victims or offenders prior to the conference, we cannot know whether these were worries which existed then (e.g. that they might meet the other party in the street) – from the questions posed at conferences, we suspect these were fairly common worries, many of which were assuaged by the process of communication at the conference.

At these follow-up interviews, which took place about ten days after the conference, both victims and offenders were very positive, both about the conference itself and about the outcomes. There were very few second thoughts about the outcome agreement. Concerns about the lack of information about what the criminal justice process itself was doing – and a lack of information about it – were beginning to rise: 'I've made lots of calls [to the police officer in the case] … but there's nobody answering the calls' (Northumbria JRC victim). The importance of facilitators following up outcome agreements and communicating the result back to victims in particular goes hand in hand with the importance of victims knowing what criminal justice outcomes were.

Innovation, standardisation and the criminal justice context

Part of the potential of restorative justice stems from its ability to move beyond 'typical' or 'standardised' responses to offending, to include items for the future which reflect the participants' particular circumstances. As we have previously remarked, each restorative justice event is unique and the participants bring different wishes and expectations to it. However, concerns have also been raised about a possible tendency toward routinisation – or 'McDonaldization' (Umbreit 1999) – when restorative justice moves into the mainstream, and in particular when it takes place against a backdrop of criminal justice. It is important to consider whether any of these issues were likely to have impacted on the schemes we were evaluating, particularly JRC. Given that considerable numbers of outcome agreements were produced, a tendency toward standardisation might have resulted. By a similar token, the emphasis in outcome agreements on the rehabilitation of offenders (which we identified above) might indicate attempts on the part of facilitators to steer participants toward the sorts of outcomes likely to make sense to, and perhaps to impact on the decisions of, criminal justice agencies.

Our first observation in this regard is that we found examples of innovative and novel items in outcome agreements in all JRC sites, with (for example) imaginative forms of reparation and resolution of family conflicts particularly apparent in Northumbria youth final warning cases and practical steps in anger management in Northumbria adult court cases. We did, however, find that there were barriers of various kinds to innovation in the form of getting 'reparative activities' into outcome agreements. In the conferences we observed, it was not uncommon for conference participants (not only victims) to suggest that the offender might consider indirect reparation (e.g. doing unpaid work) in their own or the victim's community. Suggestions included voluntary work of various kinds, from 'helping elderly people' to gardening and fundraising for victims' groups, as well as suggestions that the offender might help other people like him or herself (namely other offenders). So the notion that the offender might 'give something back' was often mooted in conferences, but as we have seen it rarely materialised in outcome agreements. This was partly because, for many offenders, reparation (beyond the symbolic level) was unrealistic, either because they were serving a prison sentence or (where conferences were held pre-sentence) because they were potentially facing one. Even where there did seem to be potential for the performance of reparative work by offenders, there was often uncertainty about how to arrange it and concerns about 'health and safety' issues – most notably in youth conferences – tended to quash ideas about appropriate reparative activities.

Another factor which we think had a bearing on the content of outcome agreements was the variety of professional backgrounds of facilitators who, in JRC, included police officers (in London and Northumbria) and (in Thames Valley) probation officers, prison staff and community mediators, the latter not allied with any particular criminal justice agency. This had mixed implications for outcome agreements. On some occasions it was clear that a facilitator was able to draw upon his or her professional knowledge of community or criminal justice resources in drawing up an outcome agreement. However, facilitators were sometimes less able to draw on their experience: such as, when conducting a conference in an unfamiliar setting, such as when a community mediator or police officer conducted a conference in a prison. Difficulties could also arise for facilitators when a conference took place pre-sentence, so that the criminal justice 'destination' of the offender – custody or community – was not known. When this happened, some facilitators adopted the practice of producing two 'provisional' outcome agreements, only one of which would be 'activated' post-sentence. We regarded this as a sensible and innovative strategy.

It was clear then that facilitators' knowledge and experience – and uncertainty, in some cases, about the offender's impending sentence – were ways in which the criminal justice setting impacted on the content of at least some outcome agreements. It is also possible that outcome agreements were influenced – either directly or indirectly – by facilitators' awareness that they might be seen by external criminal justice audiences and, in some cases, decision-makers. Whether they produced outcome agreements or not, all of the schemes had mechanisms for 'feeding forward' to criminal justice agencies information about the restorative justice event.[6] In the case of the JRC scheme, senior staff had held a number of discussions with senior members of the judiciary and prison authorities during the initial phase of the project and had been assured that control group offenders would not suffer detriment from being randomised out of the possibility of attending a conference. Nonetheless, the subsequent decision of the Court of Appeal in *Collins*[7] confirmed that being prepared to attend a restorative justice conference could be considered a mitigating factor in sentence. It is likely that aspects of outcome agreements (such as apologising, paying compensation, undertaking programmes) may also have been seen as mitigatory by sentencers (see also Edwards 2006), though only in one group was there any significant difference in the likelihood of being given a custodial sentence between the restorative justice and control groups.[8] It is also possible that in cases involving prisoners, where the conference took place during a custodial sentence, an outcome agreement might influence discretionary release decisions. It was not, however, possible for us to obtain direct evidence of whether this occurred.

Monitoring compliance with outcome agreements

As we have seen, the majority of items which appeared in outcome agreements comprised undertakings of various kinds on the part of the offender. In addition to offers of apologies (usually delivered during the conference), offenders agreed to apply for or take part in programmes of various kinds, abstain from particular behaviours and, in a smaller proportion of cases, perform reparative activities. As we noted above, these agreements could be understood as a 'contract' drawn up with the agreement of participants, but they were non-enforceable in the sense that there were no sanctions for non-compliance.

Nonetheless, there are strong theoretical grounds to expect reasonably high rates of compliance with outcome agreements produced in the context of a restorative justice event. Theoretically, high rates of compliance may be linked with high levels of perceived procedural justice, which stem from the fact that two of the key prerequisites of a restorative justice encounter are, firstly, that the offender has admitted responsibility for the offence and, secondly, that the offender must consent to take part in the process. Thus the presence in restorative justice encounters of offenders who have been coerced or who deny the offence ought to be a rarity – and offenders whom we interviewed after the process said that they had not been coerced and no one involved with criminal justice had 'told' them to take part (Shapland *et al.* 2006a). Indeed, as we have argued elsewhere, offenders on the threshold of a restorative justice encounter may be substantively different from those who are generally subjected to traditionally 'rehabilitative' interventions: that is, they are likely to include a significant proportion who are already thinking about desistance and whose motivation to take part is explicable with reference to a decision, or a desire, to desist (Robinson and Shapland 2008). This potentially sets them apart from those offenders who participate in 'correctional' programmes under a court order, where both consent and genuine motivation to participate may be questionable; it would also appear to increase the likelihood of compliance with any agreement reached in the restorative justice process.

During Phase 2 of the JRC scheme, staff began to establish procedures for monitoring compliance with outcome agreements, although follow-up work was initially not very systematic and sites developed slightly different practices and systems for recording information about compliance. The London site developed the most sophisticated recording system, which enabled us as evaluators to distinguish between (for example) non-completed items which were still pending or had not been complied with for various reasons (e.g. because a programme was not available, or because contact with the offender had been lost). Other sites' and schemes' databases, however, lacked full data on compliance and reasons for non-compliance. Where items were 'aspirational' and lacked a specified outcome or time frame, it was more difficult for the scheme, or us, to confirm rates or degrees of compliance. We have therefore had to use our judgment, to some extent, in respect of arriving at conclusions about compliance.

With this proviso, we found overall that 36 per cent of the 348 JRC Phase 2 outcome agreements were completed fully and another 52 per cent were completed at least partially, leaving just 11 per cent which were definitely not completed.[9] Timescales for review were relevant for 70 per cent of agreements: of these, 11 per cent of items were completed on the same day as the conference, 20 per cent within a month, 25 per cent within three months and 27 per cent between three and six months. However, a significant minority of items (14 per cent) took up to a year to complete and 3 per cent more than a year (Shapland *et al.* 2006a).

Completion rates for different kinds of items varied considerably. Apologies, particularly verbal apologies, were often completed very quickly and, as noted above, the majority happened during the conference: overall, 99 per cent of verbal apologies and 85 per cent of written apologies were completed. However, other, longer-term items in relation to victims proved more difficult to fulfil. Where progress letters were promised, these were written to victims in only a third of the 91 cases with such items, and definitely not written in 45 per cent of cases.[10] Similarly, as far as we were able to ascertain, compensation payments were only definitely completed in 38 per cent of relevant cases and were definitely not completed for 41 per cent of agreements (Shapland *et al.* 2006a).

Where outcome agreements included 'rehabilitative' items which offenders had agreed to explore or undertake, confirmed completion rates were in the region of 50 per cent. So, for example, we found that 53 per cent of requirements to apply to or participate in a drug programme were completed, while 17 per cent were definitely not completed, 15 per cent were not verifiable (lost contact, etc.), 6 per cent were unachievable by the offender and several were 'pending'. Very similar proportions occurred for applications to or participation in alcohol programmes (50 per cent completed), anger management programmes (41 per cent completed), counselling (40 per cent completed), participation in education (49 per cent completed), action on employment (45 per cent completed) and action on housing (54 per cent completed). But these figures should not lead us to imply that offenders had not put in the effort necessary to complete the programme or action. The definite failure rates were generally around 11 per cent to 18 per cent, with counselling (at 36 per cent) the only item having a higher failure rate. Given the seriousness of the offences, the fact that many offenders were given custodial sentences and often transferred to other establishments (which might not have relevant programmes or might not have space on the programme) and the chronic nature of many of the offenders' problems, these may be considered low failure rates (Shapland *et al.* 2006a).

Although some (n = 11) REMEDI direct mediations included outcome agreements, there was no formal process for following up items in agreements. We cannot, therefore, say overall whether items were completed.[11]

Satisfaction with outcome agreements

Compliance with outcome agreements is likely to be one element affecting participants' satisfaction with the outcomes of restorative justice. Whether outcome agreements are sufficiently specific to permit measurement of compliance is another. We have argued that when schemes are set up, review periods should be set for items in outcome agreements, as these significantly impinge on both the length of time a case may take and the potential to deem it 'completed' or not (Shapland *et al.* 2006a). We have also argued that the legitimacy of restorative justice processes, where outcome agreements are produced, will be dependent upon the effectiveness of the scheme in feeding back to participants accurate information about compliance.

In our final interviews with participants in JRC conferences, we asked individuals a number of questions about outcome agreements. In total, 81 per cent of the victims and 78 per cent of the offenders we interviewed said they remembered outcome agreements being recorded in the last part of the conference. In cases which did produce an agreement, 75 per cent of victims and 78 per cent of offenders said they were satisfied with the agreement. A relatively small proportion (9 per cent of offenders and 13 per cent of victims) felt that their views were not taken into account in deciding upon outcomes and, perhaps reflecting this, 12 per cent of victims and 10 per cent of offenders said they were not satisfied with outcome agreements that were produced in their conference (Shapland *et al.* 2007: 25, 27).

Of the (JRC) offenders we interviewed after restorative justice, 87 per cent said they had completed everything or some of what they had agreed to do, with only 8 per cent saying that they had not done anything pertaining to the agreement (Shapland *et al.* 2007: 28). These data largely reflected JRC's own records, as discussed above. However, it is worth noting that only 41 per cent of offenders recalled being contacted by scheme staff after the conference, while 56 per cent said they had not been contacted. Of the victims we interviewed, 56 per cent said they had been recontacted, while 38 per cent said they had not. Participants in the experimental (conference) group and in more serious (offence) cases were more likely to say they had been recontacted (Shapland *et al.* 2007: 29).

This meant of course that a relatively large proportion of victims were unsure about whether outcome agreements had been completed. Indeed, some 38 per cent of victims said they did not know what, if anything, had happened regarding completion of the agreement, and 19 per cent believed that it had not been completed. We have surmised that not being recontacted by the scheme following restorative justice may well have had an impact on victims' overall assessments of and satisfaction with the process (Shapland *et al.* 2007: 30). A similar conclusion was reached by Maxwell and Morris (1993) in their evaluation of family group conferencing in New Zealand: around one-third of victims reported dissatisfaction with outcomes, and one of the cited reasons for dissatisfaction among victims was that they were not informed about whether outcomes had been achieved. In contrast, because of the New Zealand experience and emerging findings from our own evaluation, particular attention has been paid to following-up progress and informing participants in the Northern Ireland statutory youth conferencing process.

There is an important learning point here: this is that where an outcome agreement has been reached, it is crucial that sufficient attention and resources are devoted to maintaining communication with and updating participants about progress towards objectives. This is particularly true for victims, who are less likely to be personally involved in many of the outcome agreement items. It appears that, for participants, being kept informed in this way after the restorative justice event contributes in an important way to procedural justice and, ultimately, satisfaction with the restorative justice process.

Outcome agreements and theoretical views of restorative justice

In this chapter we have reviewed the schemes' use of outcome agreements as part of restorative justice, which varied according to the type of restorative justice process adopted by the schemes. For JRC, which used conferencing, outcome agreements were a standard part of the restorative justice event. For the other two schemes (REMEDI and CONNECT), which practised victim-offender mediation, formal agreements were far less important and only produced rarely, when individual circumstances seemed to suggest that such a written agreement would be useful.

On the basis of available data, it is difficult to draw firm conclusions about the extent to which outcome agreements facilitated the broader objectives associated with restorative justice discussed in Chapter 2. In relation to JRC, which produced the vast majority of agreements, we found clear evidence that participants wanted conferencing to act as a 'springboard' to potentially rehabilitative interventions for offenders (Braithwaite 1999). Although the final phase of conferences was 'scripted' in such a way as to facilitate individualised and potentially novel outcome agreements, our findings in respect of the most common types of items in the agreements we analysed were consistent with a model of restorative justice influenced directly by Braithwaite's theory of reintegrative shaming, which tends to prioritise the reintegration of offenders (loosely defined) over other outcomes (see Chapter 1). We found examples of a variety of potentially 'reintegrative' items in the agreements we analysed, including both symbolic ones (e.g. the expression of apologies) and more practical ones (albeit that examples of direct reparation to victims were rare).

Most of the emphasis, in respect of practical steps toward reintegration, was on traditionally rehabilitative and correctional resources (treatment programmes, education, etc.), mostly in criminal justice contexts. This may of course have reflected the fact that the schemes we evaluated were doing restorative justice which was strongly associated with criminal justice, which for some trials led directly to criminal justice decisions (sentence, programmes of interventions for final warnings, decisions on release). It may also have been associated with those schemes dealing primarily with adult offenders and often with quite serious or very serious offences. The cultural 'justice values' (Shapland *et al.* 2006b) which participants brought with them to restorative justice events and which underpinned what participants thought were 'proper' outcomes were likely to have involved traditional ideas of criminal justice outcomes for these kinds of offences.

We found fewer examples of attempts to develop offenders' social capital (Coleman 1988) or to enable offenders to pursue 'strengths-based' approaches to rehabilitation (Maruna and LeBel 2003; Raynor 2004). Nonetheless, among conference participants there was a great deal of support for the potentially rehabilitative/reintegrative aspect of conferencing which, for many, was framed in terms of preventing future victimisation and thus as a form of 'symbolic reparation'. There were also occasions on which conferencing, in particular, provided an opportunity for offenders who were in prison at the time of the conference to be in touch with relatives, including more distant relatives whom facilitators had contacted at the request of the offender. On a few occasions, supporters agreed to help offenders to accomplish elements of the outcome agreement (e.g. by encouraging them to attend programmes, providing transport, etc.) and were happy to be mentioned on the outcome agreement as the person who would monitor that element.

Victims were also often dismayed by offenders' lack of social capital – particularly where offenders had become estranged from their immediate family – and also by their lack of human capital in terms of qualifications, likely employment opportunities, etc. Commonly, participants might decide what would be helpful in promoting desistance for that offender but needed input from facilitators or probation officers attending the conference[12] to sort out what opportunities might be available. In this way, facilitators and other criminal justice actors might act as providers of the bridging social capital that offenders (and victims) themselves often lacked as far as connections with support agencies were concerned.[13] It is for this reason that we consider that facilitators do need either some experience of the criminal justice system or access to others who can guide them toward relevant provision.

One of the most important findings of our research in respect of outcome agreements was in relation to the practice of following-up progress toward achieving the agreed outcomes. This was an area in which practice improved over time, but which could have been further developed. We have argued that restorative justice schemes need to devote sufficient resources both to the tracking of progress and to the process of keeping participants informed about what has happened toward the achievement of outcomes. Where participants are left with unanswered questions in this regard, their reflections are likely to be tinged with frustration and/or dissatisfaction, and this may ultimately diminish their support and positive regard for the restorative justice process.

10 The offenders' views: reoffending and the road to desistance

Meeting victims' needs was one of the key aims the funders set for the three schemes. Reducing reoffending was the other. Reducing reoffending, however, is arguably likely to be linked to offenders' own views and experiences of the restorative justice process. If, for example, offenders were to find the process unhelpful or unfairly denigratory, they would not be likely to react positively to it. Surprisingly, few evaluations have made a detailed study of offender expectations and reactions to restorative justice compared to the work which has been done with victims. In our evaluation, however, we determined very early on to look in as much detail at offender experiences of and reactions to the process and the outcome agreement as at those of victims. In this chapter, therefore, we start by exploring what offenders told us about their restorative justice experiences before considering, first, the extent to which offending behaviour was affected in the two years after experiencing restorative justice and then the extent to which reducing reoffending is congruent with restorative justice theoretical perspectives.

Looking back at restorative justice: overall judgments of satisfaction

To gauge offender reactions, we used exactly the same questions exploring the extent of satisfaction with restorative justice in all its aspects for offenders as for victims. The answers to the main questions about satisfaction from the final interviews with offenders looking back at the process and outcomes some months after experiencing them are shown in Table 10.1 for JRC and REMEDI. As with victims, there were too few interviews with CONNECT offenders to provide detailed results, but the offenders interviewed gave very similar reactions to those experiencing the other two schemes.[1]

The overall picture from Table 10.1 is of considerable satisfaction with both the process and the outcome for offenders, for both JRC and REMEDI. Indeed, for REMEDI, offenders were significantly more satisfied than victims.[2] Comparing reactions in the few days after the restorative justice event with those from the final interviews weeks afterwards, there was some slight diminution of

Table 10.1 Offenders' satisfaction with restorative justice events

	JRC %	*REMEDI* %
Overall, how useful did you feel the process was for you?		
Very useful	53	81
Somewhat useful	24	19
Not very useful	8	0
Not at all useful	8	0
Don't know	3	0
(n)	(152)	(21)
How satisfied or not are you now with the outcome of the conference/indirect mediation process?		
Very satisfied	45	59
Fairly satisfied	34	35
Not very satisfied	11	6
Not at all satisfied	5	0
Don't know/can't remember	1	0
(n)	(152)	(17)
Do you think that having the [conference/mediation] is a good way to deal with the offence you committed?		
A very good way	47	52
A good way	26	38
It is OK	14	10
A bad way	3	0
A very bad way	1	0
Don't know	4	0
(n)	(152)	(21)
Would you recommend restorative justice to others?		
Definitely	58	81
Probably	16	14
Not sure	11	5
Probably not	3	0
Definitely not	7	0
(n)	(152)	(21)

Source: JRC data derived from Shapland *et al.* (2007: Tables 4.1 and 4.2); REMEDI data include both direct and indirect mediation, except where specified.

satisfaction over time – so ratings from the follow-up interviews conducted a few days after the restorative justice event were higher than those from the final interviews after some months for London and Northumbria JRC – as others have found in other evaluations (Ministry of Justice New Zealand 2005). However, this diminution merely brought levels down from the extremely high levels of 80–90 per cent to those shown in Table 10.1 of 70–80 per cent.

There was very substantial inter-correlation between offenders' views on the different measures of satisfaction, in the same way as we saw in Chapter 8 for victims. For JRC, the questions about satisfaction with both the process and outcome, together with their usefulness to the offender and whether restorative justice was a good way to deal with the offence, when analysed statistically, again produced just one overall general factor – all the satisfaction measures were highly related.[3] For REMEDI, there was a similar general factor, but also a second factor associated primarily with indirect mediation and related to doubts about the principle of mediation but independent of views about the process itself. It seemed as though this second factor was reflecting concerns about the idea of mediation, which then led victims to choose indirect mediation – but this choice did not then relate to subsequent experiences of mediation or the likelihood of being satisfied or not satisfied with what happened.

Though the overall level of offender satisfaction was high, not everyone – not surprisingly – was satisfied. Some 40 JRC offenders (out of 152 interviewed) were not very satisfied or not at all satisfied on one or more of the questions about usefulness, satisfaction or recommending restorative justice to others – though only six offenders, all from JRC, were dissatisfied on all these measures. Given previous studies' findings that young offenders, in particular, may feel overwhelmed by the conference or that others taking part may be too overbearing (Daly 2003b; Hoyle *et al.* 2002) we looked carefully in terms of possible dissatisfaction at where these events were held, the age of participants and the professional background(s) of the facilitators. All but one of the six conferences with which offenders said they were dissatisfied on several measures were from Northumbria JRC and all bar one dealt with young offenders. However, looking in detail at our observations and the records we had of the conferences, they seemed very different (Shapland *et al.* 2007) and there was no common element. So, for example, though there was more than one conference where there were mental health issues, others with similar issues resulted in considerable satisfaction rather than any dissatisfaction. We also looked carefully at the ratings of the facilitators. Northumbria was the site where, overall, some respondents thought the facilitator tended to be a bit too much in control – but these conferences, again, did not show this as a particular element. As we commented in Chapter 4, police facilitators also received as good ratings as facilitators with other professional backgrounds (Shapland 2009a). We think there can certainly be a potential problem of young people feeling isolated in a room full of adults at conferences, but we do not think that this was a major factor in the conferences being organised by JRC nor a key reason for dissatisfaction. Where people were dissatisfied, it tended to be with individual elements of the case or the participants.

Overall, offenders said that they were very likely to recommend restorative justice to others in similar situations (Table 10.1). What was important to them about what went on at conferences? When asked what was the best thing about the conference, offenders spoke about 'clearing the air' and 'being able to work it out with the victim'. Elements of being able to explain what had happened, to answer questions, to apologise and to find closure were all cited. The restorative justice literature has tended to emphasise the possibility of closure for victims, but we would suggest that it is even more important for offenders. Overall, 56 per cent of JRC offenders said 'yes' when asked whether the conference had provided a sense of closure for them, while 19 per cent said they had experienced this to some extent – only 7 per cent said 'not really' and 10 per cent 'no' (Shapland *et al.* 2007). Even offenders who had spent some time in prison (prior to release from or having been given prison sentences) spoke of closure. It seemed that punishment alone was not being felt by offenders to be sufficient to pay one's debt; there was unfinished business in relation to apologising, taking steps to change one's life and in relation to the victim generally. The restorative justice conference was an opportunity to air all these things and to try to make some amends.

Indeed, for JRC offenders, though 18 per cent thought there were no particular problems which were behind their offending, 61 per cent thought the conference had made them address problems they now recognised were related to their offending. Those whose expectation of the conference was that it might help with such problems were significantly more likely to say it had helped[4] – so it is possible that expectations of, and being offered, the conference had made offenders think about what they wanted to do with their lives thereafter. This is in line with our suggestion that those who are thinking about desistance from crime are likely particularly to benefit from restorative justice (see below and Chapter 11).

Offenders in general told us they did not find the conference process easy. Asked whether the conference was difficult or painful, 28 per cent said it was very much so while 22 per cent said it was difficult to some extent (34 per cent said it was OK, 10 per cent easy or very easy). However, offenders themselves indicated that, after the conference, they themselves were generally more likely to understand more about how that offence had happened (56 per cent very much so, 24 per cent to some extent). They thought the victim did too (48 per cent very much so, 22 per cent to some extent).

Was meeting the other party better than indirect communication?

One question which this evaluation is able to start to address but which has only rarely been considered in the literature is whether participants find direct meetings or indirect mediation more helpful. Indirect mediation involves the passage of information between the parties but no direct meeting. What were offenders' views about indirect mediation? The vast majority (90 per cent) of REMEDI offenders wanted information to be passed to their victims – but in practice this tended to turn into the sending of a written apology (88 per cent), rather than any two-way communication. REMEDI offenders saw the best thing about the opportunity for restorative justice as being the making of the apology and trying to make the other party feel better – but they found the wait then to obtain information from the victim as to how it was received very difficult. Several offenders said they never found out what happened after they had written the letter. Follow-up, as in CONNECT as well, could fall down.

REMEDI mediation was not intended to tie up closely with what happened during offenders' sentences and outcome agreements were relatively rare. It is not surprising, therefore, that indirect mediation turned out not to be very future-oriented and not to provide opportunities for offenders to address problems relating to their offending, and it was not meeting many offenders' expectations or needs in relation to restorative justice.

In fact, over half the REMEDI offenders experiencing indirect mediation said that they would actually have preferred, once they had got to this stage, to meet the victim directly. All those experiencing direct mediation were sure that it was better to meet the victim directly. Asked the same question, JRC offenders, all of whom experienced a direct meeting, primarily agreed it was better to meet the victim directly (71 per cent very much so, 13 per cent to some extent – only 4 per cent said it was worse). The comparison between the schemes suggests that offenders found conferencing or direct mediation (with a meeting) more helpful than indirect mediation.

Did participating in restorative justice affect reoffending?

In line with their views about conferences affecting the problems behind their offending, 63 per cent of JRC offenders said in final interviews that they thought the conference would very much affect their likelihood of reoffending, while 16 per cent said it would have some effect. There was little difference in this between different trials and sites. Were they right? Was there an effect on reoffending?

What can we measure in terms of subsequent reoffending?

We have no means of measuring directly the exact extent of reoffending by any of those involved in the three schemes because the evaluation did not include contacting respondents again a considerable time into the future. Thus we could not ask those who had taken part directly what their extent of offending had been (self-reported offending). We can only look at the extent to which those who had taken part (in the restorative justice or control groups) had come to the attention of the criminal justice system in the subsequent period, i.e. those who had been reconvicted in the two years after the offence for which they experienced restorative justice. Reconviction is only likely to happen for a proportion of offences which an offender has committed – but there is a strong association in general between the extent of reoffending, as measured by self-report offending questions, and the extent of reconviction. Those who commit a lot of offences are likely to be caught and convicted (Farrington *et al.* 2006) – particularly those who are already known to the police as adult offenders, as almost all those in our samples were.

We also need to bear in mind that many of the offenders in these three schemes were persistent offenders with many previous convictions. This is very different from most previous studies of reconviction with restorative justice, which have been with young offenders.[5] Those studies have tended to find either positive or non-significant results on reoffending which has been measured in relation to arrests or otherwise coming formally to the attention of the police. So, for example, in relation to young offenders, the later work of the Leeds Mediation and Reparation Service, which was primarily with young offenders, showed a significant decrease in the frequency of reconviction after mediation (which was mostly indirect mediation) and also a significant decrease in the numbers of offenders who were reconvicted over a two-year period (Miers *et al.* 2001). RISE, which involved conferencing with randomly assigned groups in Australia, found a significant decrease in the frequency of offending detected by the police after one year in their youth violence group, but no significant effect in relation to shop theft and youth property offences with direct victims (Strang 2002). Statutory schemes (such as those in New Zealand and Northern Ireland) are unfortunately difficult to evaluate in terms of offending because one cannot compile a satisfactory control group.

There have been few studies of reoffending in relation to adult offenders, but one early study, the Brooklyn Dispute Resolution Centre (Davis *et al.* 1980), found no difference between randomly assigned mediation and control groups in the frequency of arrests for violence over a subsequent follow-up period (though the types of disputes involved were very minor and only just over half the mediations were completed – see Chapter 2). A pilot study involving court referrals with adults in New Zealand found offenders participating in conferences were slightly less likely to be reconvicted in the following two years, but this was not statistically significant (Triggs 2005). Two subsequent pilots using pre-trial referral and conferencing with adult offenders found a significantly lower likelihood of reconviction over one year compared to matched control samples (Maxwell and Morris 2001). In Winnipeg, Canada, reoffending was measured primarily in terms of arrest: it was found that offenders on the programme were significantly less likely to have been rearrested than a matched control group (and were also less likely to be given a prison sentence following that rearrest – though being on the programme may have been a confounding factor here) (Bonta *et al.* 1998). On the other hand, the only RISE conferencing experiment in Australia which involved adult offenders (drunk-driving offences) found an increase in reoffending as detected by the police after one year (Sherman *et al.* 2000). Sherman and Strang (2007), in their recent meta-analysis, concluded that for adult offenders restorative justice has substantially reduced repeat offending for some offenders, but not all.

Previous restorative justice with adult offenders which has measured reconviction rates has tended to involve offences which were relatively minor or did not have direct victims. There could therefore be few expectations in terms of what would be found in our own evaluation, for which offences have often been relatively serious (burglary, robbery, violence) and in which cases had reached court. Offenders themselves who experienced conferencing, as we saw above, often expected participation to result in decreased reoffending – but were they good predictors of their own conduct?

Making comparisons

At the time that we were undertaking the evaluation of reconviction, the main measure in England and Wales for adult offenders was whether or not the offender had been reconvicted in the two years following the event (Harper and Chitty 2005). The overall likelihood in terms of adult offenders who had been sentenced at court during the same time period as in the evaluation was 58 per cent (Shepherd and Whiting 2006). However, the likelihood of reconviction depends considerably on such factors as age, gender and type of offence.

It is only therefore possible to consider whether participating in restorative justice had an effect if one compares reconviction for the restorative justice group against an appropriate control group which is known to have, or can reliably be assumed to have, a similar composition on relevant variables. JRC was set up deliberately to be able to look at reconviction through its research strategy incorporating random allocation – so that only around half of the cases in which the offender and victim agreed to participate in restorative justice actually proceeded to a restorative justice conference, with the remainder being randomly allocated to the control group, which did not have the conference, outcome agreement or follow-up of whether the outcome agreement was completed.[6] However, it is important to note that this random allocation occurred only after both the offender and victim had agreed to participate in such a conference – which was of course also after the preparation process by the facilitators which introduced restorative justice and what might happen. Hence, for JRC, both restorative justice and control groups experienced the preparation and both groups were composed of people who had agreed to participate. The comparison was of everyone who had agreed to participate, whether or not they actually experienced a conference if they were in the restorative justice group.[7] The comparison is hence not really a comparison of all the experience of restorative justice against those who have no experience at all – but of those who were assigned to having a conference (and what flowed from that) against those not so assigned.

REMEDI and CONNECT in contrast did not wish to use this experimental methodology. In order to consider reoffending, it was hence necessary for the evaluators to construct a control group for the CONNECT group of offenders who had agreed to participate in mediation and for all the REMEDI groups who had similarly agreed. The details of these control groups are given in Shapland *et al.* (2008), which also contains more explanation of the methods used for the reconviction analysis and all the results from it. For CONNECT, the control group comprised offenders who had appeared at the same magistrates' courts over a different time span, matched on variables known to affect reconviction such as main offence, age range and gender. For REMEDI, details were obtained of convictions from the same approximate geographical area, matched on offence type, gender, type of disposal (prison, community sentence, etc.), age, and so on. For both schemes, this was individual matching of each offender, not the less rigorous matching of the whole group on relevant characteristics. However, for both, it was comparison of a group of offenders who had agreed to participate in restorative justice with a group of offenders for whom one could not know how they would respond if offered the opportunity to participate.

There is one further caveat we need to consider before we turn to the findings from the evaluation. The extent of the difference between the two groups will depend upon the extent of the effect of the intervention (in this case, restorative justice) upon the amount of reoffending – whether, for example, there is a 10 per cent effect on reoffending or a 20 per cent effect or a 40 per cent effect. Generally, it is very rare for criminal justice interventions to produce more than an average 10 per cent effect. So, for example, the first evaluation of cognitive skills programmes with adult male offenders in England and Wales produced a reduction in reconviction of up to 14 per cent (Friendship *et al.* 2002), but subsequent evaluations found there was no difference (just 1–2 per cent for adult males and young offenders on programme starters) (Cann *et al.* 2003). Friendship *et al.* (2003) found that there was about a 3 per cent decrease in sexual and violent reconviction rates over two years on the prison-based Sex Offender Treatment Programme in England and Wales.

However, small effects can also occur by chance and so it is important only to consider statistically significant effects.[8] If we were expecting possibly a 10 per cent effect, then we can calculate the size of the restorative justice and control groups that would be needed in order for this effect to show up as statistically significant (though the size also depends upon the base rate of reoffending likely for those kinds of offenders). As we showed in Shapland *et al.* (2008), for JRC, it would require 390 offenders in each of the restorative justice and control groups (780 in total) for there to be a significant difference. Looking back to Chapter 3, it is clear that only if one were to put all the JRC trials together across all three sites could one achieve anything like those numbers. Fortunately, because the JRC trials were run using identical methods, just on different samples from different stages of criminal justice, they can be taken together in a meta-analysis. We should not, however, expect to find significant results on any JRC individual trial. Similarly, there are quite simply insufficient numbers of cases for both CONNECT and REMEDI to expect there to be any significant results on reconviction.

As we indicated above, the traditional measure of reoffending in England and Wales has been the likelihood of reconviction over the subsequent two years. However, more recently, two new measures of reoffending have been recommended by the Ministry of Justice in England and Wales for adult offenders, which 'allow a wider understanding of re-offending' (Ministry of Justice 2008b: 3). As the report says:

> The previously published two-year actual (yes/no) measure of the proportion of the cohort re-offending, compared to the rate expected, was and remains useful information, but in terms of being able better to understand what works in reducing re-offending, this measure only allows the assessment of whether or not an offender was proven to have re-offended. It does not

take account of how many re-offences an offender may have committed (in terms of number of crimes and community safety, an offender who commits one re-offence of burglary is different to an offender who commits five re-offences of burglary), and it also does not differentiate between the type of re-offence being committed (for example, whilst the yes/no measure would show both a theft and a murder as being the same, it is clearly of a very different impact to society).

We were fortunate in being able to pre-empt this recommendation through having the opportunity to discuss our emerging methodology with researchers in the Home Office and Ministry of Justice. We have therefore used measures of frequency, seriousness and cost in our analyses of reoffending, as well as the traditional likelihood of reoffending. However, because the three schemes were primarily aimed at adult offenders, we have used a two-year period to measure reconviction rather than the one-year period now used in relation to young offenders and which is used in Ministry of Justice (2008b).

The overall findings from our evaluation on reconviction

Our findings from our evaluation of JRC, CONNECT and REMEDI on reconviction are set out in detail in Shapland *et al.* (2008). To summarise them, the overall findings were as follows:

1. There was a *significant* decrease in the *frequency* of reconviction over the following two years, looking over all the trials, schemes and groups. We can express this as: *offenders' reoffending decelerated.*
2. There were no significant effects on *severity* of reconviction, or *whether or not someone was reconvicted.*
3. Cost of convictions (cost to potential future victims plus costs of criminal justice) combines frequency and severity. All JRC groups (conferencing), summed together, showed a significantly lower *cost of convictions* versus the control groups (mediation did not).
4. The decrease in the cost of further offending was enough to make conferencing value for money – it covered the cost of running the conferences.
5. There were no significant results pointing towards any criminogenic effects. Restorative justice does not make people more likely to reoffend or increase the frequency or seriousness of their offending.
6. There was no difference on reconviction between types of offender or offence – age, gender, offence type, ethnicity showed no difference in terms of reconvictions for the restorative justice group compared to controls. So no evidence currently exists on reoffending to support targeting restorative justice.
7. However, as in previous evaluations, offender experiences of and views about JRC conferences did relate to reoffending – for adult offenders, there were significant links with:

- the extent to which the conference had made them realise the harm done;
- whether the offender wanted to meet the victim;
- the extent to which the offender was observed to be actively involved in the conference;
- how useful the offender felt the conference was.

Let us consider each of these findings in more detail.

1. *Offenders' offending decelerated*

The frequency of reconviction was measured in terms of the number of times an offender was reconvicted for an offence or offences committed on a separate occasion, where the offence was committed during the two years after the restorative justice conference/assignment to the control group.[9] We were able to find these figures from the Police National Computer for over 90 per cent of offenders in each scheme, trial and site.

The results can be seen visually. Figure 10.1 shows the meta-analysis (run using Comprehensive Meta Analysis version 2.0: Borenstein *et al.* 2004) for the frequency of reconviction for JRC only. The effect size of the difference between the restorative justice and control groups has been calculated as 14 per cent.[10]

Each line of the table refers to one of the JRC trials. As can be seen, the mid-point (represented by a square) of the difference between the restorative and control groups was in the direction of less reconviction for the restorative justice group for each trial (to the left of the zero line). However, this is only

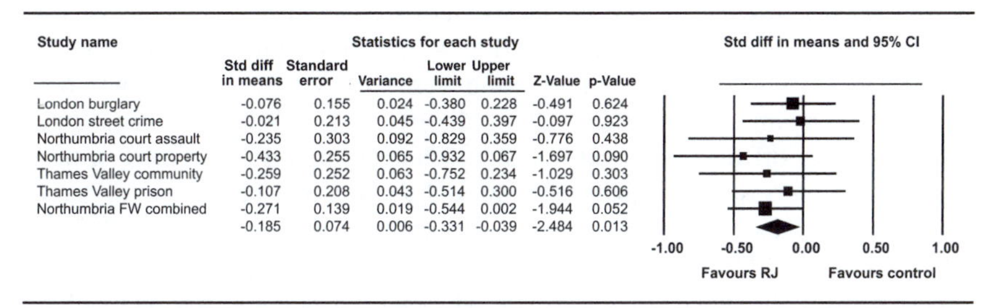

Study name	Std diff in means	Standard error	Variance	Lower limit	Upper limit	Z-Value	p-Value
London burglary	-0.076	0.155	0.024	-0.380	0.228	-0.491	0.624
London street crime	-0.021	0.213	0.045	-0.439	0.397	-0.097	0.923
Northumbria court assault	-0.235	0.303	0.092	-0.829	0.359	-0.776	0.438
Northumbria court property	-0.433	0.255	0.065	-0.932	0.067	-1.697	0.090
Thames Valley community	-0.259	0.252	0.063	-0.752	0.234	-1.029	0.303
Thames Valley prison	-0.107	0.208	0.043	-0.514	0.300	-0.516	0.606
Northumbria FW combined	-0.271	0.139	0.019	-0.544	0.002	-1.944	0.052
	-0.185	0.074	0.006	-0.331	-0.039	-2.484	0.013

Figure 10.1 Meta-analysis of the frequency of reconviction over two years comparing restorative justice and control groups for JRC trials*

*The meta-analysis was run using Comprehensive Meta Analysis version 2.0 (Borenstein *et al.* 2004). Given that it was frequency of reconviction (i.e. a continuous scale), the standardised difference in means has been run, but the skewed shape of all frequency scales means that the data had to be transformed into Ln (number of offences resulting in a sanction in the restorative justice period per year at risk + 1). In the original analysis reported in Shapland *et al.* (2008: Table 2.6) the odds ratio was used. The overall result was the same.

a significant difference for that trial on its own if the 'whiskers' do not touch the zero line, which did not occur for any trial on its own. Looking over all the trials, however (the diamond at the bottom), the diamond does not touch the zero line and so the result over all the trials as a whole is significant (at the $p = 0.013$ mark).

The JRC trials fulfil all the requirements for doing a meta-analysis. Most meta-analysis researchers would also allow the results for CONNECT and REMEDI to be considered alongside the JRC trials.[11] If we do this, the result is also significantly in favour of restorative justice (this time, at $p = 0.009$).

2. No significant effects on severity of reconviction and on whether or not the offender was reconvicted

The other two main measures of reoffending are whether or not the offender was convicted (the traditional measure) and severity of reconviction. The measure of severity of offences was taken from a scale being developed by the Home Office, ranking offences from 1 (most serious) to 10 (least serious). Offences scoring 1 were offences such as murder, the most serious possible, while offences scoring 10 included minor traffic and regulatory offences. Most standard list criminal offences, in terms of volume, would be found around levels 5, 6 or 7 (theft, criminal damage, etc.). Looking at all trials, schemes and sites, there was only one group (JRC Northumbria adult magistrates' court property offenders) which showed any significant difference on severity. That was a significant result in the direction favouring restorative justice (at $p = 0.042$: see Shapland *et al.* 2008: Table 2.4). However, groups varied as to whether they became slightly more serious or slightly less serious in their reoffending. A meta-analysis produced no significant result.

In terms of whether or not offenders were reconvicted of any offence over the subsequent two years, overall, for JRC, 47 per cent of the restorative justice group and 51 per cent of the control group were reconvicted – but this was not a statistically significant difference. One trial, the Northumbria adult magistrates' court property offenders, did show a significant difference on its own, with 61 per cent of the restorative justice group and 94 per cent of the control group being reconvicted at least once over the subsequent two years ($p = 0.005$: see Shapland *et al.* 2008: Table 2.2). No other trial showed a significant effect. The meta-analysis was not significant. For REMEDI, overall, 44 per cent of the restorative justice group and 48 per cent of the control group were reconvicted. For CONNECT, the proportions were 37 per cent and 49 per cent. None of these differences are statistically significant.

3. All JRC groups (conferencing), summed together, showed a significantly lower cost of convictions versus the control groups (mediation did not)

There is one other measure of reconviction that we can use to tease out the potential effectiveness of restorative justice. This is to compare the cost of the offending for restorative justice and control groups, comparing what they had been doing in the two years prior to the offence for which restorative justice was being considered, with what they were doing in the two years afterwards. The cost of the offending was the cost to the victim for each offence for which the offender was convicted, as calculated using Home Office economists' figures, plus the cost of using the criminal justice system for each conviction (Shapland *et al.* 2008). Essentially, such an overall cost figure combines ideas of seriousness (more serious offences cost more to both victims and criminal justice) and frequency (more offences cost more).

To give an idea of the kinds of figures involved, the average cost saving (amount in £ saved to victims and criminal justice) over all JRC sites per offender in the restorative justice group between their offending in the two years afterwards and their offending in the two years before was £19,771 (Shapland *et al.* 2008: Table 2.5). For the control group for JRC, there was a cost increase (not a cost saving) of £11,699. This was a statistically significant difference ($p = 0.039$). Individually, there was a statistically significant difference on London burglary cases ($p = 0.018$) but not on any other individual JRC trial.

The results for CONNECT and REMEDI were not so positive. For CONNECT, there was a cost *increase* for the restorative justice group (average £12,037) as well as the control group (average £1,654). So, in cost terms, the results for CONNECT were in the wrong direction (but not significant). Similarly, for REMEDI, there was a cost increase, averaging £27,201, for the restorative justice group, and also a cost increase, averaging £4,919, for the control group. Again, these results are not in the right direction. It seemed as though mediation, as opposed to conferencing, was not pushing down the cost of subsequent criminality.

4. Conferencing was value for money – the decrease in the cost of convictions covered the cost of running the scheme

As we saw above, for JRC, conferencing produced a significant decrease in the subsequent cost of reoffending (to those who would have been victimised and to criminal justice). How important was that cost decrease? Was it enough to pay for the cost of running the scheme – i.e. was it value for money? We can compare the cost reductions, as calculated above, with the cost of running the scheme, as discussed in Chapter 3.

We need to note that this is a minimalist way of measuring value for money because it concentrates on only one of the major aims of the schemes (Chapter 1) – that of reducing reoffending. It does not cover the other main aim – meeting the needs of victims. We cannot currently measure the financial benefits to victims because we do not have a measure, like quality of life for health interventions (drugs or operations), which allows us to measure how much victims benefited from restorative justice – though we know they say they have been positively affected in terms of their health and closure from the offence (Chapter 8; Strang *et al.* 2005). Developing such an economic measure for the effects on victims needs to be included in future evaluations of interventions which impact on victims as well as offenders.[12] So our figures as to whether restorative justice was value for money are very conservative ones.

Among our three schemes, only JRC, overall, produced a net reduction in the cost of convictions, comparing the cost of convictions prior to the incident for which offenders experienced restorative justice with the cost afterwards. REMEDI and CONNECT both produced overall increases in the costs of reconvictions and so could not be value for money.

The size of JRC's reduced cost of convictions was in fact very considerable. We can only compare by site – London, Northumbria and Thames Valley – because we could only add up the cost of running the JRC schemes (paying facilitators, arranging conferences, participants' expenses, venue and office space, liaising with other agencies, etc.) for the site as a whole. However, in all three sites, the cost of running restorative justice conferencing was less than the cost of the prevented reconvictions – in all three sites, conferencing, as run by JRC, was value for money (see Table 10.2[13]).

5. Restorative justice does not make people more likely to reoffend

When initiating something new in relation to criminal justice, it is important to monitor whether it might be having any negative effects on anyone participating. One such negative effect would be if restorative justice were to increase reoffending. We have already seen that one of the RISE trials in Australia, using restorative justice on drunk-driving offenders, had just that effect – it increased offending. However, that was an offence with no direct victim in these instances (the drunk driving did not lead to an accident).

The possible negative effects in relation to the schemes we were evaluating would have been (a) if there had been physical violence during any restorative justice events; (b) if restorative justice had increased revenge attacks after the event; or (c) if restorative justice had increased reconvictions. Even though the evaluations involved primarily adult offenders, often with substantial previous criminal records, and included violent offences, we can say that none of these three effects occurred. There was no violence in any restorative justice event (see Chapter 7). There was no greater frequency of intimidation from offender to victim (or victim to offender) after restorative justice events than in the

Table 10.2 JRC costs and savings

Scheme	*Cost for RJ cases over running period* £	*Money saved through decreases in offending* £
JRC London	598,848	8,261,028
JRC Northumbria	275,411	320,125
JRC Thames Valley	222,463	461,455

Source: Derived from Shapland *et al.* (2008: Table 4.8).

normal run of criminal justice in England and Wales (see above). There was no trial, group, scheme or site in the evaluation in which offenders experiencing restorative justice had significantly more reconvictions than the control group on any measure of reoffending we used (Shapland *et al.* 2008). In other words, restorative justice did not make any group worse.

6. There was no difference on reconviction between types of offender or offence

Rates of reconviction vary considerably between offenders who have been convicted of different types of offence (property, violence, sexual offences, etc.), who are of different age groups and who are of different genders (Cunliffe and Shepherd 2007). In general, property offenders, offenders in their 20s and male offenders are more likely to be reconvicted. If we were to want to target restorative justice on particular groups (for example, if there were only limited resources to implement it), then it would make most sense to target it at groups on whom it would have most benefit – so, in terms of reoffending, at groups whose reoffending is most likely to decrease. The only way to see whether there are any such groups is to control for the main demographic variables (age, gender, offence type, etc.) which are known to have considerable effects on reoffending.

We undertook such an analysis in relation to all the demographic factors on which we had reliable data (gender, ethnic groups, age group, violent/property/other offences), whether restorative justice with adult offenders was delivered pre-sentence or post-sentence, and whether the victim and offender knew each other or not.[14] Because of the numerical constraints, we could only do the analyses for JRC and so we only have results in relation to conferencing. These are all factors which are known before the restorative justice commenced. There was no significant difference in relation to any of these factors. This means that, so far, there is no evidence base from our evaluation on which one could argue that restorative justice should be targeted at particular groups or restricted to particular groups.

7. But offenders' experiences of conferencing did affect reoffending

Previous studies have found that elements of the restorative process itself can relate to the likelihood of reoffending – but all have been on youth conferencing. So, for example, Hayes and Daly (2003) in Australia found that consensus in coming to an outcome agreement and the offender showing remorse in the conference related to the likelihood of reoffending. Maxwell and Morris (2001) found that similar offender-related variables significantly affected reoffending after youth conferencing in New Zealand: the offender feeling remorseful; shaming not being stigmatising (i.e. the offender was not made to feel like a bad person); the offender feeling involved in conference decision-making and agreeing with the outcome; and the offender meeting the victim apologising to the victim and completing the outcome agreement.

For JRC, we found that aspects of the conference – as perceived by the offender – related to the frequency of reconviction for adult offenders only – but victim views were not so related. Specifically, the extent to which offenders felt that the conference had made them realise the harm done by the offence, whether the offender said they wanted to meet the victim, the extent to which the offender was actively involved in the conference and how useful the process was found to be by the offender related significantly to one or more of the measures of reconviction.[15] This means that, though it was not possible to predict prior to the conference (or offering restorative justice) which adult offenders were less likely to reoffend after experiencing conferencing, the ways in which they experienced the conference itself did relate to whether they succeeded in offending less. The process of the conference affected how offenders felt and how they then behaved afterwards. Taken with the findings in the previous literature, it suggests that offenders who come to a conference with the intention of participating – and who do actively participate – then find the process useful and it helps them to desist from offending.

Would we expect participating in restorative justice to affect reoffending?

Having found that there were, if anything, positive effects on reoffending – and since this was one of the major aims for the schemes – it may seem churlish to query whether one would expect such a reduction in reoffending (as measured by reconvictions). But it is important to recognise that not all theories of restorative justice, its aims and the ways in which it may 'work' would expect to create effects on reoffending and it is important to situate the schemes we were evaluating in the appropriate theoretical context.

In talking about reducing or ceasing offending, it is also important to recognise that this is only a relevant question if the perpetrator has a previous history of offending. (If this was a first offence, the idea of reducing offending is irrelevant.) However, for those with several previous offences it is a serious question. It is also, necessarily, a more important question for the schemes we were evaluating – which were dealing with adult offenders who had a potentially longer offending career – than for the young offenders with whom restorative justice programmes have normally worked. The specific schemes and trials which were involved in this evaluation turned out to be dealing with offenders many of whom had considerable numbers of previous convictions (which of course was a contributory factor to their cases being tried at the Crown Court or them being sent to prison). For JRC, the predicted proportion of offenders who would expect to be reconvicted within two years was on average 66 per cent for the group receiving restorative justice, while it was 44 per cent for CONNECT and 57 per cent for REMEDI[16] (Shapland *et al.* 2008: Table 2.2). This is much higher than would be expected in any general population sample.

As we saw in Chapter 2, the three schemes varied in their aims. JRC saw reducing reoffending as a key aim for the conferencing it was facilitating (alongside providing benefits for victims). CONNECT also specifically mentioned reducing reoffending, but included a wider set of objectives, such as enabling the victim to ask questions, receive reparation and apologies, increasing the offender's sense of responsibility for the offence and improving both the victim's and the offender's view of the criminal justice process. REMEDI, on the other hand, did not place so much stress on reducing reoffending, saying that 'REMEDI believes mediation may have a role to play, along with other interventions, in supporting offenders to cease or reduce their reoffending'.

The three schemes seemed to us to be reflecting different theoretical strands. JRC was clearly strongly influenced by Braithwaite's (1989) theory of reintegrative shaming, which provides a fairly damning critique of traditional criminal justice's attempts to affect reoffending and highlights the potential of restorative justice to be more effective – through inducing shame and eliciting remorse on the part of the offender, followed by reacceptance of the offender into the law-abiding community. JRC's directors have also strongly espoused Tyler and others' theory of procedural justice (Tyler 2006; Tyler and Huo 2002; see Tyler *et al.* 2007), though that theory postulates slightly different mechanisms for promoting compliance. Procedural justice suggests that offending is discouraged through the willing acceptance by citizens of authorities, providing that those authorities make decisions in ways which are judged to be fair and treat participants fairly. Both restorative justice and forms of criminal justice may meet these standards (Tyler *et al.* 2007), but the emphasis of restorative justice on all who are affected by the offence having an opportunity to talk is arguably more likely to foster the self-regulation, ascription of legitimacy to authority and feelings of responsibility to authority which are the mechanisms which procedural justice suggests would bind participants toward conformity. CONNECT's aims also clearly reflect elements of procedural justice, together with the aim to restore victims (through reparation).

REMEDI's aims, however, reflect more closely other theoretical strands of restorative justice (see Chapter 1), and in particular restoration and healing of conflict between the victim and offender. These are reminiscent of Christie's (1977) views on the need for those affected by the offence themselves to take part in resolving the conflict and also Zehr's (1990) vision of restorative justice as working towards healing and restoration. Neither Christie nor Zehr would necessarily take the view that restorative justice would directly impact on reoffending, particularly reoffending not linked to the previous offence – though clearly if any conflict is resolved it may make the perpetrator less likely to start up the conflict again. Hence for REMEDI, an effect on reoffending would, we think, be more likely to be an indirect effect.

We have argued elsewhere, however, that the process of restorative justice, particularly conferencing, may be likely to result in reduced reoffending – through different mechanisms (Robinson and Shapland 2008). We would argue that greater shame on the part of the offender, induced by the emotions expressed by the victim and/or others, may not be the key element, as reintegrative shaming has argued. Indeed, many offenders came to JRC's conferencing (and CONNECT and REMEDI's mediation) appearing already to feel shame or guilt, being prepared to admit responsibility for the offence and wishing to offer apologies, as we have seen. It is a key principle of restorative justice that offenders must consent to take part – and must have admitted the offence – and those two prerequisites tend to create the situation in which offenders may already be feeling shame and guilt.

We have suggested that offenders who agree to restorative justice may already have in mind the possibility of desisting from crime (reducing the frequency of their offending/ceasing to commit crime). They may not know how to set about it; they may doubt their ability to desist; they may only have made a very provisional decision or just entertained the possibility of leading a life characterised by less or no offending – that possibility is likely to have entered their mind, knowing that they will be explaining themselves to the victim and, in conferencing, their own supporters. As we shall argue in the next chapter, restorative justice may then provide an event at which these provisional decisions may be affirmed (by the victim, by the occasion itself, by any supporters present, by any subsequent criminal justice decision-maker) and may be facilitated through the social capital provided by means of the outcome agreement. All of these may provide means through which reoffending may be reduced. However, this can only occur if the restorative justice event is concerned with the future for that offender, as well as the offence and the effects of that offence. It is far more difficult to see how it would occur if the event only considers the past, or does not explicitly consider the reasons behind the offending and how they might change. This theoretical stance does not reject the insights of reintegrative shaming, nor procedural justice, nor conflict resolution – but it does try explicitly to consider why the elements of restorative justice might impact on reoffending.

However, we would never claim that one restorative justice process or event will always be a life-changing moment for that offender (or victim). A few hours of preparation and an hour or two in a restorative justice meeting cannot resolve the practical problems of desistance, nor provide all the emotional and cognitive support necessary. It is only one event, in what we would see as potentially a long-term, difficult and uncertain path towards reducing offending.

11 Restorative justice: lessons from practice

Restorative justice programmes have been developed in a number of jurisdictions worldwide and there is considerable interest in exploring further the potential of restorative justice in relation to crime. Yet, with some notable exceptions, there have been few large-scale evaluations and those which exist have concentrated primarily upon young offenders (for example, the evaluations of RISE, the New Zealand statutory family group conferencing and the Northern Ireland Youth Conferencing Service). The distinctive features of the evaluation results presented in this book are that the schemes focused upon adult offenders and that most of the restorative justice delivered was undertaken within the context of the main criminal justice system. Restorative justice occurred pre-sentence or during sentence (whether that be a community sentence or a prison term) and the results were fed back to criminal justice personnel. The minority of cases which were, in strict terms, diversionary (in that the case did not proceed further through the criminal justice system) were in fact also within the normal criminal justice diversionary mechanisms in England and Wales of final warnings (for young offenders) or formal cautions (for adult offenders) delivered by police officers. The result, as we saw in Chapter 1, was that the offences concerned ranged from relatively minor (theft, minor assault, damage) to very serious (robbery, causing grievous bodily harm).

Having considered the results, including the attitudes and experiences of victims, offenders and those running the schemes, we can now draw our key findings together and look at what it meant to deliver restorative justice over this wide range of offences and in different parts of the country. The lessons that the schemes and ourselves learned – and which we discussed together – bring out aspects which have not always been considered previously in restorative justice evaluations, but which are essential if one is thinking about mainstreaming restorative justice or working with adult offenders. They also need to be related to what one is seeking to do in offering restorative justice – to the theoretical rationales for restorative justice and to how it does or does not relate to criminal justice.

Why are we focusing on this restorative justice/criminal justice interface? Surely restorative justice advocates, such as Christie (1977), Shearing (2001) and Zehr (1990), have seen restorative justice as a more 'just' process producing more 'just' outcomes, but one which needs to be separate from criminal justice, its mistakes, its processing, its over-professionalisation and its punitive heart? We do not seek in any way to denigrate diversionary or community restorative justice, which we think certainly have a place within justice systems. However, where restorative justice seeks to deal with adult offending in today's relatively punitive and state-centred climate (Garland 2001), we think that considering connections with state-run criminal justice is inescapable.

There are two major reasons why we think this. The first is well set out by Christie (2009) himself, looking back at the development of restorative justice over the last 20 years: restorative justice must be voluntary on the part of offender and victim. It cannot deal with cases where the offender does not admit any responsibility for that offence. It cannot mount trials, which, for crimes, need to have the procedural, human rights safeguards of state-based and state-accountable criminal justice and the power literally to bring the offender to trial, by coercion if necessary. If there is denial of the offence, then it is state criminal justice which needs to come into play (though restorative justice may well be appropriate later in the process).

The second reason lies at the heart of the democratic, inclusive nature of restorative justice. Restorative justice should include all those affected by the offence. It is they who should discuss and deliberate what should be done. It is they who need to agree the outcome of the session and any outcome agreement. It is therefore their judgment as to what kinds of outcomes might be suitable – their 'justice values' as we have termed them (Shapland *et al.* 2006b) – which will predominate in discussions and in outcome agreements. For serious offending by adult offenders, those judgments will include the possibility of coercive sanctions such as imprisonment and unpaid work. These need to be imposed and overseen by state criminal justice personnel. Hence, either restorative justice in such cases runs alongside such state determinations (for example, the outcome agreement goes to the sentencer who takes it into account in pronouncing sentence) or restorative justice butts onto the culmination of state punishment (solely post-sentence) – or restorative justice confines itself to minor offences and young offenders.

Needing to take into account state criminal justice does not, however, imply that this is easily accomplished or that theoretical and practical questions do not arise. We would argue that it is in considering these issues that restorative justice can really consider the hard questions of what kind of justice with what values it wishes to promote. In this chapter, therefore, we look first at practical lessons from the evaluation, and at the issues which delivering restorative justice to adult offenders raises, before turning to consider how restorative justice – including future, statutory, mainstreamed restorative justice – might coexist with criminal justice.

Key lessons from evaluating restorative justice

The experience of evaluating the three schemes has pointed up a number of issues which those starting up new schemes may need to take into consideration.

As we saw in Chapter 3, all three schemes found the following.

1. They had underestimated the length of time and the effort it would take to set up agreements and protocols with other agencies in criminal justice and the courts. Protocols needed to be negotiated with all those referring cases to the scheme, with police forces in relation to obtaining victim contact details, with all the prisons where offenders were remanded or serving sentences and in which conferences might be held, with all the probation offices whose officers were preparing pre-sentence reports on offenders or supervising offenders, and with Victim Support in each locality. Being a 'new player on the block' in criminal justice in the kind of multi-agency environment which exists in England and Wales requires persistence on the part of the new agency and much goodwill from the existing agencies. Nor does an initial round of work suffice – because then the contacts made will only be personal, not institutional ones. The new service provider needs to expect to keep in contact with each agency regularly.
2. They had considerably underestimated the amount of 'environmental scoping' they would need to do to receive a sufficient flow of cases but not too many. Referrals of cases needed to be those where the offender had admitted responsibility for the offence and where there was sufficient opportunity for restorative work to take place (i.e. there were four weeks remaining before sentence, or the offender was going to be released in the next few months), as well as there being one or more named victims who were private individuals or who had been individually affected if the legal 'injured person' was corporate. These statistics are not routinely available in England and Wales and estimates needed to be made from court or prison records.
3. They had to negotiate means of acquiring the details of potential cases from existing records rather than depending upon busy court personnel or criminal justice professionals to remember to refer suitable cases. In our evaluation, the schemes 'abstracted' relevant cases from pre-sentence report requests (at the magistrates' court), from the 'warned list' at the Crown Court (cases which were expected to be heard in the next 2–3 weeks, the lists of which were sent to defence solicitors) and from police records (for diverted cases). However, these means could potentially disenfranchise victims and offenders whose cases do not fall within these categories.
4. They had not thought through in advance what kinds of data systems they were going to need to set up to provide accountability to the various stakeholders, to provide an operational database for facilitators, and to provide monitoring and evaluation data to managers. We ourselves designed the databases or helped with this for the schemes. We think that, if restorative justice is to be mainstreamed for adult offenders or developed further for young offenders, it would be helpful for an overall national database template to be developed, using easily available commercial software, which can be

customised to particular schemes' requirements. The database must be user-friendly – so that administrators and facilitators can easily input new data and record case progress.

5. If cost-benefit (value for money) analysis is to be done, then a new scheme needs to be able to separate the costs incurred in running the scheme from any other activity its parent institution may be undertaking. This proved difficult in relation to statutory criminal justice agencies, such as the police, who typically, for example, do not cost premises costs per square metre or think about the opportunity costs of officers being tasked to do different work, etc.
6. If it is required that reconviction rates be assessed, sufficient time and data need to be allowed to do this. For adult offenders in England and Wales, the standard time over which to consider reoffending is two years (with interim measures sometimes being taken over one year). However, that needs to be two years after the offender is in the community having completed the restorative justice (and, if relevant, that the associated criminal justice decision, such as sentence, has been passed). If restorative justice takes place pre-sentence, the time to sentence (and a sufficient time in the community after release from any sentence of imprisonment) needs to be factored in; if pre-release, the time to release similarly needs to be considered.

These kinds of requirements and planning may seem bureaucratic, but they are essential to the development of a smooth-running scheme which aims to take a reasonable volume of cases.

Restorative justice within criminal justice with adult offenders

Restorative justice delivered in respect of more serious offences and with adult offenders raised a number of issues – but practice demonstrated that a number of other anticipated concerns did not occur. Perhaps it is best first to clear out of the way those worries and fears which did not materialise.

Presumptions and concerns which proved to be false

1. The belief that victims will only wish to participate for minor offences and with young offenders

Because restorative justice has mostly been introduced for more minor offences and for young offenders, some were concerned at the start of the evaluation that victims might not want to participate in restorative justice with adult offenders and serious offences. However, as we saw in Chapter 3, the proportion of victims who agreed to take part in restorative justice was over half those offered it in all the different locations and trials. Victims of young offenders were indeed more likely to agree, but victims of adult offenders and serious offences still agreed in substantial proportions. Victims in all trials and locations were satisfied with the restorative justice they experienced, but victims of more serious offences who experienced JRC conferencing were significantly *more* likely than victims of less serious offences to say that the restorative justice had helped them (Chapter 8). Hence, if anything, we should seek to offer restorative justice to victims of *more* serious offences (which were those with adult offenders). Hoyle (2008) has argued similarly that restorative justice should be for medium to serious offences.

2. The concern that ensuring a safe environment for participants will be very difficult

It is very important that restorative justice should take place in a safe situation and in a respectful manner, so that there is no revictimisation of victims and that procedural justice takes place and is seen to take place. Providing that there is adequate risk assessment prior to the restorative justice event, the experience of these three schemes was that mediation or conferencing could take place for very serious offences without problems. There was no physical assault in any of the events evaluated. Safeguards for potentially more difficult conferences or mediations included: making sure there were a number of supporters there so that there was not an uneven balance of power; ensuring 'break-out' rooms for people to cool off during a 'time-out' if necessary; having more than one facilitator present; talking through facilitator anxieties prior to the event; having a member of prison staff (for a conference in prison) available nearby but out of earshot; and building up expertise through regular debriefing sessions for facilitators afterwards.

3. The view that there is a particular point at which victims should be offered restorative justice, so offering it at different stages of criminal justice will be difficult

Neither the schemes nor ourselves knew how victims and offenders would react to the offer of restorative justice during the criminal justice process (pre-sentence) or during sentence (prior to release from prison or during community sentences). In fact, all those who agreed to and experienced restorative justice said that this was the right time for them (Chapters 8 and 10). Those who were involved pre-sentence or pre-diversionary measures (the latter in relation to final warnings) found this very helpful, particularly in working out individual plans to prevent reoffending or to try to deal with problems behind offending. Offenders seemed more resistant after sentence, particularly when they had already been given a community sentence with several activities or restrictions in it. The lesson seems to be that there is no 'wrong' stage for restorative justice, but that forward-looking restorative justice is probably more helpful prior to a criminal justice decision than after it. As a corollary, restorative justice should be offered to victims and offenders at different stages – they may not feel themselves 'ready' for it at one point, but this may well change later.

4. The worry that, because some restorative justice theory has been built on reintegration into a 'community', and because there is no 'community' in Western cities, so restorative justice will not be able to access opportunities, draw in supporters or be reintegrative

The view that there is a lack of 'community' in Western countries, particularly in urban areas, is widespread and nothing that we have found in this evaluation gainsays it. Victims and offenders were often linked by nothing more than the offence which had been committed, had never seen each other previously and were likely not to meet again. However, this did not mean that restorative justice events could not successfully take place. It did mean that coordinators might have to work hard to contact potential supporters for offenders and victims (Chapter 5). Adult offenders, in particular, had often lost touch with family members, due partly to their previous offending behaviour, partly to being in custody. However, facilitators could normally find someone who was still close to the offender, though that might be an aunt or grandfather rather than mother or father. For offenders in custody, restorative justice events could be very affirming occasions, at which their own supporters welcomed what they had done in agreeing to restorative justice, apologising, etc. and were prepared to help them on a new path to desistance. Where this occurred – and it sometimes involved victims as well – offenders were in fact being reintegrated into *their* 'community' – but their community was a micro-community or 'community of care' of those who were important to them (McCold 2004) rather than a larger, more diffuse geographical community.

In one area – JRC's Northumbria adult caution events – many of the offences related to minor crimes which affected many people (in a neighbourhood, or a club, or members of an extended family) (Shapland 2009a). In this situation, events were often large (with occasionally over 20 people present) and did involve the relevant community. Outcome agreements here did include elements which aimed to reduce any further damage to the community and to think of how to defuse matters in the future (Shapland 2009a). But these kinds of community focus were very rare among the cases dealt with by the schemes.

Another difficulty where there are few or no links to a wider community is being able to access programmes or other resources for offenders after the event. Here, as has been noted as well in the US, criminal justice professionals needed to step in to provide details of what kinds of opportunities were available, how to access them and whether they might be suitable for that offender. Such programmes in England and Wales, in contrast to the US and mainland Europe, are also probably more likely to be run by state agencies rather than by voluntary sector groups.

Though these concerns about undertaking restorative justice in more serious cases were found to be relatively groundless in practice, other points pertinent to undertaking restorative justice with adult offenders did arise – and will be important to take into account in the future (see below).

Issues that emerged which will be important for future schemes

1. The need to be careful about professional conflicts of interest

As we saw in Chapter 4, it is important to consider where restorative justice schemes should be based and their management structure. Basing a scheme within another criminal justice agency has the advantages of obviating the difficulties of liaising with that agency and of being able to build on partnerships and competences that agency already has. So, for example, basing restorative justice within the police reduces difficulties in contacting victims, while basing restorative justice within the probation services obviates difficulties in contacting and working within prisons and in accessing rehabilitative and resettlement programmes. Basing restorative justice outside current criminal justice agencies, as an independent agency, has the advantage that the facilitators will be seen as neutral – but significant disadvantages in terms of needing to construct and negotiate partnership agreements and protocols with other agencies, and of needing to set up finance, human resources and such services for the scheme.

If restorative justice is based, as some is sure to be, within another criminal justice agency, then it is crucial that steps are taken to ensure the restorative service is perceived as neutral by potential participants and that conflicts of interest are minimised. For this, the management of the restorative service practitioners must not be the operational branch of the agency for that area. The restorative service needs to be separate from operational matters and able to resist operational demands (for example finding out police intelligence from restorative justice events, or to be compelled to breach or investigate participants because of minor matters admitted during restorative justice events). The values of restorative justice, as set out in international instruments – in particular that events are safe places and facilitators are neutral – require appreciation of potential professional conflicts of interest among those delivering the restorative service and other practitioners in that agency.

2. The need to develop adequate mechanisms for accountability and regulation

The growth of restorative justice internationally and its use increasingly with adult offenders have brought in their train new questions about accountability and regulation (Chapter 4). The accountability of restorative justice needs to be to all its stakeholders: participants, funders, those referring cases, partner agencies in criminal justice and communities. There is a need to develop more precise good practice guidelines for regulatory mechanisms to:

- prevent netwidening – ensuring that cases that previously would have been dealt with informally do not become 'sucked into' more formal restorative justice mechanisms;
- prevent any existing power imbalances affecting the process or outcomes of restorative justice. Power imbalances during the event can be mitigated by

ensuring support for the relevant parties and inviting supporters (deliberative accountability – see Chapter 4); potential power imbalances in outcomes require pointing out by the facilitator and participants;

- ensure good record-keeping on cases, their progress and their outcomes so that relevant stakeholders are kept informed;
- provide mechanisms for dealing with any subsequent complaints or allegations of abuse of the process. The key need here is to have a record of proceedings which can be viewed by managers of the restorative justice process and, if necessary, a judge who might be investigating such allegations;
- provide means to hold agencies accountable for the provision of programmes which feature in restorative justice outcome agreements;
- consider how to create the right balance between the necessary confidentiality and privacy of restorative justice proceedings and the need for the interests of society and the local community to be able to be taken into account in relation to outcomes. There will be no one right solution here – the best may be that if the restorative justice is diversionary from the criminal justice process overall then performance and evaluation of the scheme may suffice, without further consideration of individual cases. However, if the case is referred from the court or during a sentence of the court, it may need to be reviewed individually by the judge/penal authorities, as happens in Northern Ireland and New Zealand statutory youth conferencing.

3. The importance of a statutory basis and implications for mainstreaming

The questions discussed above can only be resolved if restorative justice is placed on a statutory footing. If restorative justice does not have such a basis, it can only deal with cases which are either diverted from criminal justice to the restorative justice provider (and do not return to criminal justice) or cases in which it offers restorative justice under the supervision and control of another criminal justice agency (and which return to that agency for decisions). For young offenders, this has been an acceptable basis in many countries, particularly those which have a tradition of diversionary youth justice. It is notable, however, that common law countries, such as New Zealand and Northern Ireland, have felt it necessary to bring restorative justice onto a statutory footing to allow referrals by courts and prosecutors of more serious cases. For adult offenders, diversionary referrals will only produce a tiny minority of cases, as was clear from the attempt to pilot conditional cautioning restorative justice in England and Wales a few years ago.[1] Restricting restorative justice to diversion will not allow most victims or offenders the ability to experience restorative justice.

The results from the evaluation of the three schemes show that considerable benefit was derived from restorative justice by victims, particularly victims of more serious offences, and by adult offenders. We would therefore argue that restorative justice for adult offenders should be put onto a statutory basis as soon as possible.

At what stage should restorative justice be available? Given that victims and offenders who experienced it at each stage of criminal justice all thought that this was the right point for them, whether it was diversionary, pre-sentence, post-sentence or pre-release, there is no reason why it should not be available at each of those stages. However, we would argue that the key stages are pre-sentence and pre-release from prison, because it is at these stages that criminal justice would itself benefit most from the outcomes and process of restorative justice. Pre-sentence, restorative justice can create individualised outcome agreements which meet victim needs and also suggest helpful possibilities for sentence. Pre-release, restorative justice can help to create agreements which will minimise the possibility of revictimisation or unhelpful encounters after release. However, immediately post-sentence it is difficult to see how participants in restorative justice can create the best solutions, given that the parameters of the sentence will already have been set, so that there are few possibilities for offenders to undertake additional activities, nor for restitution.

Conferencing or mediation?

As we saw in Chapters 1 and 2, restorative justice has evolved in many countries simultaneously, with traditions of mediation and conferencing developing to suit the requirements for particular offender groups and stages of criminal justice. There are particular traditions of mediation or conferencing in different countries. The result has been that it has been very rare for any one evaluation to be able to cover a number of different schemes in detail or to compare mediation with conferencing. We are fortunate in that, in the three schemes we were evaluating, CONNECT and REMEDI principally undertook mediation (both direct and indirect mediation) whereas JRC offered only conferencing. It is thus possible to compare some of the results between the schemes and see whether there are any differences which might be related to the choice of conferencing or mediation.

One needs to be careful, however, in attributing any resulting differences to the use of mediation or conferencing. The definitional difference between mediation and conferencing stresses *participation*: mediation is for victim and offender alone, conferencing involves victim and offender supporters as well. However, attendance or participation may not be the only differences. As one of us has set out in more detail elsewhere, the schemes also varied in the stages of the process which tended to occur, the role of the facilitator, the aims of the schemes and the types of outcomes which tended to be agreed (Shapland 2010). The key question is then whether those differences necessarily stemmed from different attendance, or whether they resulted from the different traditions from which the schemes developed.

By first comparing indirect mediation with direct meetings (mediation or conferencing), we have found that:

- When offered the choice between indirect mediation and a face-to-face meeting, more participants chose indirect mediation. However, if offered a choice only between conferencing and no restorative justice, a similar proportion of participants chose conferencing to the total of those choosing indirect mediation and a face-to-face meeting in the other sites (Chapter 5). We can also say that when offered the choice to bring supporters to a direct meeting (i.e. JRC conferencing), most participants chose to bring one or more supporters – most conferences did have supporters present, and it was the victim's/offender's choice who to bring (Chapter 7). We do not know whether, if restorative justice were mainstreamed, more would choose to participate if offered indirect mediation after they had turned down the opportunity of conferencing.

- It was the perception of facilitators that where there was some disparity in the power balance/loquaciousness between participants, having supporters present (and having a greater number of supporters present – up to a limit) tended to reduce that disparity, because supporters could encourage more taciturn or nervous participants (Chapters 4 and 7). Strang (2002) has found similar processes occurring.
- There was more restricted communication between participants in indirect mediation: outcome agreements were less common and communication only rarely covered the future but concentrated on circumstances surrounding the offence, the effects of the offence and an apology by the offender (Chapters 7, 8, 9). We think this was not a result of the particular model operated by the mediation schemes but an intrinsic consequence of indirect mediation. Basically, the extent of communication can suffer if all has to be relayed through a third party, with delays inevitably occurring between the question and the answer.
- The disjunctions in communication in indirect mediation could cause some participants to doubt the impartiality of the mediator(s) (Chapter 7) – not because the mediators lost their neutrality, but perhaps because the answers received may not have matched participants' expectations and the person receiving the answer could not then quickly put a question back or cross-examine the respondent. As a result there was lower satisfaction – and some participants wished afterwards they had opted for a direct meeting.
- The results in relation to reconviction from indirect mediation were significantly worse than those for conferencing. There were insufficient numbers of direct mediations to be able to tell whether these were worse or better than indirect mediation (Chapter 10). However, the scheme which undertook, quantitatively, most indirect mediations (REMEDI) did not see itself primarily as aiming to reduce reoffending.

We can conclude that communication through indirect mediation was less satisfactory to participants than communication in a direct meeting. However, we cannot conclude whether the limited communication afforded by indirect mediation is better than experiencing no restorative justice at all.

We can next turn to comparing the results between direct mediation and conferencing. We found that:

- Supporters (conferencing) participated actively in the meeting, though their role was secondary to that of victims and offenders (Chapter 7). They talked about the effects of the offence on them, as well as on their main participant, and also contributed to the outcome agreement.
- Outcome agreements were more common in conferencing and contained more separate items (Chapter 9). In direct mediation, as operated by REMEDI, the topics which were discussed were the topics the victim and offender decided to raise at the meeting – though we cannot know how far the topics were those discussed with the mediators during preparation for the meeting or influenced by what the mediators said then. Victims and offenders, left to themselves, tended not to tackle the future. We suspect this was not because they were not interested in the future – their expectations of mediation were remarkably similar to the expectations of those agreeing to conferencing (Chapter 5). JRC, in contrast, operated a three-stage model, in which the third stage, 'What should happen now to make things better?' (or a similar question), was clearly future-oriented and designed to lead to an outcome agreement. We suspect this gave 'licence' to the participants to think creatively about the future – which they may well have felt they needed, given that this was decision making in close relation to criminal justice, an area which English participants may well have felt should be talked about only by professionals. Hence they needed encouragement to give their input about the future. The difference between JRC conferencing and REMEDI mediation in relation to talking about the future was clear. What is less obvious, however, is whether mediation intrinsically finds it difficult to create discussion about the future or whether this was the effect of the particular model being operated. We suspect – but have no proof – that it may be easier to talk about the future with several people present, but that models of mediation might be developed which do emphasise the possibility of discussion of the future.
- Supporters contributed actively to discussion of the outcome agreement in conferencing and could make creative suggestions because they were aware of the particular circumstances of their key participant (Chapter 9). They also were prepared to encourage the offender, in particular, to think what would help in changing his or her life in the way the offender wished (as were victims). Victim supporters were also active in encouraging the offender to live a less offending lifestyle and so to rejoin the community they represented. If offenders were inclined towards desistance, this support by those close to the offender (and offender supporters were normally family or close friends – Chapter 7) would tend to act to encourage the wish to desist.
- Offender supporters were often prepared to offer to play a role in facilitating or monitoring particular items in outcome agreements (Chapter 9). In this they were offering social capital to the offender.
- The results in terms of decreasing the frequency of reconviction and the cost of reoffending were significantly better for conferencing than mediation

> (there was no significant difference in relation to the propensity to be reconvicted or seriousness of reconvictions) (Chapter 10). The decrease in the frequency of reconviction was such that JRC conferencing represented value for money, in that the costs of running the scheme were less than the moneys saved in decreased reoffending. Were these results due to JRC using conferencing, as opposed to mediation? What would have happened if the mediation had been as future-oriented as the conferencing experienced by JRC participants? We cannot provide a definitive answer, but we suspect that the presence and contribution made by supporters not only at the conference but in the months afterwards were material in helping some offenders to tread the path towards desistance.

Essentially, therefore, conferencing seemed to encourage more discussion and allow more input than mediation. It seemed to be more future-oriented and to encourage formal agreements signed by everyone. However, should mediation wish to move further in these directions, there seems to be no reason why similar results should not occur. Some mediation schemes, for example those in Scandinavia and Belgium, are future-oriented and strongly encourage the making of reparation agreements between offender and victim (Gunther Moor *et al.* 2009). Mediators there clearly indicate to participants that this might be a good idea and participants duly follow this lead. Though we think that having more participants may make discussion of the future easier and more fruitful, what matters most is probably what schemes, and participants' expectations and aims are rather than who attends.

When comparing mediation and conferencing, we also have to bear in mind what the aims are (Chapter 2). Some restorative justice aims at conflict resolution, some at mitigating the effects of the offence and restoring participants, some at problem-solving, some at reducing reoffending – and most seek to achieve more than one of these. Different methods and processes will be needed to accomplish each of these outcomes.

We think it is now very important that restorative justice schemes should consider their own model and decide what they most want to accomplish with different client groups and how this might best be achieved. Though it has been said that restorative justice is more evaluated than practised, there is a clear need for more comparative evaluation of different models and their effects in terms of processes and outcomes. We need detailed study of models and clear exposition of what is said and how facilitators work. It will then be possible to share good practice. It is highly likely that slightly different models or processes may be more helpful for some participants or offences, others for others. Currently we have only a few indications as to which processes and facilitator inputs create which outcomes. However, those indications strongly suggest that, given the element most desired by participants is communication (Chapter 5), a direct meeting is more useful and more appreciated than indirect mediation. And participants, when offered the choice, seem to prefer to bring a supporter or two.

Working with criminal justice

Restorative justice theorists have sometimes despaired of restorative justice retaining its own individual voice and values within the juggernaut of criminal justice. They have suggested that the punitiveness which they see as characterising criminal justice sentencing and the inflexibility in terms of who is allowed to participate will deaden and eventually render impotent the creativity, inclusiveness and communication which characterise restorative justice meetings and outcomes. The three schemes which we evaluated were working in close proximity to criminal justice. Is this what happened to them?

When we asked those running the schemes, they were not so defeatist (see Chapter 3). They said that it was possible to organise effective restorative justice meetings with victims and offenders present – and, where these were supposed to be conferences, with supporters present as well. They said that criminal justice practitioners and sentencers were very interested in the outcomes of the meetings and readily took them on board in terms of future criminal justice decisions and processes. But they agreed it was not easy to accomplish this.

We think that there is a need to distinguish between those aspects of criminal justice which may, sometimes, be inimical to the processes or outcomes of restorative justice and those aspects which reflect the normal working of criminal justice 'insiders' (practitioners and the judiciary). We found that there were very few of the former which caused any real difficulty to creating restorative justice alongside criminal justice – but quite a number of the latter, particularly those which disturbed the normal routine working patterns of professionals. Christie (1977, 2009) has made similar distinctions – his worries about the 'steamrolling' tendencies of criminal justice stem from concern about the over-influence of professionals rather than about the 'justice' of criminal justice.

Two main aspects of criminal justice itself might, potentially, come into conflict with restorative justice. One is that restorative justice is not suitable for 'trying' criminal cases (i.e. determining guilt or innocence where this is disputed between the parties). Both Christie (2009) and all three of the schemes would agree that cases can only start with conferencing or mediation (at least if they are criminal cases involving adults) if the offender admits responsibility for the offence to a criminal standard of proof. The second is that if a sentence of the court is required, this must be passed by a judge or other person who represents the overall society, not only those affected directly by the offence or the local community. Today's criminal justice is state criminal justice rather than local criminal justice. This means that an outcome agreement cannot be the sentence of the court without being agreed by a judge (or equivalent person). It also implies that those who are gathered in the restorative meeting do not have the sole right or power to determine the outcome of the matter in all its aspects. They only have the right and power to determine it in respect of that meeting and the participants at it.

The latter position, we would argue, is not against the tenets of restorative justice. Restorative justice has never sought to bind people not present at the meeting by the decisions of that meeting. A conference cannot bind a non-present judge, nor prevent a third party bringing a civil suit in relation to a linked matter. If society is prepared to delegate its power to the meeting (as with diversionary conferencing or mediation), then there is no problem with the restorative justice outcome being the overall outcome (as long as the human rights of the participants have been respected in the process). If it is not – and society is unlikely to give up its power in relation to serious criminal matters or adult offenders – then the restorative justice outcome will be an element of the overall result, though it may well be the major driving force for it. In such cases, the total criminal justice sentence, disposal or outcome will be more than those of the restorative justice element.

Taking this position, however, is quite different from agreeing that the current working practices of criminal justice practitioners are suitable for restorative justice. In relation to the three schemes, though criminal justice was usually trying to be a friend to restorative justice, it was not a very flexible friend. If magistrates thought that they might fall foul of criminal justice time targets for processing cases by adjourning a case for restorative justice, they tended not to adjourn but to pass sentence immediately. If they thought imprisonment might be merited, they tended to pass an immediate sentence rather than to see what the restorative justice outcome agreement might suggest. Though clerks and probation officers were genuine in meaning to refer cases to restorative justice, under the pressure of time in a normal working day they might forget about the scheme. Time limits tended to be set according to when probation officers might be able normally to produce pre-sentence reports rather than when victims might be available to meet with offenders. Prison officers might not be available to escort people to conferences. All of these are not actions which indicate animosity towards restorative justice – they were symptomatic of the managerial values which tend to dominate criminal justice, which are to get through the maximum number of cases as quickly as possible without breaching legal rules (most of which are, rightly, to do with the human rights of the offender and do not mention the victim).

It may be that the professionalisation of criminal justice (prosecution, defence, judiciary, probation, etc.) is intrinsically antithetical to restorative justice values of inclusivity, as Christie would argue. Professionalisation can go hand in hand with power and with the belief that it is the professional who makes the best decisions. Professionalisation also tends to carry with it the belief that speed rather than allowing everyone to be present and to have their say may be a greater virtue. It is also possible, however, to have professionals who adopt different balances of values: that there is importance in creating solutions to problems and in promoting a more lasting resolution and the integration of potentially warring parties. It may be that the points at which criminal justice and restorative justice are painfully rubbing up against each other today are the results of a system in which justice has become impoverished: towards the immediate or the fast solution, in which there is no time for victims or communities. Professionalisation also brings costs, in that the time of professionals is valuable and expensive. It is then possible to see that there might be trade-offs in terms of reoffending and lasting solutions – but they may be trade-offs which require slightly more time, the expertise of lay people and challenging standard outcomes with individuality to make them relevant to those people and that offence.

Inspiring and transforming criminal justice: legitimacy and problem-solving

A number of restorative justice theorists have suggested that restorative justice may have the potential to transform criminal justice (for example, Zehr 1990). They have primarily been thinking either about doing away with criminal justice – or about a separate restorative justice scheme feeding back into criminal justice and inspiring its procedures so that they are more victim-sensitive and friendly, more creative in terms of sentences and more linked to the community. These theorists have primarily been considering the Anglo-American common law tradition of criminal justice, characterised by an oppositional stance between prosecution and defence. The Anglo-American system also tends to result in what one may call 'normalised justice', in which the pressure is to treat cases very similarly and routinely in order to conserve resources and speed up case processing, reducing the possibility for either 'side' to use time as a tactic (see Sudnow 1964; McConville *et al.* 1994; Shapland *et al.* 2003). The problem with such normalised justice is that, when it comes to sentencing, it tends to turn into impoverished justice, in which sentences become standardised, the use of reports is minimised, there is little time for victims to be contacted and creative solutions to imprisonment (particularly short sentences of imprisonment) become harder to find (Dignan 2000; Holdaway *et al.* 2001). The routinisation of pre-trial negotiation can turn into the routinisation of sentencing and youth justice proceedings (Zernova 2007a).

We think that the likelihood of osmosis of creativity, legitimacy and victim sensitivity from a *separate* restorative justice to criminal justice is small – and so far has not been very visible on the youth justice side, where restorative practice has been mainstream for many years in England and Wales. Criminal justice is just too large and too resistant due to the conflicting tensions within it of processing and due process. However, were restorative justice to be run as part of and alongside criminal justice, the potential for increasing the overall creativity, victim sensitivity, legitimacy and effectiveness of the whole system would be much greater. We have seen in this evaluation that victims were more satisfied with the performance of the criminal justice system as a whole if they had experienced restorative justice conferencing. Where restorative justice outcome agreements were given to sentencers, they did inform sentencing and the result seemed satisfactory to both victims and offenders (and, from the few interviews we were able to do with sentencers, to the judiciary as well). Similar reactions have occurred where restorative justice has been mainstreamed pre-sentence, in Northern Ireland (Campbell *et al.* 2005) and in New Zealand (Consedine and Bowen 1999).

If, then, we are to speak about the transformative power of restorative justice, we need to think carefully through the questions of transformative for whom and how, and whether there are any downsides. A core value of restorative justice is that it should be democratic, bringing together those affected by the offence, including the victim, the offender and the local community. In terms of criminal justice, we must add society. We need to think through whether restorative justice is transformative for each of these participants.

Considering first the victim, restorative justice within criminal justice can provide a voice to ask questions of the offender, to provide information about the effects of the offence, to reduce feelings of revenge, and potentially to decrease the insecurity associated with the offence for the victim and those around the victim. Offences cause ripples of disquiet not only to direct victims but to those around them and those who hear from them what the criminal justice has done (or failed to do) (Shapland 2009b; Shapland and Hall 2010). These are benefits for victims themselves, but they also include benefits for sentencers (restorative justice proceedings are likely to produce better information than victim personal statements) and for the local community and society in terms of reducing insecurity and the potential for revenge. Victim sensitivity is not only related to victims' views about legitimacy and confidence in criminal justice but also to the job of sentencing.

Some, however, would argue that such a transformation, which would give the victim an active voice and participation, is wrong and unfair (for example, Ashworth 1993). Why should what offenders are given as sentences depend on their victims? We are not sure whether this argument is because of a deep-seated view that the interests of victims are always inimical to those of offenders. If so, it is clearly disproved by the experiences of the victims and offenders from mediation and conferencing in this evaluation – here both had similar interests, centring on decreasing the likelihood of reoffending. Or, alternatively, the argument may arise from the view that sentencing is a professional matter in which victim views have no part, the point of view antithetical to that of Christie (1977) but similar to human rights principles and discourse about sentences needing to be passed by a properly constituted court, as already discussed. This is where what happens after the restorative justice event is crucial. If all restorative justice is diversionary (and so the outcome agreement is the final outcome), then it is clear that restorative justice cannot deal with serious offences or most adult offenders. Society itself will demand that crimes (meaning major crimes) are dealt with by criminal justice means. However, if restorative justice outcome agreements can be then considered by the properly appointed representatives of criminal justice for society – the judiciary – then it is for that judiciary to consider what form the criminal justice sentence should take, having considered what all those affected by the offence have said. The victim voice acquires a greater, not a lesser, legitimacy.

If now we consider the local community, we have seen that restorative justice in England and Wales, at least as seen in this evaluation, is not very accommodating. Unless the offending has impinged on several people in that community, those invited by victims, offenders or facilitators to the restorative justice event are not usually elders or pillars of the local community (the 'responsible people' to whom victims often reported minor offences in villages, as found by Shapland and Vagg (1988)). However, where the conduct took place over time in the context of people who were acquainted with each other or in a small geographical locality, it was much more likely that the local police officer, or faith leader, or youth leader, or schoolteacher was there (Shapland 2009a). So restorative justice in the context of criminal justice seems only rarely to be transformative in terms of bringing in the local community. Criminal justice, though, does not seem to have fared better. Nor does restorative justice in other parts of the world, unless the community concerned is a closely-knit community with clear leaders (Bartkowiak and Jaccoud 2008; Maxwell and Morris 2001). The problem may be not the failure of justice, but the failure of community to be seen as a legitimate and respected party to adjudicate upon problems of anti-social behaviour and crime.

Finally, we should turn to consider whether restorative justice can transform the potential of justice to influence offenders. If it is correct that desistance requires the active agency of the offender – and the most recent longitudinal work on desistance suggests strongly that this is correct (Bottoms and Shapland 2011; Farrall and Calverley 2006; Laub and Sampson 2003; Maruna 2000) – then the most fruitful activity for encouraging desistance is likely to be that which actively engages the offender, which offenders see as helping them to desist and which they see as relevant to their problems. Imprisonment can (and does) incapacitate offenders and reduce reoffending – but it does not show how to lead a non-offending or a less offending life when offenders are released. In Chapter 10 we suggested that restorative justice has the potential to aid offenders to desist by:

- involving offenders and (in conferencing) those who are important to them;
- creating individualised means which may help to solve the problem of how to lead a desisting life in the community;
- helping to provide bridging capital towards resources necessary for this;
- underlining and supporting their desire to provide symbolic reparation through turning their lives around, with that support coming both from the victim and offender supporters;
- encouraging the use of a process perceived as legitimate and fair, which allows both offenders and victims their own voice and enables offenders to pay back to victims something through answering victims' questions.

Of course, these processes will not usually occur if the offender has no desire at all to desist or change his or her life. However, even then, the restorative justice meeting may start to change offenders' views of the extent to which they have caused harm and strengthen the desire to desist. We suspect it is only the very cynical, very cold offender who will be prepared to admit responsibility, answer questions, apologise and contribute to an agreed outcome agreement, while not meaning any of it. We further suspect that this would happen only very rarely (Robinson and Shapland 2008). Those offenders who agree to go through restorative justice processes are a selective sample of offenders.

The significant reduction in reoffending frequency seen in this evaluation supports the idea that restorative justice (within the framework of criminal justice) encourages desistance. It also makes clear that the path to desistance is an uncertain one – not everyone will complete their outcome agreement, not everyone will be able to resist the siren call of offending (excitement, easy money), not everyone will move smoothly towards desistance. But having an individualised, resourced plan for desistance is likely to be more effective than having a plan which offenders have to create and undertake all by themselves, or, worse still, a plan to which they have not contributed and which has been imposed upon them by a criminal justice professional.

Though it is a great vision to have, we suspect that restorative justice will not reach over and transform criminal justice. However, we think that mainstreamed, properly resourced restorative justice alongside criminal justice for more serious offences does have the potential to transform the ways in which justice treats victims and offenders – and to create much better outcomes. The different needs and demands of victims, offenders, the community and society mean that, to do so, we need not just a simple lens to create this transformation, but a carefully-crafted prism that highlights the complex ways that people are affected by offending – and also the ways that they themselves can contribute to a legitimate, transformed means of solving the problems offending creates.

Notes

1 Setting the scene

1. As Dignan (2005) has pointed out, Eglash used the term 'restorative justice' to imply 'restitution' in a way with which most advocates of restorative justice today would perhaps not identify.
2. Dignan and Lowey (2000: Chapter 3) describe four possible models of implementation ('implementational strategies') for restorative justice reforms in the context of criminal justice. These are the subsidiary model, the stand-alone model, the partially integrated model and the fully integrated model. The latter two models are distinguished by statutory authorisation and are relatively rare; the subsidiary model does not conform to most notions of restorative justice, comprising court-ordered reparative sanctions. The stand-alone model involves restorative justice as a supplement to existing criminal justice processes.
3. Originally intended to run for a decade, the CRP in fact ran from 1999 to 2002 (see Maguire 2004 for an analysis of the CRP).
4. CONNECT proposed to use a New Zealand family group conferencing model, while JRC planned to deploy the 'Wagga Wagga' model, albeit with a range of facilitators including, but not exclusively, police oficers.
5. Introduced in England and Wales in 2000 under the 1998 Crime and Disorder Act, the final warning scheme replaced the old-style juvenile caution with a system of reprimands and final warnings for 10–17-year-old offenders, aimed at preventing reoffending.
6. Government reorganisation in summer 2007 created a new Ministry of Justice and responsibility for restorative justice policy passed from the Home Office to the new Ministry at that point.
7. Permission to use the cases for the evaluation research was obtained from all victims and offenders by schemes when they initially contacted participants. Permission to observe the conference was again sought (and granted in almost every case) prior to observation.
8. Following mediators as they met individually with either the victim or the offender would have been extremely intrusive. For similar reasons, we did not directly observe the preparatory phase for conferencing, in which facilitators met with each party separately and discussed cases with them over the telephone. We did, however, attend meetings where facilitators discussed difficult cases between themselves and also looked at case files for indirect mediation cases.
9. Pre-conference interviews were not conducted with participants after the initial pilot period, when cases were subject to a randomised controlled trial (see further in Chapter 3).

10. The impossibility of observing indirect mediation and the limited numbers of cases of direct mediation observed for CONNECT and REMEDI means that we cannot also present single case studies for the other two schemes.

2 Setting the schemes in context: a review of the aims, histories and results of restorative justice

1. The recent Criminal Justice and Immigration Act 2008 for England and Wales says that, in sentencing young people under 18, the court must have regard to the principal aim of the youth justice system – to prevent offending (or reoffending) – as well as to the welfare of the young person (s. 9) and the principles of sentencing for adult offenders, which are the punishment of offenders, the reform and rehabilitation of offenders, the protection of the public and the making of reparation by offenders to persons affected by their offences (s. 142, Criminal Justice Act 2003).
2. Funding cuts led probation to cease funding the scheme, which then effectively collapsed because of the lack of money to pay the coordinator or mediators.
3. In 74 cases the outcome was unknown.
4. See www.westmidlands-probation.gov.uk/wmps/about/victims.asp (accessed 9 December 2008).
5. The *marae* is the community centre and meeting house for Maori people in that area.
6. Results were in the same direction in both sites, but sample sizes or size of effect did not lead to significant effects in both on all measures.
7. 'Restorative justice under threat', *Law Times*, at www.lawtimesnews.com/Headline-News/Restorative-justice-under-threat (accessed 9 December 2008).
8. Earlier reports do not emphasise the aim of victim satisfaction (Sherman *et al.* 1997a, 1998). RISE itself is still continuing.
9. All findings reported in this paragraph were at the $p < 0.001$ level of significance, a very high level.
10. Currently, mediation is more widespread in the United States (Umbreit *et al.* 2000) and in mainland Europe, while conferencing has tended to be used in Australia and New Zealand. In England and Wales, youth services tend to use indirect mediation or the writing of letters of apology for criminal offences, but family group conferences for youth problems (the latter not normally including victims) (Holdaway *et al.* 2001; Zernova 2007a).
11. Unfortunately, the results presented in Strang *et al.* (1999) do not separate those aged under 18 and those aged over 18.
12. The court has discretion to refer for indictable only offences (such as manslaughter, rape and robbery) but must refer all other cases.
13. The Explanatory Notes are written by the relevant government department for all Acts at: www.opsi.gov.uk/acts/acts2002/en/02en26-b.htm.
14. See Morris (2002), who comments particularly that there has been a considerable problem with the provision of programmes for offenders in relation to youth conferencing in New Zealand, despite the fact that the introduction of youth conferencing has led to fewer young offenders appearing in court or going into custody, which has resulted in major cost savings to the state.
15. At the $p < 0.01$ level. The findings for offender satisfaction omitted one programme which was run post-sentence and which produced results completely out of line with the other programmes.
16. The first set of interviews was with 59 people in relation to JRC, 9 for CONNECT and 9 for REMEDI. The second set was with 48 for JRC, 7 for CONNECT and 7 for REMEDI. Interviews took between 40 minutes and 2 hours and covered

respondents' understanding and experiences of the aims of the schemes, how it was running and particular benefits and difficulties.

3 Setting up and running restorative justice schemes

1. Dedicated drugs courts are criminal courts/judges which aim to deal with drugs-related crime prosecutions and sentencing so that offenders' progress during sentence can be monitored in terms of drugs usage and other problems, with the aim being to ensure consistency in who hears the case and to concentrate specialist expertise on drugs.
2. This did not mean pleading guilty immediately or at the first court appearance. Schemes found that, particularly for violence offences and at the Crown Court, offenders tended routinely, on legal advice, to plead not guilty initially, in order to obtain fuller summaries of the evidence from the prosecution and to allow time for consideration of the case by defence lawyers. Sometimes guilty pleas were only tendered on the morning of a planned trial (see Hall 2009 for a discussion of pleas and the progress of cases at the magistrates' court and Crown Court). Cases involving young offenders tend to be completed in a slightly shorter time (Shapland *et al.* 2003; Ministry of Justice 2008a) and for cases diverted from prosecution, an admission of responsibility, such as an adult caution or youth final warning, is often tendered quickly.
3. The prime reason was that there was little experience in the use of restorative justice with adult offenders (and often adult victims) and these categories of case were considered to pose additional, potentially difficult issues, particularly in relation to potential power imbalances. Schemes also intended to take only cases with a direct individual victim and so initially all omitted homicide offences. However, CONNECT was asked, after about a year of operation, by relatives of homicide victims, via a Probation Liaison Unit, to take some such cases and decided it had amassed sufficient experience to do so. Facilitators undertook additional training from a person experienced in dealing with homicide cases before expanding their remit in this way.
4. We ourselves later undertook these analyses in relation to JRC London and CONNECT and provided them with the results.
5. In order to compile attrition tables, these data refer to cases received by the schemes between the start of the randomisation phase ('Phase 2') and 1 December 2003 for JRC, so that most cases had been finished by the end of the evaluation data period around Easter 2004. All cases referred or taken up to 1 April 2004 for REMEDI and all CONNECT cases are included.
6. JRC used a computerised randomisation process with a fairly wide margin for equivalence between the restorative justice and control groups, but aiming at a 50 : 50 split numerically. Randomisation was done by JRC in the United States, normally by means of a telephone call immediately after victim consent had been gained.
7. JRC did a considerable amount of environmental scanning during the set-up phase on the adult magistrates' court cases to find out what was happening to the cases.
8. Further details can be found in Shapland *et al.* (2004a, 2006a).
9. Similar problems of very low case flow affected the subsequent initiative (outside the scope of our evaluation) for conditional cautions in London involving restorative justice.
10. Only the mediation cases have been counted in Table 3.1. Victim impact work per se (which might be done in groups or individually) does not fall under the definition of restorative justice used by the schemes and the evaluation because it did not involve individual victims (see Chapter 1).

11. The figures are taken from Table 3.1 of Shapland *et al.* (2006a).
12. Operating restorative justice pre-sentence cannot be entirely 'voluntary', in the sense of having no consequences, given that taking responsibility for the offence, expressing remorse, etc. are mitigatory factors for sentence. Young (1989) has seen this as problematic and that offenders might agree for instrumental reasons. However, in these schemes, the courts had previously agreed that cases randomised to the control group would not receive any greater sentence.
13. Shapland *et al.* (2004b) argue that, because of the complexity of their jobs, it is only where there are consequences for criminal justice practitioners for failing to make referrals, allow time for restorative justice, etc. that there is a swift take-up and implementation of change in criminal justice. Statutory changes and orders create that necessary impetus and consequences, discretionary ones do not. This is one reason for the rapid implementation of youth justice reforms (Holdaway *et al.* 2001; Newburn *et al.* 2002) but the slow pace of implementation of victim and witness facilities until the requirements in the Criminal Justice and Youth Evidence Act 1999.
14. These are valid percentages, omitting 'don't know' or 'can't remember' responses.
15. Apart from one victim who said they didn't know.
16. Being housed visibly within an existing agency can also help with referrals from that agency, as REMEDI workers found with the Youth Offending Team in one town.
17. However, police officers, who are required by statute to attend conferences and participate in restorative work (in fact, they undertake much of the follow-up work from outcome agreements), are seconded to the Agency (Campbell *et al.* 2005).
18. Though a core team of paid facilitators, with a manager and administrative staff, is essential.
19. We ourselves wrote the programmes for one scheme and were the main advisors on another.
20. Details of costs for all schemes are given in Shapland *et al.* (2007). Costs quoted in this book have all been adjusted to 2005/6 levels.
21. Although those attending restorative justice events were paid travel expenses, they were not reimbursed for their time: there was no equivalent to witness expenses. This is something which needs to be considered if restorative justice is mainstreamed.
22. In criminal justice, for example, it would be normal to calculate costs per crime recorded by the police, per offender prosecuted, per offender convicted and per offender sentenced to prison.
23. Assuming that the cost of holding the conference and follow-up for conferenced cases was the same as for London.

4 Accountability, regulation and risk

1. Also see the discussion on potentially dominating facilitators in Chapter 3.
2. Pavlich similarly argues against a general theory of ethics and the possibility of unchanging, unsituated expressions of moral values: restorative processes cannot 'operate in the name of supposedly universal principles of harm, or absolute conceptions of general community interests' (2002: 5).
3. In particular, see Braithwaite and Mugford (1994), Roche (2003), Van Ness (2003).
4. Just as human rights instruments, such as the European Convention on Human Rights, most of which were drafted in the first half of the twentieth century, reflect

the preoccupations of that time, particularly the need to protect offenders against a powerful state – and have little to say about victims or other lay participants in criminal justice.

5. Van Ness (2003) comments that it was a deliberate decision not to define restorative justice, because it was not intended to deal with restorative justice at an overall policy or vision level, but instead to consider restorative justice programmes.
6. Children, Young Persons, and Their Families Act 1989, as amended to 1 October 2008.
7. Justice (Northern Ireland) Act 2002.
8. See *Deweer* (European Court of Human Rights, judgment of 27 February 1980, Series A, No. 35). A case which is sent to restorative justice but remains within the criminal process and the governance of the court (e.g. pre-sentence or post-sentence restorative justice) would presumably not be problematic, because the court still has control.
9. Though net-widening is a perennial problem in youth justice (Decker 1985).
10. However, the roles only remain fixed in so far as the participants determine they should: a fight or neighbourhood conflict in which both parties have engaged may result in a very fluid conference in terms of roles (Shapland 2009a).
11. At least in states which espouse democracy and believe criminal justice should be in touch with public views, as does the UK (Home Office 2009; Hough and Roberts 2004). Authoritarian states pursue criminal justice processes which lack public confidence and legitimacy at their own peril.
12. An exception which illustrates the potential power of such accountability has occurred in relation to the provision of offending behaviour programmes for offenders serving indeterminate sentences in England and Wales, whose cases could not be considered for release until they had been on a programme (see also Padfield 2009). Unfortunately, programmes were not available at all prisons in which such offenders were held: the High Court ruled that such detention was unlawful (see The *Guardian*, 1 August 2007, at: www.guardian.co.uk/uk/2007/aug/01/ukcrime.prisonsandprobation1 (accessed 5 March 2009)) and this was upheld by the Court of Appeal (see www.irwinmitchell.com/PressOffice/PressReleases/CourtOfAppealUpholdsDecisionOnCoursesForPrisonersServingIPPSentences.htm (accessed 5 March 2009)).
13. Criminal justice decision-makers giving reasons for their decisions (including at sentence) is a requirement under the Human Rights Act 1998.

5 Approaching restorative justice

1. Of the questionnaires, 157 were returned from offenders, 50 from victims. The disparity is due to victims normally only being approached after offenders had agreed, whereas offenders were given questionnaires after the pre-mediation meeting with mediators, whether or not they subsequently agreed. We cannot calculate an exact response rate as we do not know how many participants were given questionnaires, but this is at least 26 per cent of offenders and 19 per cent of victims, calculated from the numbers reaching the preparation phase. Further details of both interviews and questionnaires are given in Shapland *et al.* (2006a). Percentages given in this chapter are percentages of those answering the particular question in the interview or a questionnaire (i.e. valid percentages).
2. Full results for JRC and REMEDI participants are given in Shapland *et al.* (2007: Tables 2.1 and 2.2), from which Table 5.1 here is derived. There were insufficient CONNECT responses to be able to analyse them. REMEDI respondents had two extra statements in their questionnaire.

3. A principal components analysis allows us to look at the inter-correlations or statistical relationships between reasons, without making any presumption about what they might be. For the interviews/questionnaires prior to the restorative justice event, two separate analyses were done, both combining victims and offenders, one for JRC (total variance accounted for was 71 per cent) and one for REMEDI (66 per cent). All interviews were entered, using the reasons the participant gave, plus whether this was an adult or youth offender case and, for JRC, the JRC site. For the post-event interviews, additionally, for JRC, whether this was the conference or control group and whether this was a JRC group with more serious offences were also entered. For REMEDI, due to the smaller number of interviews, interviews with victims and offenders had to be combined. Factors were isolated for eigenvalues greater than 1. Variables are listed which related at correlations of 0.3 or above with the factor. For more details see Shapland *et al.* (2006a, 2007).
4. The additional statements, only available to REMEDI respondents in the pre-restorative justice questionnaires, were available to both JRC and REMEDI respondents in post-restorative justice interviews.
5. There was a significant difference between JRC offender and victim ratings in both the conference group and control group (conference group: likelihood ratio = 15.8, df = 4, $p = 0.003$; Mann-Whitney U = 12755, $p < 0.001$; control group: likelihood ratio = 12.7, df = 4, $p = 0.013$; Mann-Whitney U = 7069, $p = 0.001$) – offenders were more nervous than victims. The difference at REMEDI between offenders and victims was in the same direction but just not significant.
6. Further details about the ways in which participants were approached and their reactions are given in Shapland *et al.* (2006a, 2007).

6 Through a different lens: examining restorative justice using case studies

1. We are very grateful to Marie Howes, who undertook much of the work acquiring and analysing this case study material.
2. Miller and Blackler (2000) include three short conference case studies. For case studies of victim-offender mediation see, for example, Messmer (1990) and Flaten (1996).
3. Note that we had no direct access to proceedings or parties prior to the conference for the main, randomly assigned, phase of JRC. In some cases involving multiple victims (including two of the cases selected for this analysis) it was not possible to conduct final follow-up interviews with all of them.
4. Trust is a fundamental part of a restorative justice conference and merits a study of its own. More than once the issue of what happens to sensitive information was raised (see Chapter 4; Dignan *et al.* 2007).
5. There was no expectation that judges would reflect outcome agreements for JRC cases, in contrast to the statutory provisions for youth conferencing cases in Northern Ireland, for example (Campbell *et al.* 2005).
6. The only caveats were from David (case 3) relating to the time involved and from George (case 4) who did not think it appropriate for a 'really serious' crime.

7 During restorative justice events

1. In the 130 referral panels dealing with young offenders observed by Crawford and Newburn (2003) at which at least one offender attended, only 16 had a personal victim present and one a corporate victim (13 per cent). Their analysis of YOT records showed that, of the 1,760 cases closed, in just 67 (4 per cent) was a victim

present. Angus (2009), in a very recent study observing three YOTs' practice in relation to child victims, found that child victims were very rarely contacted or invited to attend.

2. Note that Northumbria and Thames Valley conferences could have more than one offender, while London conferences were restricted to single offenders.
3. CONNECT mediation might have more than one offender and more than one victim. There was usually only one mediator present.
4. It is difficult to compare participation rates directly between youth conferencing in Northern Ireland and JRC, because all JRC offences had personal victims (meaning an individual was directly victimised – though sometimes this direct victimisation might be in the course of their work), whereas youth conferencing in Northern Ireland is for all offences which are not indictable only, thereby including offences with commercial or organisational victims and offences, such as public order offences, with no named victim.
5. The effects of imprisonment (and many of the adult offenders who participated in JRC restorative justice were imprisoned, either on remand or because the trial was prior to release: Shapland *et al.* 2006a) on offenders' families and on offenders' bonds with their families are now well-known (Liebling and Maruna 2006; Murray 2005).
6. Observers did not, however, rate REMEDI or CONNECT mediators as dominant during the process.
7. Personal communication, mediators based in the city of Leuven.
8. CONNECT only dealt with cases involving adult offenders.
9. Percentages given here relate to the main randomised phase of JRC conferencing and so do not include the adult caution cases. Where there was more than one offender, victim, offender supporter or victim supporter, they relate to the main person in each case.
10. Telephone contacts were not recorded, so we cannot say how many contacts there were overall.
11. Some victims, mainly corporate victims, only had telephone contact with the scheme.
12. See Shapland (2009a) for a further discussion of this question.
13. Of JRC victims, only 75 per cent of those who had attended a conference and 69 per cent of those who were in the control group (experiencing criminal justice only) knew of the criminal justice outcome in their case (sentence etc.) at the time they were interviewed for our evaluation several months later (Shapland *et al.* 2007).
14. Restorative justice processes were on average rated more highly on procedural justice, but the authors suggest not sufficiently so to produce effects on behaviour when measured two years later.
15. Seventy-two per cent of conference victims and 60 per cent of control victims were very or fairly satisfied (likelihood ratio = 10.6, df = 4, p = 0.032: Shapland *et al.* 2007).
16. Likelihood ratio = 12.3, df = 4, p = 0.015.
17. Mann-Whitney U = 6389, p = 0.01.
18. See Shapland and Hall (2007) for a review of what we know about the effects and time course of victimisation on adult victims. In JRC conferences, observers rated victims as saying they were affected 'a lot' or 'quite a lot' by the offence (as opposed to 'some', 'a little' or 'not affected') in 65 per cent of conferences.
19. In JRC conferences, observers rated offenders as saying they had been affected 'a lot' or 'quite a lot' by the offence in 22 per cent of conferences.
20. They were given a five-point Likert scale from very safe to not at all safe.
21. Chi-squared = 10.755, df = 1, p < 0.001.

22. McConville *et al.* (1994) have shown how defence solicitors engage in a process of managing defendants' expectations and demands. Adult defendants do not speak in court in mitigation unless they are not legally represented, in which case they may give very short statements, often containing an apology (Shapland 1981). The inglorious and patchy history of victim personal statements, which are still not offered to many victims, shows how, even when there is significant political will to implement participative measures for victims, this does not manage to surmount the barriers of professional legal cultures (Hall 2009; Shapland and Hall 2010).
23. See Vanfraechem (2009) for an analysis of the principles mediators follow in Belgium.
24. Social capital, for Putnam, is defined as: 'The core idea in social capital theory is that social networks have value … social contacts affect the productivity of individuals and groups … [social capital refers] to connections amongst individuals – social networks and the norms of reciprocity and trustworthiness that arise from them' (Putnam, 2000: 18–19).

8 The victims' views: satisfaction and closure

1. There were insufficient final interviews with CONNECT victims to display the data numerically in any meaningful fashion. The number of interviews with REMEDI victims is quite small, so results should be treated with caution. There were insufficient numbers of interviews with direct mediation victims to present these results separately.
2. The principal components analysis accounted for 63 per cent of the variance and included both offender and victim data.
3. The first factor accounted for 62 per cent of the variance and was associated primarily with being a victim (0.47 loading; both offender and victim satisfaction data were included). Feeling the process was useful loaded 0.86, recommending restorative justice to others 0.76, whether you would take part in mediation again 0.71 and whether mediation is a good way to deal with the offence 0.67.
4. Likelihood ratio = 21.806, df = 12, p = 0.040.
5. Likelihood ratio = 23.801, df = 12, p = 0.022.
6. Likelihood ratio = 19.087, df = 12, p = 0.086.
7. If any victim suggested they might need someone to talk to at greater length or if they appeared to need support with practical or emotional effects, facilitators always gave them details of Victim Support. This was also mentioned in the follow-up telephone calls made by facilitators a few days after the conference for JRC.
8. Revenge feelings were measured by the questions 'Would you do some harm to the offender yourself if you had the chance?' (RISE) or 'Do you wish you could physically retaliate against the offender now?' (JRC London).
9. Self-blame was measured by the questions: 'Do you blame yourself or place any responsibility on yourself for the crime?' (JRC London) or 'Do you sometimes think that the incident might have been prevented if you had been more careful or less provoking' (RISE).
10. This is a very stringent test, because the randomisation only occurred after the preparation phase and when all parties had agreed to restorative justice, so the only difference was that the conference group experienced the conference itself.
11. The results for anger approach significance: chi-squared = 3.441, df = 1, p = 0.064.
12. Unlike with RISE, where conferencing involved diversion from criminal justice and so was an alternative.
13. Chi-squared = 8.926, df = 1, p = 0.003.

14. Rombouts and Parmentier (2009) make this point even more persuasively in relation to victims of abuse of power and of war crimes: often the state of 'before' no longer exists (villages are destroyed, relatives have died) or lasted so long that it cannot be remedied (because education was not received as a child, etc.).
15. Likelihood ratio = 31.7, df = 16, p = 0.011 (Shapland *et al.* 2007).

9 Outcome agreements and their progress

1. Occasionally arrangements were made to send copies of outcome agreements to participants after the conference: this happened most often in the Northumbria youth final warning RCT, in which only 77 per cent of agreements were signed by participants directly after the conference.
2. Once they started to follow up the completion of items on outcome agreements more systematically, JRC staff in London (and subsequently Thames Valley) adopted the acronym SMART PS to describe the ideal outcome agreement: Specific, Measurable, Achievable, Relevant, Timed, Proportionate and Supervised.
3. The unit for our analysis of outcome agreements is the offender rather than the conference/case, because on some occasions a conference/case involved more than one offender and in these cases separate agreements were drawn up for individual offenders.
4. It is worth noting, however, that the absence of an apology in the outcome agreement did not necessarily indicate that an apology had not been expressed during the conference.
5. This argument throws into doubt practices such as excluding victims from discussion of what may happen in the future through requiring them to leave the conference after having talked about the effects of offences upon them (Zernova 2007a). It seems that one reason for the exclusion of victims is the adoption by facilitators of a zero-sum ideology, whereby victims' needs are assumed to be potentially incompatible with those of offenders or the overarching needs of society/their agency to reduce crime. On the basis of our evaluation, it would appear that this assumption does not seem to be correct for the majority of victims.
6. For JRC cases, outcome agreements were routinely provided to courts in pre-sentence cases, to Youth Offending Teams in final warning cases for young offenders, and to probation officers in the Thames Valley probation community trial and where relevant in the prison trial. For REMEDI cases, where referrals originated with the National Probation Service, written feedback (in the form of a report to the offender's probation officer) was provided by REMEDI staff. In common with JRC, the CONNECT scheme provided reports to court (though not outcome agreements, since none were produced) in cases where mediation took place pre-sentence.
7. [2003] EWCA Crim 1687.
8. It is difficult to interpret this, given that it did not occur in the more numerous other group in London (burglary cases) – see the discussion in Shapland *et al.* (2006a: Chapter 3).
9. For adult caution cases, which did not form part of Phase 2 of the experiment, 68 per cent of the 28 agreements were completed fully and 4 per cent at least partially, with 29 per cent not being completed.
10. Incomplete databases meant that we were not able to specify exactly what happened in all cases.
11. For further information about follow-up by REMEDI staff after mediation, see Shapland *et al.* (2006a: 68–9).
12. Conferences in prison often had a probation officer attending as liaison, to fetch participants and guide them through the security, make refreshments, etc., but these

probation officers normally did not speak in the conference unless the facilitator or another participant directly asked for their assistance.

13. See McNeill and Whyte (2007) for further discussion of how probation officers can provide bridging social capital to offenders to aid in desistance, such as by reassuring potential (and actual) employers. They also refer to probation officers as potential agents to engage with families to strengthen family ties and social capital.

10 The offenders' views: reoffending and the road to desistance

1. The number of interviews with REMEDI offenders is quite small so results should be treated with caution. Where CONNECT offenders' reactions differed from those of JRC and REMEDI offenders, this is stated in the text. We have omitted the question about whether problems caused by the offence were solved because this has a rather different meaning in an interview with offenders to its meaning for victims.
2. Mann-Whitney $U = 77.5$, $p = 0.029$.
3. The principal components analysis for JRC offenders accounted for 73 per cent of the variance and was associated primarily with whether the offender was satisfied with the outcome of the conference (loading of 0.93). All loadings were at 0.78 or above.
4. Chi squared = 57.29, $df = 20$, $p < 0.001$.
5. All the schemes referred to at this point are discussed in more detail in Chapter 2.
6. The use of such an experimental methodology is seen as the 'gold standard' in looking at reoffending.
7. This is the standard method used in medicine, etc. where one compares 'intention to treat' groups whether or not the treatment group actually manages to get the treatment – in our own evaluation, there was in fact minimal drop-out between agreement and those who actually had a conference (see Chapter 3). However, there is no possibility of using the preferred medical 'double-blind' methodology with restorative justice or any other social science intervention which involves talking to people because the participants know what they are participating in and know which group they are in (as do those running the scheme once randomisation has taken place).
8. In our evaluation, we only use the term 'statistically significant' if the results would be produced at a rate of 1 in 20 times (5 per cent) or less by chance.
9. For indirect mediation the end of the restorative justice process was taken as the last contact with the scheme. Because the frequency of reconviction is also going to be affected by the length of time an offender is out in the community (and so could commit offences) during these two years, we did the analysis for offenders who had any time at all out in the community and offenders who had at least six months out in the community. Unless otherwise stated below, the results were identical for the two analyses.
10. We are very grateful to Miguel Goncalves of the Ministry of Justice for calculating the effect size, using the standardised mean difference between the two groups, from our data. The calculation shows the log transformed difference in the means to be about 0.12 and the standard deviation 0.70, with the standardised mean difference between the two groups being 0.19, which is a reduction in log transformed frequency of reoffending for a restorative justice offender of 8 percentage points, and so frequency of reoffending of 14 percentage points.
11. All the schemes were set up prospectively and have at least individually matched control groups.

12. Dolan *et al.* (2007) have shown how such a measure could be created, using methods developed from those of health economics.
13. Details of costs and calculations can be found in Shapland *et al.* (2008).
14. We undertook loglinear analyses between restorative justice and control groups on reconviction over two years for offenders who had spent any time in the community in relation both to likelihood of reconviction and frequency of reconviction (Shapland *et al.* 2008).
15. See Shapland *et al.* (2008) for details.
16. Predictions were made using the nationally calibrated reconviction index OGRS2, which is primarily affected by previous convictions (as well as the type of offence, etc.).

11 Restorative justice: lessons from practice

1. The pilot in London, for example, ended prematurely because of an inadequate flow of referrals to the restorative justice conditional cautioning scheme.

References

Allen, J., Edmonds, S., Patterson, A. and Smith, D. (2006) *Policing and the Criminal Justice System – Public Confidence and Perceptions: Findings from the 2004/05 British Crime Survey*, Home Office Online Report 07/06. London: Home Office, at www.homeoffice.gov.uk/rds/pdfs06/rdsolr0706.pdf (accessed 25 August 2009).

Angel, C. (2005) *Crime Victims Meet Their Offenders: Testing the Impact of Restorative Justice Conferences on Victims' Post-Traumatic Stress Symptoms*. PhD dissertation, University of Pennsylvania.

Angus, S. (2009) *Youth Justice and Child Victims*. PhD thesis, Middlesex University.

Ashworth, A. (1993) 'Some doubts about restorative justice', *Criminal Law Forum*, 4: 277–99.

Balahur, D. and Kilchling, M. (eds) (forthcoming) *Directions of Restorative Justice in Europe*. Brussels: Office for Publications of the European Communities.

Bartkowiak, I. and Jaccoud, M. (2008) 'New directions in Canadian justice: from state workers to community "representatives"', in J. Shapland (ed.), *Justice, Community and Civil Society*. Cullompton: Willan.

Bennett, T. (1990) *Evaluating Neighbourhood Watch*. Aldershot: Gower.

Blader, S. and Tyler, T. (2003) 'A four-component model of procedural justice: defining the meaning of a "fair" process', *Personality and Social Psychology Bulletin*, 29 (6): 747–58.

Bonta, J. (1996) 'Risk-needs assessment and treatment', in A. T. Harland (ed.), *Choosing Correctional Options That Work*. London: Sage.

Bonta, J., Wallace-Capretta, S. and Rooney, J. (1998) *Restorative Justice: An Evaluation of the Restorative Resolutions Project*. Ottawa: Solicitor General Canada.

Borenstein, M., Hedges, L., Higgins, J. and Rothstein, H. (2004) *Comprehensive Meta Analysis, version 2*. At: http://meta-analysis.com/.

Bottoms, A. E. (1995) 'The philosophy and politics of punishment and sentencing', in C. Clarkson and R. Morgan (eds), *The Politics of Sentencing Reform*. Oxford: Clarendon Press, pp. 17–50.

Bottoms, A. E. (2003) 'Some sociological reflections on restorative justice', in A. von Hirsch, J. Roberts, A. E. Bottoms, K. Roach and M. Schiff (eds), *Restorative Justice and Criminal Justice: Competing or Reconcilable Paradigms?* Oxford: Hart.

Bottoms, A. and Dignan, J. (2004) 'Youth crime and youth justice: comparative and cross-national perspectives', *Crime and Justice: A Review of Research*, 31: 21–183.

Bottoms, A. E. and Shapland, J. (2011) 'Steps towards desistance among male young adult recidivists', in S. Farrall, R. Sparks, S. Maruna and M. Hough (eds), *Escape*

Routes: Contemporary Perspectives on Life after Punishment. Abingdon: Routledge, pp. 43–80.

Bradford, B., Jackson, J. and Stanko, E. (2009) 'Contact and confidence: revisiting the impact of public encounters with the police', *Policing and Society*, 19 (1): 20–46.

Braithwaite, J. (1989) *Crime, Shame and Reintegration*. Cambridge: Cambridge University Press.

Braithwaite, J. (1994) 'Thinking harder about democratising social control', in C. Alder and J. Wundersitz (eds), *Family Conferencing and Juvenile Justice: The Way Forward or Misplaced Optimism?* Canberra: Australian Institute of Criminology, pp. 199–216.

Braithwaite, J. (1996) *Restorative Justice and a Better Future*, The Dorothy J. Killam Memorial Lecture, Australian National University/Dalhousie University, 17 October. Online at: www.anu.edu.au/fellows/jbraithwaite/pubsbyyear/index.php; reprinted in E. McLaughlin, R. Fergusson, G. Hughes and L. Westmorland (eds) (2003) *Restorative Justice: Critical Issues*. London: Sage.

Braithwaite, J. (1998) 'Restorative justice', in M. Tonry (ed.), *Handbook of Crime and Punishment*. New York: Oxford University Press.

Braithwaite, J. (1999) 'Restorative justice: assessing optimistic and pessimistic accounts', *Crime and Justice: A Review of Research*, 25: 1–127.

Braithwaite, J. (2002a) *Restorative Justice and Responsive Regulation*. Oxford: Oxford University Press.

Braithwaite, J. (2002b) 'Setting standards for restorative justice', *British Journal of Criminology*, 42: 563–77.

Braithwaite, J. and Braithwaite, V. (2001) 'Part I. Shame, shame management and regulation', in E. Ahmed, N. Harris, J. Braithwaite and V. Braithwaite (eds), *Shame Management Through Reintegration*. Melbourne: University of Cambridge Press, pp. 1–69.

Braithwaite, J. and Mugford, S. (1994) 'Conditions of successful reintegration ceremonies: dealing with juvenile offenders', *British Journal of Criminology*, 34: 139–71.

Braithwaite, J. and Strang, H. (2001) 'Introduction: restorative justice and civil society', in H. Strang and J. Braithwaite (eds), *Restorative Justice and Civil Society*. Cambridge: Cambridge University Press.

Campbell, C., Devlin, R., O'Mahony, D., Doak, J., Jackson, J., Corrigan, T. and McEvoy, K. (2005) *Evaluation of the Northern Ireland Youth Conference Service*, NIO Research and Statistical Service Report No. 12. Belfast: Northern Ireland Office, at: www.nio.gov.uk/evaluation_of_the_northern_ireland_youth_conference_service.pdf.

Cann, J., Falshaw, L., Nugent, F. and Friendship, C. (2003) *Understanding What Works: Accredited Cognitive Skills Programmes for Adult Men and Young Offenders*, Home Office Research Findings 226. London: Home Office.

Christie, N. (1977) 'Conflicts as property', *British Journal of Criminology*, 17: 1–15.

Christie, N. (1986) 'The ideal victim', in E. Fattah (ed.), *From Crime Policy to Victim Policy*. Basingstoke: Macmillan.

Christie, N. (2009) 'Restorative justice: five dangers ahead', in P. Knepper, J. Doak and J. Shapland (eds), *Urban Crime Prevention, Surveillance, and Restorative Justice: Effects of Social Technologies*. Baton Rouge, FL: CRC Press, pp. 195–204.

Cohen, S. (1985) *Visions of Social Control*. Cambridge: Polity Press and Blackwells.

Coleman, J. S. (1988) 'Social capital in the creation of human capital', *American Journal of Sociology*, 94, Supplement: S95–S120.

Consedine, J. and Bowen, H. (1999) *Restorative Justice: Contemporary Themes and Practice*. Lyttleton, NZ: Ploughshares Publications.

Cook, K. (2006) 'Doing difference and accountability in restorative justice conferences', *Theoretical Criminology*, 10: 107–24.

Council of Europe (1999) *Mediation in Penal Matters: Recommendation No. R(99)19 and Explanatory Memorandum*. Strasbourg: Council of Europe.

Crawford, A. (1998) *Crime Prevention and Community Safety: Politics, Policies and Practices*. Harlow: Longman.

Crawford, A. (2002) 'The state, community and restorative justice: heresy, nostalgia and butterfly collecting', in L. Walgrave (ed.), *Restorative Justice and the Law*. Cullompton: Willan, pp. 101–29.

Crawford, A. (2003) 'Contractual governance of deviant behaviour', *Journal of Law and Society*, 30 (4): 469–505.

Crawford, A. and Burden, T. (2005) *Integrating Victims in Restorative Youth Justice*. Bristol: Policy Press.

Crawford, A. and Newburn, T. (2003) *Youth Offending and Restorative Justice: Implementing Reform in Youth Justice*. Cullompton: Willan.

Crime and Justice Research Centre, with Triggs, S. (2005) *New Zealand Court-referred Restorative Justice Pilot: Evaluation*. Wellington: New Zealand Ministry of Justice.

Cunliffe, J. and Shepherd, A. (2007) *Re-offending of Adults: Results from the 2004 Cohort*, Home Office Statistical Bulletin 06/07. London: National Statistics.

Daly, K. (2000) 'Revisiting the relationship between retributive and restorative justice', in H. Strang and J. Braithwaite (eds), *Restorative Justice: Philosophy to Practice*. Dartmouth: Ashgate.

Daly, K. (2001) 'Conferencing in Australia and New Zealand: variations, research findings and prospects', in A. Morris and G. Maxwell (eds), *Restorative Justice for Juveniles: Conferencing, Mediation and Circles*. Oxford: Hart.

Daly, K. (2002) 'Restorative justice: the real story', *Punishment and Society*, 4 (1): 55–79.

Daly, K. (2003a) 'Making variation a virtue: evaluating the potential and limits of restorative justice', in E. Weitekamp and H.-J. Kerner (eds), *Restorative Justice in Context: International Practice and Directions*. Cullompton: Willan, pp. 23–50.

Daly, K. (2003b) 'Mind the gap: restorative justice in theory and practice', in A. von Hirsch, J. Roberts, A. E. Bottoms, K. Roach and M. Schiff (eds), *Restorative Justice and Criminal Justice: Competing or Reconcilable Paradigms?* Oxford: Hart, pp. 219–36.

Daly, K. (2004) 'Pile it on: more texts on RJ', *Theoretical Criminology*, 8 (4): 499–507.

Daly, K. and Curtis-Fawley, S. (2004) 'Restorative justice for victims of sexual assault', in K. Heimer and C. Kruttschnitt (eds), *Gender and Crime: Patterns in Victimization and Offending*. New York: New York University Press, pp. 230–68.

Daly, K. and Hayes, H. (2001) *Restorative Justice and Conferencing in Australia*, Australian Institute of Criminology Trends and Issues in Crime and Criminal Justice No. 186. Online at: www.aic.gov.au/publications/tandi/tandi186.html (accessed 10 December 2008).

Daly, K. and Immarigeon, R. (1998) 'The past, present, and future of restorative justice: some critical reflections', *Contemporary Justice Review*, 1: 21–45.

Davis, G. (1992) *Making Amends: Mediation and Reparation in Criminal Justice.* Abingdon: Routledge.

Davis, R. C., Tichane, M. and Grayson, D. (1980) *Mediation and Arbitration as Alternatives to Prosecution in Felony Arrest Cases: An Evaluation of the Brooklyn Dispute Resolution Center (First Year).* New York: Vera Institute of Justice.

Day, P. and Klein, R. (1987) *Accountabilities: Five Public Services.* London: Tavistock.

Decker, S. (1985) 'A systemic analysis of diversion: net-widening and beyond', *Journal of Criminal Justice*, 13: 207–16.

Dignan, J. (2000) *Youth Justice Pilots Evaluation: Interim Report on Reparative Work and Youth Offending Teams.* London: Home Office.

Dignan, J. (2005) *Understanding Victims and Restorative Justice.* Maidenhead: Open University Press/McGraw-Hill.

Dignan, J. and Lowey, K. (2000) *Restorative Justice Options for Northern Ireland: A Comparative Review.* Belfast: Northern Ireland Office.

Dignan, J., Atkinson, A., Atkinson, H., Howes, M., Johnstone, J., Robinson, G., Shapland, J. and Sorsby, A. (2007) 'Staging restorative justice encounters against a criminal justice backdrop: a dramaturgical analysis', *Criminology and Criminal Justice*, 7 (1): 5–32.

Doak, J. and O'Mahony, D. (2006) 'The vengeful victim? Assessing the attitudes of victims participating in restorative youth conferencing', *International Review of Victimology*, 13: 157–78.

Doak, J. and O'Mahony, D. (2009) 'State, community and transition: restorative youth conferencing in Northern Ireland', in P. Knepper, J. Doak, J. and J. Shapland (eds), *Urban Crime Prevention, Surveillance and Restorative Justice: Effects of Social Technologies.* Boca Raton, FL: CRC Press.

Dolan, P., Netten, A., Shapland, J. and Tsuchiya, A. (2007) 'Towards a preference-based measure of the impact on well-being due to victimisation and the fear of crime', *International Review of Victimology*, 14: 253–64.

Duff, A. (2003) 'Restoration and retribution', in A. von Hirsch, J. Roberts, A. E. Bottoms, K. Roach and M. Schiff (eds), *Restorative Justice and Criminal Justice: Competing or Reconcilable Paradigms?* Oxford: Hart.

Duff, R. A. (2002) 'Restorative punishment and punitive restoration', in L. Walgrave (ed.), *Restorative Justice and the Law.* Cullompton: Willan, pp. 82–100.

Edwards, I. (2006) 'Restorative justice, sentencing and the court of appeal', *Criminal Law Review*, February, pp. 110–23.

Eglash, A. (1977) 'Beyond restitution: creative restitution', in J. Hudson and B. Galaway (eds), *Restitution in Criminal Justice.* Lexington, MA: D. C. Heath.

Elonheimo, H. (2003) *Restorative Justice Theory and the Finnish Mediation Practices.* Paper presented at the Third Annual Conference of the European Society of Criminology, Helsinki, 27–30 August.

Farrall, S. and Calverley, A. (2006) *Understanding Desistance from Crime: Emerging Theoretical Directions in Resettlement and Rehabilitation.* Maidenhead: Open University Press/McGraw-Hill.

Farrington, D. P., Coid, J., Harnett, L., Jolliffe, D., Soteriou, N., Turner, R. and West, D. J. (2006) *Criminal Careers Up to Age 50 and Life Success Up to Age 48*, Home Office Research Study No. 299. London: Home Office.

Flaten, C. L. (1996) 'Victim-offender mediation: application with serious offenses committed by juveniles', in B. Galloway and J. Hudson (eds), *Restorative Justice in International Perspectives.* Monsey, NY: Criminal Justice Press.

Friendship, C., Mann, R. and Beech, A. (2003) *The Prison-Based Sex Offender Treatment Programme – An Evaluation*, Home Office Research Findings No. 205. London: Home Office.

Friendship, C., Blud, L., Erikson, M. and Travers, R. (2002) *An Evaluation of Cognitive Behavioural Treatment for Prisoners*, Home Office Research Findings No. 161. London: Home Office.

Garland, D. (1996) 'The limits of the sovereign state: strategies of crime control in contemporary society', *British Journal of Criminology*, 36: 445–71.

Garland, D. (2001) *The Culture of Control: Crime and Social Order in Contemporary Society*. Oxford: Oxford University Press.

Gehm, J. (1998) 'Victim-offender mediation programs: an exploration of practice and theoretical frameworks', *Western Criminology Review*, 1 (1). Online at: http://wcr.sonoma.edu/v1n1/gehm.html (accessed 21 August 2009).

Gray, P. (2005) 'The politics of risk and young offenders' experiences of social exclusion and restorative justice', *British Journal of Criminology*, 45: 938–57.

Gunther Moor, L., Peters, T., Ponsaers, P., Shapland. J. and van Stokkom, B. (eds) (2009) 'Restorative policing', *Journal of Police Studies*, no. 2.

Hall, M. (2009) *Victims of Crime: Policy and Practice in Criminal Justice*. Cullompton: Willan.

Hallett, C. and Murray, C. with Jamieson, J. and Veitch, B. (1998) *The Evaluation of Children's Hearings in Scotland*, Vol. 1. Edinburgh: Scottish Office Central Research Unit.

Harris, N. (2003) 'Evaluating the practice of restorative justice: the case of family group conferencing', in L. Walgrave (ed.), *Repositioning Restorative Justice*. Cullompton: Willan.

Harris, N., Walgrave, L. and Braithwaite, J. (2004) 'Emotional dynamics in restorative conferences', *Theoretical Criminology*, 8: 191–210.

Harper, G. and Chitty, C. (2005) *The Impact of Corrections on Reoffending: A Review of 'What Works'*, Home Office Research Study No. 291. London: Home Office. Online at: www.homeoffice.gov.uk/rds/pdfs04/hors291.pdf (accessed 10 February 2009).

Hayes, H. and Daly, K. (2003) 'Youth justice conferencing and reoffending', *Justice Quarterly*, 20: 725–64.

Holdaway, S., Davison, N., Dignan, J., Hammersley, R., Hine, J. and Marsh, P. (2001) *New Strategies to Address Youth Offending: The National Evaluation of the Pilot Youth Offending Teams*, Home Office Occasional Paper. London: Home Office. Online at: www.homeoffice.gov.uk/rds/pdfs/occ69-newstrat.pdf (accessed 8 January 2009).

Home Office (1997) *No More Excuses – A New Approach to Tackling Youth Crime in England and Wales*, Cm 3809. London: The Stationery Office.

Home Office (2001) *Home Office Crime Reduction Programme: Restorative Justice. Project Specification*. London: Home Office.

Home Office (2009) *Public Confidence in the Police and their Local Partners: Results from the British Crime Survey Year Ending September 2008*, Home Office Statistical News Release. Online at: www.homeoffice.gov.uk/rds/pdfs09/pubcon-bcs-snr.pdf (accessed 5 March 2009).

Hough, M. and Roberts, J. (1998) *Attitudes to Punishment: Findings from the British Crime Survey*, Home Office Research Report No. 179. London: Home Office.

Hough, M. and Roberts, J. (2004) *Confidence in Justice: An International Review*, Home Office Research Findings No. 243. London: Home Office. Online at: www.homeoffice.gov.uk/rds/pdfs04/r243.pdf (accessed 5 March 2009).

Hoyle, C. (2008) *Commission on English Prisons Today*, Restorative Justice Working Group Discussion Paper. London: Howard League. Online at: www.howardleague.org/fileadmin/howard_league/user/pdf/Commission/Howard_League_RJ_Working_Group_Discussion_Paper.pdf (accessed 21 May 2010).

Hoyle, C., Young, R. and Hill, R. (2002) *Proceed with Caution: An Evaluation of the Thames Valley Police Initiative in Restorative Cautioning*. York: Joseph Rowntree Foundation.

Hoyle, C., Cape, E., Morgan, R. and Sanders, A. (1998) *Evaluation of the 'One Stop Shop' and Victim Statement Pilot Projects*, Home Office Occasional Paper. London: Home Office. Online at: www.homeoffice.gov.uk/rds/pdfs/occ-one.pdf.

Hudson, B. (2003) 'Victims and offenders', in A. von Hirsch, J. Roberts, A. E. Bottoms, K. Roach and M. Schiff (eds), *Restorative Justice and Criminal Justice: Competing or Reconcilable Paradigms?* Oxford: Hart.

Iivari, J., Sakkinen, S. and Kuoppala, T. (2009) *Rikos-ja riita-asioiden sovittelu 2008* (*Mediation in Criminal and Civil Cases 2008*), Statistical Report 6/2009. Helsinki: National Institute for Health and Welfare.

Joint Inspection Team (2004) *Joint Inspection of Youth Offending Teams of England and Wales: Report on Sheffield Youth Offending Team*. London: Home Office.

JUSTICE (1998) *Victims in Criminal Justice. Report of the JUSTICE Committee on the Role of Victims in Criminal Justice*. London: JUSTICE.

Kant, I. (1795) 'Perpetual peace', in H. Reiss (ed.), *Kant's Political Writings*. Cambridge: Cambridge University Press, pp. 93–130.

Kearney, N., Kirkwood, S. and MacFarlane, L. (2005) 'Restorative justice in Scotland: an overview', *British Journal of Community Justice*, 4: 55–65.

Kenney, J. (2004) 'Human agency revisited: the paradoxical experiences of victims of crime', *International Review of Victimology*, 11: 225–58.

Kirkwood, S. (2010) 'Restorative justice cases in Scotland: factors related to participation, the restorative process, agreement rates and forms of reparation', *European Journal of Criminology*, 7: 107–22.

Kruissink, M. and Verwers, C. (1989) *Halt: een alternatieve aanpak van vandalisme*. Arnhem: Gouda Quint.

Lamb, M., Hershkowitz, I., Orbach, Y. and Esplin, P. (2008) *Tell Me What Happened: Structured Investigative Interviews of Child Victims and Witnesses*. Chichester: John Wiley & Sons.

Latimer, J., Dowden, C. and Muise, D. (2001) *The Effectiveness of Restorative Justice Practices: A Meta-analysis*, Report RR2001-6e. Ottowa: Department of Justice Canada, Research and Statistics Division.

Latimer, J., Dowden, C. and Muise, D. (2005) 'The effectiveness of restorative justice practices: a meta-analysis', *Prison Journal*, 85: 127–44.

Laub, J. H. and Sampson, R. J. (2003) *Shared Beginnings, Divergent Lives*. Cambridge, MA: Harvard University Press.

Liebling, A. and Maruna, S. (eds) (2006) *The Effects of Imprisonment*. Cullompton: Willan.

Lilies, H. (2001) 'Circle sentencing: part of the restorative justice continuum', in A. Morris and G. Maxwell (eds), *Restorative Justice for Juveniles: Conferencing, Mediation and Circles*. Oxford: Hart.

Lind, E. and Tyler, T. (1988) *The Social Psychology of Procedural Justice*. New York: Plenum Press.

Lyness, D. (2008) *Northern Ireland Youth Re-offending: Results from the 2005 Cohort*, Research and Statistical Bulletin 7/2008. Belfast: Northern Ireland Office.

McCold, P. (2000) 'Toward a holistic vision of restorative juvenile justice: a reply to the maximalist model', *Contemporary Justice Review*, 3 (4): 357–414.

McCold, P. (2003) 'A survey of assessment research on mediation and conferencing', in L. Walgrave (ed.), *Repositioning Restorative Justice*. Cullompton: Willan.

McCold, P. (2004) 'What is the role of community in restorative justice theory and practice?', in H. Zehr and B. Toews (eds), *Critical Issues in Restorative Justice*. Monsey, NY: Criminal Justice Press, Chapter 13.

McCold, P. and Wachtel, B. (1998) *Restorative Policing Experiment. The Bethlehem Pennsylvania Police Family Group Conferencing Project*. Pipersville, PA: Community Service Foundation.

McConville, M., Hodgson, J., Bridges, L. and Pavlovic, A. (1994) *Standing Accused: The Organisation and Practices of Criminal Defence Lawyers in Britain*. Oxford: Clarendon Press.

McNeill, F. and Whyte, B. (2007) *Reducing Reoffending: Social Work and Community Justice in Scotland*. Cullompton: Willan.

Maguire, M. (2004) 'The Crime Reduction Programme in England and Wales: reflections on the vision and the reality', *Criminal Justice*, 4 (3): 213–37.

Maguire, M. and Corbett, C. (1987) *The Effects of Crime and the Work of Victims Support Schemes*. Aldershot: Gower.

Marshall, T. F. (1984) *Reparation, Conciliation and Mediation*, Home Office Research and Planning Unit Paper 27. London: Home Office.

Marshall, T. (1999) *Restorative Justice: An Overview*, Home Office Occasional Paper. London: Home Office. Online at: www.homeoffice.gov.uk/rds/pdfs/occ-resjus.pdf.

Marshall, T. and Merry, S. (1990) *Crime and Accountability: Victim and Offender Mediation in Practice*. London: HMSO.

Maruna, S. (2000) *Making Good*. Washington, DC: American Psychological Association.

Maruna, S. and LeBel, T. (2003) 'Welcome home? Examining the "re-entry court" concept from a strengths-based perspective', *Western Criminology Review*, 4: 91–107. Online at: http://wcr.sonoma.edu.

Matrix Knowledge Group (2008) *Dedicated Drug Court Pilots: A Process Report*, Ministry of Justice Research Series 7/08. London: Ministry of Justice. Online at: www.justice.gov.uk/docs/dedicated-drug-courts.pdf (accessed 10 February 2009).

Maxwell, G. and Morris, A. (1993) *Families, Victims and Culture: Youth Justice in New Zealand*. Wellington: Institute of Criminology, Victoria University of Wellington and Social Policy Agency, Wellington.

Maxwell, G. and Morris, A. (2001) 'Putting restorative justice into practice for adult offenders', *Howard Journal*, 40: 55–69.

Messmer, H. (1990) 'Reducing the conflict: an analysis of victim-offender mediation as an interactive process', in B. Galaway and J. Hudson (eds), *Restorative Justice in International Perspective*. Monsey, NY: Criminal Justice Press.

Miers, D., Maguire, M., Goldie, S., Sharpe, K., Hale, C., Netten, A., Uglow, S., Doolin, K., Hallam, A., Enterkin, J. and Newburn, T. (2001) *An Exploratory Evaluation of Restorative Justice Schemes*, Crime Reduction Research Series Paper 9. London: Home Office.

Miller, S. and Blackler, J. (2000) 'Restorative justice: retribution, confession and shame', in H. Strang and J. Braithwaite (eds), *Restorative Justice: Philosophy to Practice*. Aldershot: Ashgate.

Ministry of Justice (2008a) *Time Intervals for Criminal Proceedings at Magistrates' Courts*, Ministry of Justice Statistical Bulletin. Online at: www.justice.gov.uk/docs/time-intervals-criminal-proceedings-september-2008.pdf (accessed 14 January 2008).

Ministry of Justice (2008b) *Re-offending of Adults: New Measures of Re-offending 2000–2005*, Ministry of Justice Statistics Bulletin. London: Ministry of Justice.

Ministry of Justice, New Zealand (2005) *Evaluation of the New Zealand Court-Referred RJ Pilot for Adults*. Wellington: Ministry of Justice. Online at: www.iustice.govt.nz/pubs/reports/2005/nz-court-referred-restorative-justice-pilot-evaluation/index.html.

Ministry of Justice, New Zealand (2007) *Restorative Justice*. Wellington: Ministry of Justice. Online at: www.justice.govt.nz/pubs/courts-publications/118-restorative-justice.html (accessed 5 December 2008).

Ministry of Justice, New Zealand (2008) *Crime Prevention Unit. Restorative Justice – General Information*. Online at: www.iustice.govt.nz/cpu/restorative-justice/index.html (accessed 5 December 2008).

Morris, A. (2002) 'Critiquing the critics: a brief response to critics of restorative justice', *British Journal of Criminology*, 42: 596–615.

Morris, A. and Maxwell, G. (1998) 'Restorative justice in New Zealand: family group conferences as a case study', *Western Criminology Review*. Online at: http://wcr.sonoma.edu/v1n1/morris.html (accessed 17 December 2008).

Morris, A. and Maxwell, G. (2000) 'The practice of family group conferences in New Zealand: assessing the place, potential and pitfalls of restorative justice', in A. Crawford and J. Goodey (eds), *Integrating a Victim Perspective within Criminal Justice*. Aldershot: Ashgate.

Morris, A. and Maxwell, G. (2003) 'Restorative justice for adult offenders: the New Zealand Case', in L. Walgrave (ed.), *Repositioning Restorative Justice*. Cullompton: Willan.

Murray, J. (2005) 'The effects of imprisonment on families and children of prisoners', in A. Liebling and S. Maruna (eds), *The Effects of Imprisonment*. Cullompton: Willan, pp. 442–64.

Nergard, T. (1993) 'Solving conflicts outside the court system: experiences with the Conflict Resolution Boards in Norway', *British Journal of Criminology*, 33: 81–94.

Newburn, T., Crawford, A., Earle, R., Goldie, S., Hale, C., Masters, G., Netten, A., Sanders, R., Hallam, A., Sharpe, K. and Uglow, S. (2002) *The Introduction of Referral Orders into the Youth Justice System: Final Report*, Home Office Research Study No. 242. London: Home Office. Online at: www.homeoffice.gov.uk/rds/pdfs2/hors242.pdf (accessed 15 January 2009).

Norris, F. H. and Kaniasty, K. (1994) 'Psychological distress following criminal victimization in the general population: cross-sectional, longitudinal and prospective analyses', *Journal of Consulting and Clinical Psychology*, 62: 111–23.

O'Mahony, D. and Doak, J. (2004) 'Restorative justice: is more better? The experience of police-led restorative cautioning pilots in Northern Ireland', *Howard Journal*, 43: 484–505.

Padfield, N. (2009) 'Parole and early release: the Criminal Justice and Immigration Act 2008 changes in context', *Criminal Law Review*, pp. 166–87.

Parker, C. (1999) *Just Lawyers: Regulation and Access to Justice*. Oxford: Oxford University Press.

Pavlich, G. (2002) 'Towards an ethics of restorative justice', in L. Walgrave (ed.), *Restorative Justice and the Law*. Cullompton: Willan, pp. 1–18.

Peachey, D. E. (1989) 'The Kitchener experiment', in M. Wright and B. Galaway (eds), *Mediation and Criminal Justice: Victims, Offenders and Community*. London: Sage.

Putnam, R. (2000) *'Bowling Alone': The Collapse and Revival of American Community*. New York: Simon & Schuster.

Raynor, P. (2004) 'Rehabilitative and reintegrative approaches', in A. Bottoms, S. Rex and G. Robinson (eds), *Alternatives to Prison: Options for an Insecure Society*. Cullompton: Willan.

Restorative Justice Consortium (2007) *Voluntary Code of Practice for Trainers and Training Organisations of Restorative Practices Facilitator Training*. London: Restorative Justice Consortium, at: www.restorativejustice.org.uk/Resources/Code_&_Trainers_List/RJC%20Voluntary%20Code%20of%20Practice.pdf (accessed 10 February 2009).

Review of the Criminal Justice System in Northern Ireland (2000) *Report of the Criminal Justice Review Team*. Belfast: HMSO.

Roberts, A. and Umbreit, M. (1996) 'Victim-offender mediation: the English experience', *Mediation*, 12 (3). Pamphlet reprint.

Robinson, G. and Shapland, J. (2008) 'Reducing recidivism: a task for restorative justice?', *British Journal of Criminology*, 48 (3): 337–58.

Roche, D. (2003) *Accountability in Restorative Justice*. Oxford: Oxford University Press.

Roche, D. (2006) 'Dimensions of restorative justice', *Journal of Social Issues*, 62 (2): 217–38.

Roche, D. (2007) 'Retribution and restorative justice', in G. Johnstone and D. Van Ness (eds), *Handbook of Restorative Justice*. Cullompton: Willan.

Rombouts, H. and Parmentier, S. (2009) 'The International Criminal Court and its Trust Fund are coming of age: towards a process approach for the reparation of victims', *International Review of Victimology*, 16: 149–82.

Ruddick, R. (1989) 'A court-referred scheme', in M. Wright and B. Galaway (eds), *Mediation and Criminal Justice: Victims, Offenders and Community*. London: Sage.

Shapland, J. (1981) *Between Conviction and Sentence: The Process of Mitigation*. London: Routledge & Kegan Paul.

Shapland, J. (2003) 'Bringing victims in from the cold: victims' role in criminal justice', in J. Jackson and K. Quinn (eds), *Criminal Justice Reform: Looking to the Future*. Belfast: Queen's University Belfast, pp. 48–69.

Shapland, J. (2009a) 'Restorative justice conferencing in the context of community policing', in L. Gunther Moor, T. Peters, P. Ponsaers, J. Shapland and B. van Stokkom (eds), 'Restorative policing', *Journal of Police Studies*, no. 2, pp. 119–38.

Shapland, J. (2009b) 'Key aspects of restorative justice alongside adult criminal justice', in P. Knepper, J. Doak and J. Shapland (eds), *Urban Crime Prevention, Surveillance and Restorative Justice: Effects of Social Technologies*. Boca Raton, FL: Taylor & Francis, pp. 123–48.

Shapland, J. (2010) *Conferencing in Relation to Criminal Offences: Evaluation Results Internationally*. Invited plenary presentation to the 6th Biennial Conference of the European Forum for Restorative Justice, Bilbao, 17–19 June.

Shapland, J. (forthcoming a) 'Evaluating restorative justice', in D. Balahur and M. Kilchling (eds), *Directions of Restorative Justice in Europe*. Brussels: Office for Publications of the European Communities.

Shapland, J. (forthcoming b) 'Victims and criminal justice in Europe', in P. Knepper (ed.), *Handbook of Victimology*. Boca Raton, FL: Taylor & Francis.

Shapland, J. and Hall, M. (2007) 'What do we know about the effects of crime on victims?', *International Review of Victimology*, 13: 175–218.

Shapland, J. and Hall, M. (2010) 'Victims at court: necessary accessories or centre stage?', in A. E. Bottoms and J. Roberts (eds), *Hearing the Victim: Adversarial Justice, Crime Victims and the State*, Cambridge Criminal Justice Series. Cullompton: Willan, pp. 163–99.

Shapland, J. and Vagg, J. (1988) *Policing by the Public*. Abingdon: Routledge.

Shapland, J., Willmore, J. and Duff, P. (1985) *Victims in the Criminal Justice System*. Aldershot: Gower.

Shapland, J., Johnstone, J., Sorsby, A., Stubbing, T., Hibbert, J., Howes, M., Jackson, J. and Colledge, E. (2003) *Evaluation of Statutory Time Limit Pilot Schemes in the Youth Court*, Home Office Online Report 21/03. London: Home Office. Online at: www.homeoffice.gov.uk/rds/pdfs2/rdsolr2103.pdf (accessed 14 January 2008).

Shapland, J., Atkinson, A., Colledge, E., Dignan, J., Howes, M., Johnstone, J., Pennant, R., Robinson, G. and Sorsby, A. (2004a) *Implementing Restorative Justice Schemes (Crime Reduction Programme): A Report on the First Year*, Home Office Online Report 32/04. London: Home Office. Online at: www.homeoffice.gov.uk/rds/pdfs04/rdsolr3204.pdf.

Shapland, J., Atkinson, A., Atkinson, H., Chapman, B., Colledge, E., Dignan, J., Howes, M., Johnstone, J., Pennant, R., Robinson, G. and Sorsby, A. (2004b) *Restorative Justice: An Independent Evaluation*. Paper given to the conference on 'Restorative Justice at the Coalface: Working with Victims, Offenders and Stakeholders in Crime', Newcastle-upon-Tyne, 23–24 June.

Shapland, J., Atkinson, A., Atkinson, H., Chapman, B., Colledge, E., Dignan, J., Howes, M., Johnstone, J., Robinson, G. and Sorsby, A. (2006a) *Restorative Justice in Practice: The Second Report from the Evaluation of Three Schemes*, University of Sheffield Centre for Criminological Research Occasional Paper 2. Sheffield: Faculty of Law. Online at: http://ccr.group.shef.ac.uk/papers/pdfs/Restorative_Justice_Report.pdf.

Shapland, J., Atkinson, A., Atkinson, H., Chapman, B., Colledge, E., Dignan, J., Howes, M., Johnstone, J., Robinson, G. and Sorsby, A. (2006b) 'Situating restorative justice within criminal justice', *Theoretical Criminology*, 10: 505–32.

Shapland, J., Atkinson, A., Atkinson, H., Chapman, B., Colledge, E., Dignan, J., Howes, M., Johnstone, J., Robinson, G. and Sorsby, A. (2006c) *Restorative Justice in Practice: Findings from the Second Stage of the Evaluation of Three Schemes*, Home Office Research Findings No. 274. London: Home Office. Online at: www.homeoffice.gov.uk/rds/pdfs06/r274.pdf.

Shapland, J., Atkinson, A., Atkinson, H., Chapman, B., Dignan, J., Howes, M., Johnstone, J., Robinson, G. and Sorsby, A. (2007) *Restorative Justice: The Views of Victims and Offenders*, Ministry of Justice Research Series 3/07. London: Ministry of Justice. Online at: www.justice.gov.uk/docs/Restorative-Justice.pdf.

Shapland, J., Atkinson, A., Atkinson, H., Dignan, J., Edwards, L., Hibbert, J., Howes, M., Johnstone, J., Robinson, G. and Sorsby, A. (2008) *Does Restorative Justice Affect Reconviction? The Fourth Report from the Evaluation of Three Schemes*, Ministry of Justice Research Series 10/08. London: Ministry of Justice. Online at: www.justice.gov.uk/docs/restorative-justice-report_06-08.pdf.

Shearing, C. (2001) 'Transforming security: a South African experiment', in H. Strang and J. Braithwaite (eds), *Restorative Justice and Civil Society*. Cambridge: Cambridge University Press.

Shepherd, A. and Whiting, E. (2006) *Re-offending of Adults: Results from the 2003 Cohort*, Home Office Statistical Bulletin 20/06. London: National Statistics.

Sherman, L. (1993) 'Defiance, deterrence and irrelevance: a theory of the criminal sanction', *Journal of Research in Crime and Delinquency*, 30: 445–73.

Sherman, L. W. and Strang, H. (2007) *Restorative Justice: The Evidence*. London: Smith Institute.

Sherman, L. W., Strang, H. and Woods, D. J. (2000) *Recidivism Patterns in the Canberra Reintegrative Shaming Experiments (RISE). Final Report*. Canberra: Centre for Restorative Justice, Australian National University. Online at: www.aic.gov.au/rjustice/rise/recidivism/ (accessed 2 December 2008).

Sherman, L. W., Braithwaite, J., Strang, H., Barnes, G., Christie-Johnston, J., Smith, S. and Inkpen, N. (1997a) *Experiments in Restorative Policing – Reintegrative Shaming of Violence, Drink Driving and Property Crime: A Randomised Controlled Trial*. Canberra: Australian National University. Online at: www.aic.gov.au/riustice/rise/progress/1997.html (accessed 2 December 2008).

Sherman, L.W., Gottfredson, D., MacKenzie, D., Eck, J., Reuter, P. and Bushway, S. (1997b) *Preventing Crime: What Works, What Doesn't, What's Promising*. Washington, DC: US Department of Justice.

Sherman, L. W., Strang, H., Barnes, G., Braithwaite, J., Inkpen, N. and Teh, M. (1998) *Experiments in Restorative Policing: A Progress Report on the Canberra Reintegrative Shaming Experiments (RISE)*. Canberra: Australian National University. Online at: www.aic.gov.au/rjustice/rise/progress/1998.html (accessed 2 December 2008).

Sherman, L., Strang, H., Angel, C., Woods, D., Barnes, G., Bennett, S. and Inkpen, N. (2005) 'Effects of face-to-face restorative justice on victims of crime in four randomised, controlled trials', *Journal of Experimental Criminology*, 1 (3): 367–95.

Skogan, W. G. (1994) *Contacts Between Police and Public: Findings from the 1992 British Crime Survey*, Home Office Research Study No. 134. London: HMSO.

SmartJustice (2006) *Crime Victims Say Jail Doesn't Work*. Durham: SmartJustice.

Strang, H. (2002) *Repair or Revenge: Victims and Restorative Justice*. Oxford: Clarendon Press.

Strang, H. and Braithwaite, J. (eds) (2000) *Restorative Justice: Philosophy to Practice*. Aldershot: Ashgate.

Strang, H. and Sherman, L. (2003) 'Repairing the victim: victims and restorative justice', *Utah Law Review*, pp. 15–42. Online at: www.sas.upenn.edu/jerrylee/research/rj_utah.pdf (accessed 21 August 2009).

Strang, H., Barnes, G., Braithwaite, J. and Sherman, L. (1999) *Experiments in Restorative Policing: A Progress Report on the Canberra Reintegrative Shaming Experiments (RISE)*. Canberra: Australian National University. Online at: www.aic.gov.au/rjustice/rise/progress/1999.html (accessed 2 December 2008).

Strang, H., Sherman, L., Angel, C., Woods, D. J., Bennett, S., Newbury-Birch, D. and Inkpen, N. (2005) 'Victim evaluations of face-to-face restorative justice conferences: a quasi-experimental analysis', *Journal of Social Issues*, 62 (2): 281–306.

Stuart, B. (1996) 'Circle sentencing: turning swords into ploughshares', in B. Galaway and J. Hudson (eds), *Restorative Justice: International Perspectives*. Monsey, NY: Criminal Justice Press.

Sudnow, D. (1964) 'Normal crimes: sociological features of the penal code in a public defender office', *Social Problems*, 12: 255–76.

Tarling, R., Dowds, L. and Budd, T. (2000) *Victim and Witness Intimidation: Key Findings from the British Crime Survey*, Home Office Research Findings No. 124. London: Home Office. Online at: www.homeoffice.gov.uk/rds/pdfs/rl24.pdf (accessed 24 August 2009).

Tavuchis, N. (1991) *Mea Culpa: A Sociology of Apology and Reconciliation*. Stanford, CA: Stanford University Press.

Transformative Justice Australia (2002) *Transformative Justice Australia Conferencing Facilitators' Manual: How to Run a TJA Conference*. Sydney: TJA.

Triggs, S. (2005) *New Zealand Court-referred Restorative Justice Pilot: Two-Year Follow-Up of Reoffending*. Wellington: New Zealand Ministry of Justice. Online at: www.justice.govt.nz/pubs/reports/2005/nz-court-referred-restorative-justice-pilot-2-year-follow-up/nz-court-referred-restorative-justice.pdf (accessed 4 December 2008).

Tyler, T. (1990) *Why People Obey the Law*. New Haven, CT: Yale University Press.

Tyler, T. R. (2006) 'Restorative justice and procedural justice: dealing with rule breaking', *Journal of Social Issues*, 62 (2): 307–26.

Tyler, T. and Huo, Y. (2002) *Trust in the Law: Encouraging Public Cooperation with the Police and Courts*. New York: Russell Sage Foundation.

Tyler, T., Sherman, L., Strang, H., Barnes, G. and Woods, D. (2007) 'Reintegrative shaming, procedural justice, and recidivism: the engagement of offenders' psychological mechanisms in the Canberra RISE drinking-and-driving experiment', *Law and Society Review*, 41 (3): 553–86.

Umbreit, M. (1999) 'Avoiding the marginalization and "McDonaldization" of victim-offender mediation: a case study in moving towards the mainstream', in G. Bazemore and L. Walgrave (eds), *Restorative Juvenile Justice: Repairing the Harm of Youth Crime*. Monsey, NY: Criminal Justice/Willow Tree Press.

Umbreit, M., Bradshaw, W. and Coates, R. B. (1999) 'Victims of severe violence meet the offender: restorative justice through dialogue', *International Review of Victimology*, 6: 321–43.

Umbreit, M. S., Coates, R. B., Kalanj, B., Lipkin, R. and Petros, G. (1995) *Mediation of Criminal Conflict: An Assessment of Programs in Four Canadian Provinces*. St Paul, MN: Centre for Restorative Justice and Mediation, University of Minnesota.

Umbreit, M. S., Greenwood, J., with Fercello, C. and Umbreit, J. (2000) *National Survey of Victim-Offender Mediation Programmes in the United States*. St Paul, MN: Office for Victims of Crime.

Van Dijk, J. and de Waard, J. (2009) 'Forty years of crime prevention in the Dutch polder', in A. Crawford (ed.), *Crime Prevention Policies in Comparative Perspective*. Cullompton: Willan.

Van Ness, D. (2003) 'Proposed basic principles on the use of restorative justice recognising the aims and limits of restorative justice', in A. von Hirsch, J. Roberts, A. E. Bottoms, K. Roach and M. Schiff (eds), *Restorative Justice and Criminal Justice: Competing or Reconcilable Paradigms?* Oxford: Hart.

Van Ness, D. and Strong, K. H. (1997) *Restoring Justice*. Cincinnati, OH: Anderson.

Vanfraechem, I. (2009) 'Restorative policing: in pursuit of principles', in Gunther Moor, L., Peters, T., Ponsaers, P., Shapland, J. and van Stokkom, B. (eds), 'Restorative policing', *Journal of Police Studies*, no. 2, pp. 39–64.

Vincent-Jones, P. (1997) 'Hybrid organization, contractual governance, and compulsory competitive tendering in the provision of local authority services', in S. Deakin and J. Michie (eds), *Contracts, Co-operation and Competition: Studies in Economics, Management and Law*. Oxford: Oxford University Press.

von Hirsch, A., Roberts, J., Bottoms, A. E., Roach, K. and Schiff, M. (eds) (2003) *Restorative J*[illegible] *and Criminal Justice: Competing or Reconcilable Paradigms?* Oxford: H[illegible]

Walgrave, [illegible] *Repositioning Restorative Justice*. Cullompton: Willan.

Walgra[illegible] *ative Justice, Self-interest and Responsible Citizenship*. C[illegible]

W[illegible] 'Can mediation be therapeutic for crime victims? An [illegible] es in mediation with young offenders', *Canadian Jo*[illegible] *al Justice*, 47: 527–44.

Wozniak [illegible] – *The Reality in Poland after the Framework Decisi*[illegible] r on Developments in Restorative Justice in relation [illegible] the Implementation of Restorative Justice in Poland [illegible] Sheffield, 12 May.

Wright, M. (19[illegible] *rs: A Restorative Response to Crime*. Buckingham: [illegible]

Wynne, J. (1996) '[illegible] ion Service: ten years' experience with victim-offender m[illegible] y and J. Hudson (eds), *Restorative Justice: International Perspe*[illegible] NY: Criminal Justice Press, pp. 445–61.

Young, R. (1989) 'Repar[illegible] igation', *Criminal Law Review*, pp. 463–72.

Young, R. (2001) 'Just co[illegible] ng "shameful" business? Police-led restorative justice and the lessons of research', in A. Morris and G. Maxwell (eds), *Restorative Justice for Juveniles: Conferencing, Mediation and Circles*. Oxford: Hart.

Youth Justice Board (2009) *Working with Victims*. London: Youth Justice Board. Online at: www.yjb.gov.uk/en-gb/practitioners/WorkingwithVictims/RestorativeJustice/Targets.htm (accessed 6 March 2009).

Zehr, H. (1985) *Retributive Justice, Restorative Justice*. Elkhart, IN: Mennonite Central Committee, US Office of Criminal Justice.

Zehr, H. (1990) *Changing Lenses: A New Focus for Crime and Justice*. Scottdale, PA: Herald Press.

Zehr, H. (2002) 'Listening to victims', *Te Ara Whakitika: Newsletter of the Court-Referred Restorative Justice Project*, October/November, issue 12, as cited in Crime and Justice Research Centre, with S. Triggs (2005) *New Zealand Court-referred Restorative Justice Pilot: Evaluation*. Wellington: New Zealand Ministry of Justice.

Zernova, M. (2007a) *Restorative Justice: Ideals and Realities*. Aldershot: Ashgate.

Zernova, M. (2007b) 'Aspirations of restorative justice proponents and experiences of participants in family group conferences', *British Journal of Criminology*, 47: 491–509.

Zernova, M. and Wright, M. (2007) 'Alternative visions of restorative justice', in G. Johnstone and D. Van Ness (eds), *Handbook of Restorative Justice*. Cullompton: Willan.

Index